I0475141

The Dynamic Manager's Guide To Creative Selling:

How To Make More Sales And Build A Super Sales Career

By Dave Donelson

THE DYNAMIC MANAGER'S GUIDE
TO CREATIVE SELLING:
How To Make More Sales And Build A Super Sales Career

Published and printed in the United States of America
by Donelson SDA, Inc.

For information, contact Donelson SDA, Inc.
44 Park Lane, West Harrison, NY 10604

FIRST EDITION

ISBN-10: 1460929667
ISBN-13: 978-1460929667

Chapters 1 – 28 are available as an eBook, The Dynamic Manager's Guide To Sales Techniques
Chapters 29 - 51 are available as an eBook, The Dynamic Manager's Guide To More Sales

Acknowledgements
Some of the material in this book originally appeared in various forms
in one or more of these publications:

Accessory & Performance Retailer
Automotive Aftermarket
Autographics
Broadcasting & Cable
Central NY Business Journal
The Christian Science Monitor
Club Industry
Convenience Store Decisions
Distribution Sales & Management
Distribution Channels
Electronic Media
Entrepreneur
Fabricator
Family Business
Gift Basket Review
LP Gas Magazine
NFIB's MyBusiness
Niche Magazine
NSGA Retail Focus
Nursery Retailer
Performance Business
Pizza Today
Professional Builder
Restyling
Ward's Dealer Business
Westchester Magazine
Woodworker's Journal
Woodshop News

Table of Contents

About This Book

My very first sales call was a debacle. The general manager of the radio station where I worked picked a listing out of the yellow pages—he chose a neighborhood restaurant named "Ma's Diner." Then he handed me a map showing that our signal covered most of two states and told me to go sell the diner's owner a $300 package of radio spots. Other than that, my sales training consisted of his advice, "Don't leave until Ma says 'no' three times."

Being young and foolish, not to mention eager to earn the $36 commission from that $300 order, I sallied forth into a career in sales. If you guessed that I didn't make that sale, you'd be right. In fact, Ma literally chased me out of the diner waving a very dangerous-looking spatula. I took that for the third "no."

After more than a few calls like the one on Ma's Diner, I started learning how to sell—a process that continues to this day. Along the way, I developed the Creative Selling System, a simple method that turned selling into an enjoyable and satisfying experience for both me and my customers. I also made a pretty good living at it, if I do say so myself, although I never did sell anything to Ma.

The Creative Selling System came about through trial and error. I kept using different sales techniques on my own prospects and accounts until I found the ones that worked best for me. Later in my career, I observed the salespeople I hired, trained, and managed as they sold in different ways, a study that confirmed my beliefs about selling creatively. Finally, I dissected the best sales methods and turned them into a step-by-step sales training program that I marketed quite successfully throughout the United States.

That sales training program served as the basis for my first book, *Creative Selling: How To Boost Your B2B Sales* (Entrepreneur Press, 2000). Some of the material in that book has been updated and included here. *The Dynamic Manager's Guide To Creative Selling* also includes columns and case studies that I wrote for the national business and trade publications you'll find listed in the bibliography.

The first part of this book covers basic sales techniques from how to introduce yourself to a new prospect to how to close the sale. The second goes beyond the basics to give some insights into maximizing good customer relationships and turning them into increased revenue for your company.

This book isn't about theory—it's about doing. It's a how-to book outlining the steps to a successful sales career and some of the alternative strategies you can use along the way. There are a couple of ways you can use this book. First, I suggest you learn by doing. Read a chapter, then apply the techniques in it as you sell to your customers. If you take about a week to absorb and practice each chapter, you'll better understand the process and use it more effectively. Participants in my training programs were required to use each step with a real prospect before they could go on to the next one. It takes a little more time to do it that way, but the results were spectacular. If you are a sales manager, you can guide your staff through the process in this way.

The really great thing about Creative Selling is that it gives you control over your own success. Creative Selling works in good economies and bad, whether you're selling widgets or financial services, roaming a nationwide territory or confined to a retail store. That because Creative Selling isn't about hoping a willing customer will come along and listen to your pitch, it's about making your own luck in a simple, straightforward way. Good salespeople seize every opportunity that comes along. *Great* salespeople don't wait—they create opportunities for themselves.

No matter what you do, don't just read about Creative Selling. Do it! Unleash your creative sales power. You'll make more sales and have a lot more fun.

—Dave Donelson

Chapter 1
Creativity In Sales

"Creative selling enables you to find needs even when the prospect doesn't know he has them."

In business, creativity is often thought of as an exciting, dangerous thing. The word itself conjures up images of wild-eyed people dressed in black doing strange things that have little to do with making a profit. But aren't salespeople creative? I think so, since the really good ones create things all the time. Like opportunity. And demand for products and services. And customer satisfaction. What about wealth? The best salespeople certainly create wealth not only for themselves and their companies, but often for their customers as well.

The nature of the sales process itself is creative. A good salesperson creates demand where it doesn't exist. He or she creates a message (the sales pitch) using various media (face-to-face calls, telephone pitches, PowerPoint presentations) that alters the thinking of the audience (the prospect). A salesperson explores new territories in their craft through cold calls, brings new ways of thinking to their audience by persuading prospects, and makes the world a better place by providing customer satisfaction.

These may not sound like the things you or your salespeople do. Lots of perfectly productive salespeople are nothing more than harvesters of existing business. They take orders, fill out the necessary forms, collect their commissions and go home. They never break rules and they hate new products and changes because they disrupt the orderly nature of their existence. To them, new customers are generally a pain in the behind because it takes so much work to make them into old customers. Besides, it's much more profitable to service existing accounts anyway.

Salespeople like that used to play an important role in our economy. Today, of course, they are well along the road to extinction. Just ask your local bookseller what Amazon has done to their business. Or your stockbroker how he or she has been affected by online trading. If a salesperson isn't looking for new customers or better ways to serve existing ones, he's doomed. On the other hand, there will always be a need for people who have the energy, fearlessness, and drive to create new sales opportunities.

The Creative Selling System

I've had the immense pleasure of studying, practicing, and teaching creative selling for many years. I've worked closely with, managed, and observed thousands of salespeople, both creative and not. I found that selling creatively unleashes your idea power—your ability to make more sales and create more personal wealth by selling ideas for solutions instead of products. That's what the system is about.

And it is a system: the repeated application of proven techniques to accomplish a desired end. My system repeatedly applies creative selling to the goal of producing more sales. It is also a framework that enables you to be a more effective, efficient salesperson. When you work within that framework, you apply creative techniques to every step of the selling process from prospecting new accounts to servicing old ones. You use your personal creative talents (and we all have them) to solve problems and create opportunities for your customers to use your products or services—and for you to make more sales.

Just as in my training programs, we begin with the basic assumption that you are a pretty effective communicator, know your product or service, and are interested in professional growth, job satisfaction, better customer service, and making more money. These are pretty safe assumptions because almost everybody in sales has these qualities.

We also assume you are willing to invest your time, money, and effort to achieve these goals. Nothing good happens without effort, especially in sales. Learning to use the Creative Selling System is the same. As I have advised thousands of salespeople, if you're not willing to invest the time and effort to practice, you'll never reap the rewards. If you're one of those people looking for an effortless way to get rich through sales, stop reading and go do something you really want to do. Life's too short.

Still reading? Great! That means you have an open mind. And an open mind is the single most important component of creativity.

Creating New Business

In this book, our focus will be on developing new business. Not because existing accounts aren't important, but the same techniques you use to sell new accounts will work even better on the ones you already have. It's also because, as every salesperson knows, you have to constantly work on new accounts because your old ones are never 100 percent secure. Their plans change. Their business changes. Their own customers change their habits. Their competitors "zig," causing your customer to "zag" in response. And every change in your customer's business has the potential to change their relationship with you and their need for your products and services. If you sell retail, your best customers have an irritating habit of moving away, or their kids grow up, they retire, or they lose their job. All those things cause them to change what they buy and why they buy it—not to mention where they go to shop besides your store.

Your competitors are always there, too, nibbling like ducks at your existing customers. Contradicting what you say, bringing in new products, even—horror of horrors—undercutting your prices! Even the smallest competitor can hurt you by taking away an account here and there. And a big one can devastate your sales and income like an elephant stepping on a grasshopper.

If you're not constantly working on bringing in new accounts, your sales and commissions are going to wither away. And that may not be a problem that's way out over the horizon. In some industries, customer loyalty is so tenuous that they experience 40 percent account turnover year-to-year. In other words, they have to replace nearly half of their account base every year just to stay even.

In most companies, there's another reason the salesperson should be developing new business. That's because it's their job. Almost every sales job description includes the direct or implied function of introducing new users to the company's products. If the orders just came in, there wouldn't be any need for salespeople. All you'd need would be an order-processing department. So you should think of new business development as job insurance.

But the main reason you should work on new accounts is that it's *fun*. The work, the challenges, the risks of failure are tremendous. But there's little in life that matches the excitement, the edge-of-the-seat suspense, the joyful exhilaration of creating an opportunity and closing a new account. You created it. And creativity is *fun*.

Creative Selling Principles

Now, down to business. There are three principles to creative selling that guide every strategic and tactical decision you make in the Creative Selling System.

The first principle is to focus your efforts on the largest potential prospects. Obvious, isn't it? If you only sell the biggest accounts, you'll sell more and work less. But many salespeople gravitate toward smaller accounts. Sometimes they think it's easier to get a small order than a big one. Or they're intimidated by a big account and the layers of bureaucracy that often comes along with that territory. There are other reasons for this tendency, but if you have it, lose it! It's just as easy to ask for "one hundred thousand" as it is to say "a thousand" and the rewards are obviously much greater. You'll also find there are many other reasons to concentrate on the largest potential prospects that we'll get into later. At this point, trust me: it's important.

Principle two is that you must know the customer's business before you can effectively sell them. Sure, you can stumble across some people who need your product if you make enough calls. But you're not really selling them, are you? You're just filling the order they were waiting to give you. To accomplish one of the goals of creative selling—changing your prospects' perception of their needs—you have to know what's going on in their minds to start with. You have to know enough about their business to identify needs that they didn't even know they had until you made your presentation.

The third principle is that you must sell ideas instead of product. What do I mean by ideas? They're solutions. They're ways for the prospect to use your services. They're the benefits the prospect gets from using your product instead of the features of the product. Selling ideas instead of selling product means you have to present your product in the context of the prospect's needs, not just lay out a list of its components.

A participant in my training program once called this system "consultive selling with a bang," which I thought was a pretty apt description. Just as in consultive selling, you start with a needs analysis (see principle two:

know your customer). The difference lies in the way the needs analysis is done—my method is much more accurate—and the application of the creative process to finding solutions for the customer.

The biggest difference, though, is that creative selling enables you to find needs even when the prospect doesn't know he has them. Then you create solutions to those needs even if your company doesn't sell a specific product or service that directly applies. It's close to making something out of nothing—a truly creative process.

One of my most successful personal investments was in a company I helped start with a partner who demonstrated that anyone—even an engineer—could be a creative seller. The entrepreneur was Madison (Matt) Batt and the company was Tower Engineering Consultants. The company specialized in the structural analysis of communications towers, a numbers-driven and formula-ruled service if there ever was one. Matt's ability to go beyond those boundaries to identify needs his prospects didn't know they had and to persuasively present solutions to them made his new company a winner.

One of the first times I saw him sell creatively was with a prospective client responsible for the public structures (everything from playground equipment to bridges) owned by a county government. The prospect sent out an RFP (request for proposals) for inspection of the county's communications towers, which are used for two-way radios and other communications systems. Usually, the sale is made in these situations by the lowest bidder—and there's not much room for doing anything other than meeting the technical specifications of the bidding process.

Matt looked past the RFP at the entire assortment of structures his prospect managed. Then, instead of just submitting a proposal for inspection of the communications towers, he added a section that explained that the county bridges were subject to the same structural stresses that towers were (weather, materials deterioration, wind, etc.). Even more importantly, he pointed out that they presented the same kinds of dangers to the public if there were structural problems. Then Matt proposed to inspect and analyze the county's bridges using the same rigorous professional methods his firm applied to towers. As Matt said, "From an engineering analysis standpoint, there isn't much difference between the two. A bridge is more or less just a tower laid on its side."

Bridges weren't covered in the RFP, but Matt made the sale by creating a perceived need that didn't exist in the prospect's mind when he started. He then created a solution to the need by designing a service that his firm didn't normally provide (bridge engineering). My partner's mind was open to the possibilities—and he used creative selling techniques to create an opportunity.

Matt didn't do this just once; he did it time and time again. What makes creative selling so successful isn't the one instance when it's used to bring in a new piece of business. It's when the system is used over and over again to create a stream of new business. When the creative process becomes not the exception but rather the rule itself. When your customers start relying on you as a continuous source of ideas to help their business. That's when you really create something of note, mainly a whole lot of satisfied customers and a great deal of wealth.

The Macintosh computer may have made Steve Jobs rich, but it didn't make him a legend. It was his entire body of work—the iPod, the iPhone, the iPad, etc.—that made him a superstar. It is repetitive success in sales that will do the same for you. It's also worth noting that there will be some failure along the way—anybody remember the Newton? But that's what happens when you create things. It's your willingness to take risks and bounce back from a few failures that enables you to create a stream of successes.

Chapter 2

Tactical And Strategic Advantages

"Satisfied customers are repeat customers, the most profitable customers of all."

There are many advantages to using the Creative Selling System. It's not product-driven. It's not even market-driven. It goes beyond that to become a market driver itself. The company that consistently practices creative selling repeatedly widens its market by creating new opportunities in the undiscovered needs of its customers. Creative sellers don't respond to the needs of the marketplace—they create new ones.

And what does that do to the competition? They're out of the race before they even know it has begun. How can they compete to satisfy a need the customer doesn't even know exists? The competition is forced to play a continual game of "catch-up" and "me-too" in response to the sales that the creative seller is making.

The creative seller builds something else of immense value: a super-strong relationship with the customer. When the prospect realizes that you're there to talk about their needs (not about your need to sell something), they're much more open to listening to your proposal. When they see the amount of *your time* invested in *their success*, they'll be willing to hear you through completely. And when they discover that you're also bringing them an idea to use—giving them something of value before they give you any money—their minds will open even wider.

This relationship will build on itself, creating (there's that word again) a bond between the buyer and seller based on the seller's ever-increasing value to the buyer. The creative seller gets easier access to decision-makers, moves earlier into the decision-making process, and is seen not as an adversary but as an ally. The creative seller becomes the idea resource for the customer. The buyer turns to the seller not for more products, but for more ideas on how they can enhance their own life or business.

Ideas are powerful things. They're scarce. They don't exist until someone creates them. They can be copied, but only after the original idea has been created and sold. And because 1) they are in short supply and 2) the competition can't come into the market until after the initial sale, the price of an idea is determined solely by the perceived value in the buyer's mind. No competitive bidding. No price shaving for market share. Just the seller's ability to create perceived value through understanding the customer's needs and persuasively presenting an idea to meet those needs.

There are some great tactical advantages to selling this way, too. One of my favorites is that the prospect can reject your solutions. That's right, the ease with which the customer can say "no" is actually an advantage to idea selling. Let me explain.

Traditionally, sellers walk into the prospect with a presentation listing the many reasons their product should be bought. They present their case to the prospect, giving arguments and evidence much like a lawyer in a courtroom. They then listen to the opposing case (the objections from the prospect) and rebut them as best they can. The whole process becomes about winning a courtroom debate with the prospect. Sound familiar?

Now, in my limited experience in a courtroom, there are basically three parties involved in a typical case: the judge, who hands down a decision based on the merits of the arguments which are presented by the other two people, the plaintiff and the defendant. What's different about selling is that the "judge," or prospect, also happens to be the "opposing attorney!" He's responsible not only for making a decision, but for arguing against it. Not that he can't be objective, but the odds aren't with you. That's one reason closing ratios are typically so low for many salespeople.

But losing the case—or getting a "no" from the prospect—isn't the toughest part. It's the fact that once this "judge" hands down the decision, it's pretty final. There's not really any appeal in traditional sales and it's pretty hard to come up with a new case and get back into the courtroom with it. You usually give *all* your best reasons to buy during the first presentation. To get a second chance to pitch your product, you have to first overcome the prospect's attitude that he's "heard it all before." You have to offer something new to get back in the door.

When you sell ideas, though, you've always got a reason for the prospect to see you again—because you can always come up with a new idea. Remember that an idea isn't a product—it's a use, a solution to a discovered need. So, as long as you can come up with different ideas, you'll be able to get back in to see the prospect with them. You're not coming back to make the same old pitch; you're offering something new.

Of course, part of your presentation includes the reasons your product will satisfy the prospect's needs. You *do* need to make your arguments. But if you structure your presentation the way I suggest, the prospect will focus on the desirability of your idea instead of on the reasons for buying your product or service. Your "arguments" will go unanswered. And you'll have the opportunity to present them again as you come back over and over again with new ideas. Same arguments every time, just new ideas to get you in the door.

Another tactical advantage to selling ideas is how the prospect responds to them. The traditional seller makes a presentation full of information about his company's product or service. So what does the prospect talks about? The *seller's* company or his products, of course.

But when you talk about an idea—one that is unique to the prospect—they'll talk about how the solution applies (or not) to *their* business or personal needs. Which is what you the seller really want them to talk about. You want to hear the prospect talk about their needs, concerns, desires, and objectives. The more they talk about their needs, the better you'll be able to shape your solutions to meet them. It's a powerful feedback loop that works in your favor.

Creative Customer Relationships

I've found in years of working with clients in dozens of different lines of business that they all want and need ideas. I've yet to meet a businessperson that's truly not interested in hearing an idea that will make them more money or solve a problem they've been struggling with. They'll present plenty of obstacles to the salesperson, of course, but deep inside nearly every business manager or owner there is a desire to do better. And a willingness to beg, borrow, steal, or even buy ideas on how to do better from any source available.

When you become identified as the "idea seller" by your prospects, you'll be surprised at how many doors are opened to you. You'll stand head and shoulders above the dozens of salespeople clamoring for attention from your prospects. And that's an enviable position to be in.

The more ideas you present to a given prospect, the more feedback you'll get. The more you learn about their business from that feedback, the more needs and opportunities you'll see, which in turn will lead you to even better ideas to sell them. And the stronger your ideas become, the better they will work for the customer and the more satisfied your customer will be. Satisfied customers are repeat customers, the most profitable customers of all.

Creative selling isn't the exclusive domain of a few wild eyed sales fanatics. You don't have to know how to use brushes and paints to be creative. Anyone with a set of ears and eyes connected to an open mind can become a creative seller. All you need is the desire to learn and the willingness to try new things. And the personal motivation to practice them until they work for you.

Chapter 3
Selling A Basket Of Solutions

"The creative part of the sales process is finding new uses for the product."

Let's see how a creative sale actually gets made.

Remember, there are two kinds of salespeople, order processors and idea sellers. The first one serves a certain function in any business, but it's the second one that will make the business boom.

Who are idea sellers? Salespeople who size up a prospect's business and take them a proposal for a product or service to meet their needs. They plant the idea for the solution to a need in the prospect's mind even though the prospect may never have acknowledged that need to start with. By doing so, the idea seller creates demand for his or her products.

Here's an example: Let's say the prospect is an insurance agency and you, the idea seller, have a small business making gift baskets—those elaborate assortments of gourmet foods, trinkets, and colorful goodies that solve a lot of gift-giving problems. As a real idea seller, you will take a look at the insurance agency and think up ways they could use gift baskets to sell more insurance. They could buy a basket every week to award the agency's top producer, for example, or send a basket to every new client as a way to say thanks. Maybe they could reward clients who go three years without a claim or send a gift basket to prospective customers as a door opener. In other words, there are lots and lots of ways the insurance agency could use gift baskets.

But if no one suggests it, the insurance agency probably would never think of it themselves. That's where the idea seller steps in. You pitch one of these ways the agency could use the product and gives them a specific proposal (how many—of what—at what cost) on which to act. That's idea selling in a nutshell. It's very creative.

Gift basket makers are generally very creative people, so they should be very good at this. The key is to put some of the same wonderful creativity that goes into designing baskets into ways that your prospective customers can use them. I'm sure you noticed that the "ideas" mentioned for the insurance agency aren't different types of gift baskets—they're different applications for the gift basket product. It's conceivable, in fact, that the same gift basket design could be used in all four—or more—ways mentioned above. The creative part of the sales process is in finding new uses for the product.

How do you find ideas?

Brainstorming is the best way I know of to come up with new ideas. In this case, you'd start by making a list of every way that every customer you've ever had used a gift basket. Make that list as long as possible, because, when you're brainstorming, quantity comes before quality.

Next, review the ideas and combine or extend them, creating new ideas. Again, don't be judgmental. It's not time to throw out bad ideas. This combining and extending process should add ideas to your list, not remove them.

Now that you've come up with the ideas, pick one and pitch it. That's right, pick one—any one. It doesn't matter which idea you choose as long as you know your company can deliver it. You can't choose one based on your knowledge of the customer's likes and dislikes because you haven't met the prospect—so just pick one and go with it.

There is one final check to make before preparing the presentation of your idea: See if you can clearly express your idea in a sentence or two. Try to say it aloud without taking a breath. If you can't, re-examine the idea to see if it's too complicated. Overwhelming a prospect with a proposal that you can't explain in simple terms is a sure way to lose a follow-up call.

Learning While You Sell

Now make your pitch. At every opportunity, stop and ask the insurance agency decision-maker for feedback in a way that draws out information you can use to better shape this and subsequent proposals. Begin with a brief explanation of what your gift basket idea is designed to accomplish: promote customer retention, reward employee performance, open the doors to new markets, or one of the many other needs your unique product can fulfill. Then ask a question like

- Is that a goal for your business?
- Does that sound like something you'd want to do?
- Are we going in the right direction?

If the prospect says "yes," proceed with your pitch as planned. But if they say "no," pause and ask the good salesperson's favorite question, "why?" Odds are that the prospect will tell you what needs he or she really has, in which case you can change the rest of your presentation to address them. The most important thing you can do at this point (and every other) is to listen to what they're saying and make sure you fully understand it before plunging ahead with the pitch.

Then show them your sample basket and explain how it will meet the needs you've just discussed. Go into some detail about the contents, decoration, and design, and try to relate each item to what the prospect wants to accomplish. Whenever possible, ask a question:

- Isn't that appealing?

- Does it make sense to include __________?
- Do you think this will accomplish your goal?

Again, if the answers are positive, you can proceed. If not, probe more deeply to find out what the prospect would like to see changed. Remember, the design you've brought in may be the best one you've ever done, but it's only wonderful if *this* prospect buys it. If the customer wants it different, make it different!

On-The-Spot Response

But watch out for the impulse to "go back to the drawing board" when the prospect throws you a curve. Inside, you're dealing with your own desire to get out of a stressful situation when the prospect says that he or she has a need you haven't anticipated or wants a different design element in the basket you're offering. You'll want to retreat and regroup and come back another time with a different proposal, but resist the temptation. You are a professional, you know your product inside and out, so be ready to make changes!

Only after the prospect agrees that your gift basket program will meet his or her needs are you ready to bring up the subject of price and ask for the order. If you never get agreement on your product's ability to satisfy the prospect's needs, the price won't make any difference, so don't rush into it. Ask your questions, really listen to the answers, then ask the prospect to buy.

Creative sellers with open minds have an endless market for their gift baskets or anything else. Some of us, though, actually have lots of ideas but are hesitant to use them because we're afraid they won't be good enough. The problem with that kind of thinking is that it puts the onus of judgment on the wrong person. The salesperson shouldn't judge the merits of an idea—leave that to the prospect. If the customer thinks it's good—it's good! Put your idea in front of him or her using the best presentation skills you have, and let the prospect make the final judgment.

You'll be surprised how often they decide they like your bright idea.

Chapter 4
Sell On The First Call

"Most prospects expect the seller to have done their homework before they come in the door."

One of the great myths about selling is that you need to make a series of calls on a prospect to determine their needs before you can make a proposal to them. If you're selling anything less complicated than enterprise computing systems, this is time-wasting nonsense based on a misunderstanding of consultive selling. Why wait? You'll speed up the prospect's decision-making process and save yourself hours and hours of selling time (which you can use to make more sales) if you present a specific proposal on your very first call.

This suggestion invariably sends traditional consultive sellers into convulsions and they say things like, "How can you make a proposal without ascertaining the need?" "Won't the prospect think you're arrogant to come in with a proposal the very first time you meet them?" "What if your proposal is wrong?"

This response comes from a lack of understanding of my method. You'll notice that I want you to make a proposal on the first call—but that doesn't necessarily mean that that call will be the first time you've visited the prospect. Nor does it mean that you haven't done a needs analysis. In fact, the time and effort you put into needs analysis (before the first call) will dwarf that of a typical consultive seller who goes into the first call with questionnaire in hand. And your needs analysis will be more accurate, which will mean a more accurately targeted proposal.

Selling on the first call isn't as simple as it sounds, of course. It's not a matter of taking the same product to as many prospects as possible in hopes that you'll stumble across someone that needs to buy something today. Nor does it mean that you ignore the prospect's individual needs and try to sell them a one-size-fits-all product. To make a sale on the first call, you need to research the prospect in advance, ask probing questions during your presentation, and be ready to change your design or other elements of your proposal—on the spot. It takes preparation and a set of ears finely tuned to what the customer is saying.

Consultive selling, about which shelves full of books have been written and decades' worth of seminars presented, is based on the principle that you need to understand the prospect's needs before you can make a sale. Nothing wrong with that. But some practitioners of the approach believe the first step is to set up a meeting to ask the prospective customer a series of questions, the ever-popular "needs analysis" call. By answering those questions, the theory goes, the customer will tell you what they need or want to buy. Then you can come back with a proposal on the next call. There's certainly nothing wrong with the intentions of that approach, but in my experience it seldom works out quite so neatly.

The Truth About Consultive Selling

For one thing, few prospects will give you the time to answer your questions unless they're already interested in your product, which sounds good until you realize that making presentations only to those people means you've eliminated a large group of prospects who won't give you the first appointment. I'll grant that pre-qualifying prospects this way may be a good time management method, but I can't help but believe that the "not interested" prospects could be a very valuable source of new business.

And that number grows every day because the "needs analysis" approach is hugely over-worked as more and more prospects refuse to invest *their* time in it. Business operators are bombarded with offers to study their financial needs, manufacturing systems, advertising plans, and insurance programs. "It's a valuable study without any obligation to buy" is an offer they've heard so many times that they've become immune to the pitch.

What can be even more discouraging is that, in many industries, the same prospect has undergone the consultive needs analysis multiple times with the same company because the vendor has such high turnover in its sales force. And they've gotten nothing in return except another proposal to buy which looks suspiciously like the last proposal they got from that company's previous salesperson. In other words, fewer and fewer prospects are falling for the "needs analysis" gambit.

But what about those who *do* let you in the door to answer your questions? While generalizations can be dangerous, I don't believe that they're going to give you the best, most accurate information on which to base your proposal. They wouldn't be seeing you unless they already had some pre-conceived notion of what they would like to buy from you. This, in turn, will tend to color the answers they give to your needs analysis questions. Not that the prospect would lie to you, it's just that when someone already knows the answer, they tend to interpret the question to fit it. And their interpretation of your question may not be the same as yours, with some possible confusion over the answer as a result.

And that's assuming they're fully cooperative to start with. What are the things you want to learn when you conduct the needs analysis? Most of the questionnaires I've seen can be boiled down to two questions: 1) How can the prospect best use my product and 2) How much money can they spend on it? The variations on the first question will get some fairly accurate answers, but the second will often generate purposefully wrong answers because most people are pretty sensitive about giving out financial information to perfect strangers.

And that's what you are, after all—a stranger. Since this is the first call on the prospect, by definition you don't know them and, even more importantly, they don't know you. All the prospect knows is that you're there to get something from him (information and time) and he'll get something in return (a proposal) sometime in the future. You should look on every sales call as a transaction in which items of value change hands. Even if a sale doesn't occur, information changes hands—and that's an item of value. In a solid transaction, items of equal perceived value are exchanged in a two-way process. On the consultive sell first call, though, the prospect gets nothing of value in return for his or her time and cooperation.

I worked with a furniture store in Texas whose owner told me the story of how her local newspaper advertising department came to do a needs analysis for her. She was a big advertiser with them already, but the rep told her they could do an even better job for her store if their team could spend some time with her studying the situation. Sounds good, doesn't it?

The newspaper's team consisted of the ad sales rep, the retail ad sales manager, a layout artist, and two other people whose functions were never completely clear. Their "study" consisted of the ad manager asking a series of questions about who her target customer was and which were her busiest months. While he and the sales rep were asking the questions, the other three team members wandered around the store. When the questions had all been asked and the answers dutifully written down, the team left, promising a report within a week.

This needs analysis interview took up two hours of my client's time. The "report" she got back consisted of a proposal for doubling her space contract for the next year, delivered to her by her sales rep. She never did find out what the people wandering around the store were looking for.

The point of the story isn't that this needs analysis process was poorly handled, it's that this is a fairly typical *perception* of the process by most of your prospects. They've either had this happen to them or know someone who has, so they are very hesitant to give you the time to conduct your needs analysis "study."

Prospect Priorities

In the Creative Selling System first call, the seller "pays" for the prospect's time with an idea. And ideas are valuable.

What you get for your payment is information about the prospect. That information comes in the form of responses to your proposal—not as answers to your direct questions. Since the responses are spontaneous and voluntary, they're generally more accurate than answers to questions. For the same reasons, the prospect will often give you a greater amount of information because they're not limited by the specific subject of your question.

If you're in business-to-business sales, you know where you and your product generally rank on the list of priorities of most prospects. It's usually way down there near the bottom of the list simply because a business operator or manager has so many situations clamoring for their attention every day.

Start with personnel (the biggest headache of all) and all the issues that go with it: hiring, firing, motivating, compensating, absenteeism, benefits, training, and on and on. Then there is the cost of goods if the business is a retail establishment or the cost of materials if it's a manufacturer. These contribute directly to the profit margins, which are thin and getting thinner in most businesses today. There's the "infrastructure" of the business—

overhead items like rent, utilities, computer systems, debt service, and insurance. There are partners and shareholders to deal with, not to mention the most important of all, the customers. And then there's that old bugaboo: taxes in all their myriad forms.

With all these matters weighing on the prospect's mind, is it any wonder that it's tough to get an appointment—especially one to ask a bunch of questions?

It's even tougher when you factor in the competition—other salespeople. And I'm not just talking about your direct competitors. I'm referring to the army of salespeople peddling items and services that deal with all the above issues. Vendors, manufacturer's reps, insurance agents; the list is endless. They all want a few minutes of the prospect's time every day. If the prospect saw them all, they'd never get anything else done. If you want an appointment, you have to break through the clutter. You should pay the prospect for his time, not expect him to pay you.

These days most prospects expect the seller to have done their homework before they come in the door. They barely have time to do their own jobs, much less educate every salesperson who wants to sell them something. So, do the research first, then come up with a product or service that will meet the needs you think the prospect might have. Now, instead of calling the prospect and asking for some of their valuable time to educate you, you can offer to give them something of value—an idea to help their business in some way. Approached that way, the prospect is much more likely to give you a few minutes to make your pitch.

Chapter 5
Prospect Knowledge

"The more you know about your prospects, the more sales you'll close."

I'm sure you get the message: make an idea-based proposal on the first call. Back to the question at hand, though, which is how do you come up with an idea without doing a needs analysis? You don't, of course. What the creative seller does is invest some time and energy into research about the prospect's potential needs using every available resource *except* a first call questionnaire. I suggest that you ask yourself a series of questions about the prospect and see if you can get the answers from any of the many available sources. Believe it or not, you can learn just about everything you need to know, including who makes the decisions, what needs does the prospect probably have, and even how big their budget is without directly asking them. And you can do it in advance so that your first call proposal will seem perfectly reasonable to them.

I like to build a file for each prospect that contains everything I can find that pertains to their business. That file doesn't have to only contain items related to your product or service, either. It should cover anything you can find about the prospect's business, his market, and his customers. It should be very wide in scope because you never know where an idea is going to come from. And the information should always be gathered as if you were the prospect himself. You want to know what he wants to know. Ideally, you'll learn to think like him or her.

There are three basic things you need to know about your prospects. The first two, who makes the decision and why do they buy, I'll talk about now. The third, how much money can they spend, will be covered in the next chapter.If you know these three things, you can open doors to new accounts, increase sales to existing ones, and grow your income accordingly.

Who Decides?

When someone walks into your store or calls to place an order, you're *sometimes* dealing with the decision maker. Often, though, that person is simply carrying out the instructions of the real buyer. The sales manager's secretary who orders "Top Producer" awards from a trophy store, for example, may decide what kind of plaque to buy, but the decision to make the purchase in the first place was made by the manager. If you want to sell more, you have to persuade that person—the original decision maker—to buy them.

To sell completely new accounts, of course, you absolutely have to find the person who can say "yes." When you approach a new potential customer on your own initiative, it's very easy to get stuck dealing with an underling who may or may not be able to give you an order. You need to at least try to see the prime decision maker when you make your first contact. So how do you know who they are?

One way to find out, of course, is to ask. Before you knock on the door with a presentation, call the company and ask for the name of the president, the marketing director, the human resources manager, or whomever you think is most likely to be the person who controls the budget you want to tap. You can also find names on company websites or from services like Dun & Bradstreet. Their reports not only provide data like address and phone numbers, but also whether you are dealing with a headquarters location. Facts you can use include the number of employees nationwide and locally as well as annual sales, both of which can help you estimate how much potential the account has. You'll also find the names of various executives, a.k.a. decision makers. One nifty feature allows you to store this company's name online in a tracking folder and be notified of changes.

To carry your sleuthing a step further, type the executive's name into Google. Do the same with the company name itself. If they've been in the news, you might learn that they're just announced a new product that your product or service could help their sales force introduce. Or you might find that they're active with a church, youth activities, or a local non-profit, which gives you a way to open the door by offering to support their favorite cause. Other places to check include your local newspaper's website, which often contains a search feature that will pull up past stories about your prospect from their archives.

Why Do They Buy?

Who they are is only part of the story. Why they buy (or might buy) is the other half. You can always ask them, of course, once you've gotten in their front door. But having that information when you knock on the door will make it open a lot easier because you can tell them you've got something to help them with a certain specific area of concern when you call to ask for the appointment. Instead of calling to say, "I'd like to meet with you to show you our line," you can say "I'd like to show you a product that will help improve your employee's morale." If you were on the other end of the phone, which one would you rather meet?

A good place to start is with a little background reading about the issues facing your prospect's industry. If one widget maker has a problem, his competitor often has the same one. Industry trade publications are excellent sources and there seems to be at least one for every type of business in the world. The Tradewriter's Resource Center (tradewriter.freeservers.com)

lists 25 magazines serving the financial industry, for example. Since many of those magazines offer at least some of their editorial content online for free, you can quickly check a title for hints about what's on the decision maker's mind when they go to their office in the morning.

Another good place to look are trade association websites. Like trade magazines, nearly every kind of business has one—or more. A trade association often has information about the issues their members are facing and may also offer statistics like industry sales trends that are extremely useful in planning your sales presentation.

If you want to know the dollar volume of the prospect's market, visit the US Census Bureau. They publish the census of retail trade, wholesale trade, manufacturing, and agriculture with data gathered every five years. It's available by SIC code and broken down into county and even three-digit zip cells, which can give you a pretty accurate estimate of the size of the prospect's market. It's a good starting place and it's free.

This kind of prospect research can seem aimless and enormously time consuming, and it can be unless you know what you're looking for. What you want to know is whether there are any problems (or opportunities) facing your prospect's industry that you can help solve by selling them your products or services. Do businesses like your prospect's need to work on customer retention because account turnover is a problem in their industry? Are there new competitors entering their market trying to weaken their customer base? Do they need to acquire new customers for growth? How about employee morale problems? If industry productivity is slipping, they may want to encourage higher production with employee awards. If employee turnover (which cuts into profitability) is a factor, your product might help reduce it.

Information And How To Use It

Researching an entire business category is actually a very efficient way to gain and use prospect knowledge. Once you've learned that the widget makers of America are competing with a flood of imported widgets, for example, you can devise a proposal they can give them a tool to combat it. When you offer that same program to all the widget makers in your area, you've spread the time invested in the original research over numerous potential accounts. For a list of prospects for your program, just look in the Yellow Pages under "widget makers."

You can often find other useful information by taking a little drive around the market, checking out the relative size of the prospect's and competitors' locations. Count the number of cars in the parking lots. Take a tour if they offer one. If your prospect is a retailer, stroll through the store and mentally count the number of employees. See which of your competitor's products you see on the shelves or which of their delivery trucks you see at the loading dock. You don't have to be 100 percent accurate, but you'd be surprised at how much information you can gather just by keeping your eyes and ears open.

Regardless of the type of business the prospect operates, ultimately they sell something to someone. While you're out and about, observe the prospect's customers if you can, since that is the next general area for research. You should find out who their customers are, why they buy this type of product or service, what steps they take in the decision-making process, what alternative sources of need satisfaction do they have, how long is the buying cycle, etc.

Once again, securing this information is mostly a matter of common sense and a little time. When appropriate, do a little "mother-in-law" research, which consists of informally surveying your friends and relatives about their impressions of the prospect and his competitors. Look at the prospect's advertising. Who are they trying to reach? What appeals are they making?

Even if this information isn't directly related to the product or service you're selling, it's important information to the prospect so it should be important to *you*. It's the kind of information that they use directly or indirectly as a basis for their purchasing decisions.

For you, it's all useful information that will help you shape your proposal without bothering the prospect with a "needs analysis." You'll use this information in a number of ways, not the least of which is pre-qualifying the prospect. You'll also use it to conduct what I call a one-person brainstorm, which is the process of translating the information you've gained into a set of goals for the prospect to achieve through purchase of the idea you present to them.

Prospect knowledge doesn't come without a price—usually time. It's a solid investment, though, and will save you time in the long run by helping you better qualify your prospects, reach the real decision makers, and make better, more customer-need-focused presentations. The more you know about your prospects, the more sales you'll close.

Chapter 6
How Much Can They Spend?

"You'll be working smarter, not harder, when you estimate how much the prospect is worth before you call on them."

The first question I hear when I start explaining how to estimate a prospect's budget is, why estimate when I can just ask them? There are several reasons, some pretty apparent and some not so obvious. The simplest reason is that you want to make a sales pitch on your very first call on a new account so you *can't* ask beforehand.

The second reason, though, is just as compelling. As I said before, most new prospects are less than eager to talk about their money with someone they've just met for the first time. I've also found that when they do give you a figure, it may or may not be accurate—either on purpose or accidentally.

Potential Vs. Budget

Most importantly, though, what matters isn't how much money the client *currently* spends—it's how much they could *potentially* spend. Many businesses significantly under-spend in certain product and service categories. This is at least partly due to salespeople who concentrate on getting their share of the status quo rather than on creating new dollars by presenting new ideas to the prospect. In my experience, if you give a client a good reason to spend more, they will, whether it's "in the budget" or not. That's why you estimate their *potential* spending—not just their current budget.

Estimating the potential gives you a target to aim for—a tangible "real money" target that serves as a compelling reason for you to invest your time in this client. The estimate will help you shape the scope of your proposal in terms of both total dollars and value to be offered. And an accurate, well-founded estimate also gives you a mental starting point for future negotiations.

So what happens if your estimate is wrong? After all, you're really just preparing an educated guess—and guesses can be off the mark. Let's look at the two possibilities: estimates that are too low and those that are too high.

Estimating Too Low

If you estimate too low, you might leave some money on the table. Your competitors have a chance to lay their hands on it and that's obviously not good. But there are some other, not so obvious dangers to estimating too low. You also may inadvertently insult the prospect by bringing them a proposal that's beneath their consideration. You'd be surprised at how often this happens. Or you try to pitch the top decision-maker only to discover that your proposal is so small that it gets delegated to a lower-level subordinate.

When you believe the client doesn't have much potential, you also tend to price your product lower than its true value in order to make it more affordable. A combination of these factors leads to the biggest problem with under-estimating, which is that you sell the client too little and the satisfactions they get from your product or service are just that—too little. Don't estimate too low—you're not playing it safe, you're just playing it cheap.

Estimating Too High

How about estimating too high? Are there any dangers there? Yes, but fewer than you think. There is always an outside possibility that you can make a proposal so big that it scares the prospect away. Believe it or not, this happens so rarely that it's not a real consideration except in very extreme circumstances. The biggest danger of estimating too high is that you spend too much of your valuable time on a client who doesn't warrant it. But that's a time management problem that's quickly and easily corrected once you make your first call on the prospect.

One of the biggest "sell-in" problems I face when coaching salespeople in my training programs is the widespread fear of pitching a proposal that's too high. I remember Jerry, an advertising salesperson I was working with in Michigan, who just couldn't believe that any of his prospects could spend more than $10,000 annually. Since he believed that, of course, that's the maximum amount he would ever propose—and his prediction became a self-fulfilling prophecy.

In my training programs, I usually work with the salesperson on specific prospective accounts they've chosen. Jerry had targeted a local dairy for this work. I didn't know much about the prospect, so I did some quick and dirty research. Jerry and I walked through a couple of the grocery stores in town and checked the dairy case, where we saw that his prospect had about half of the facings! I did a little quick math, estimating the dollar volume of the diary's products sold based on the number of stores in the market, my guesstimate of the wholesale value of the product, and its share of the facings in the stores.

This process gave us a potential advertising budget for the dairy of $60,000 annually. When I told Jerry that he should make a proposal for that amount, he turned pale and staggered as though he were going to faint.

"He'll kill me," Jerry said. "I couldn't ask him for that much money. He'll think I'm a crook." I couldn't figure out what Jerry's honesty (or lack thereof) had to do with the size of the proposal, but the fact he said it certainly reflected on his state of mind. Since Jerry didn't believe that this (or any) prospect could spend more than $10,000, he thought he would be talking them into something that wasn't financially healthy if he proposed more than that amount. And that the prospect would get mad if he tried. This raises all sorts of questions about Jerry's prospect knowledge, faith in his own product, and other issues of course, but I won't go into that here.

"Our estimate might be off, but not by much," I said. "Besides, what do we have to lose?"

Against his better judgment, Jerry put together an idea-based proposal for $60,000. Since he was actually physically afraid to make the presentation by himself, I went with him—but only as an observer. Jerry overcame his fear and made a good presentation until he got to the point where he was supposed to ask for the $60,000. He froze and couldn't say anything.

The dairy owner looked at the amount of money on the page and did some quick calculating in his head. Jerry started to squirm in his seat next to me, so I put my hand on his arm. Finally, the prospect spoke.

"This is about what I spend on *all* my advertising and promotion, Jerry," he said. "I'm not really comfortable putting all my eggs in one basket, which is what I'd be doing if I bought your plan. Could I schedule your ads every other week? Would that cut my costs in half?"

Jerry was still paralyzed, so I answered with a resounding "yes" for him. Then I thanked the dairy owner for his business, took Jerry by the arm, and led him out to the car. He had just made a sale three times larger than any he had previously closed. Jerry became a believer in the worth of estimating a prospect's potential *before* making the first proposal.

Estimating Methods

The best way to avoid the dangers of estimating too high or too low, of course, is to prepare an accurate estimate in the first place. I recommend that you use two or more methods and then compare the results to improve your accuracy. The methods I use most often center on first estimating the prospect's gross sales, then applying an expense-to-sales ratio to determine the spending potential.

So how do you estimate the prospect's gross annual sales? You can use several sources. One of my favorites is the US Census Bureau, which I mentioned before. Every five years, the Census Bureau conducts a census of retail trade and one of service industries, as well as the census of agriculture, wholesale trade, manufacturing, etc. You can get data from the most recent census at your public library or from the census bureau's web site (census.gov). The data available includes annual sales, number of establishments, and number of employees for literally hundreds of business categories. What's more, it's available for every county in the United States—so you can retrieve the actual sales for your prospect's market within a five-year time frame.

Let's look at an example of some Census of Retail Trade data and use it to prepare an estimate using three different methods. Assume your prospect is a retail garden shop with one location. According to the Census of Retail Trade in the county I arbitrarily selected, there are 14 retail nurseries and lawn and garden shops with collective annual sales of $10,660,000. As a group, they have 76 employees.

Given these three figures, you can estimate your prospect's sales three different ways. First, you can make an educated guess as to their market share based on the size of their store relative to the other stores in the county. You may need to do a little driving to find out how big the stores are, but it's not rocket science. Just go to the stores, casually pace off the width and length of the sales areas to estimate their square footage, then calculate your prospect's share of the total. That will give you a rough approximation of their share of the market. If your survey of the 14 stores leads you to believe that the prospect garners a 20 percent share of the market, their annual sales would be a little more than $2 million. $10,660,000 times 20% = $2,132,000

Another way is to calculate the average sales in this category, which simply means dividing the sales by the number of stores. This method yields an average annual sales figure of $761,000. You then adjust that figure up or down, again depending on whether the prospect's store is larger or smaller than the others in the market. If your view of the 14 competitors' stores shows that the prospect's location is 50 percent bigger than the average, you would estimate their sales at slightly more than $1 million. $761,000 plus 50 percent equals $1,141,500).

The third method is to calculate the sales per employee ($10,660,000 divided by 76), then multiply it by the number of employees in the prospect's store. Again, you can get a quick and dirty count of the prospect's work force by strolling through the store and keeping your eyes open. In this example, that works out to $140,000 per employee in the category. If your prospect has 20 full-time employees—or their equivalent in part timers—you would estimate annual sales of $2,805,000.

If you're dealing with a multiple store prospect, don't forget to adjust your figures by multiplying the per-location estimate by the number of outlets. And I'm sure you've noticed that each method requires you to be familiar with the prospect's store—and their competition. Some reconnaissance before you make that first proposal is always a good idea when preparing for a new client. In fact, you can't make an accurate estimate using any method without it!

These three methods yielded a range of estimated annual sales from $1,141,000 to $2,805,000. Averaging the three numbers gives you a pretty safe bet of $2,026,000.

Remember, you're not planning manned space flight here. You're just trying to determine the size of the ballpark your prospect plays in. You want to come up with an estimate of their spending potential that will be realistic to them: not too high, not too low, but in a range they will be comfortable talking about.

Once you've estimated the sales, use one of the readily available compilations of expense-to-sales ratios to calculate the prospect's potential budget. Of particular interest is the Small Business Administration's web site (sba.gov), which is full of practical if dry information about all sorts of businesses. There are several studies available at most public libraries or from various trade associations such as the National Auto Dealers' Association. They will break down expense categories for types of businesses—sometimes for geographic regions—and calculate the ratios you need. They'll tell you things like the average retail garden shop spends 4.3 percent of its annual sales on advertising and promotion. Or that liability insurance costs for a widget manufacturer are 1.5 percent of gross sales. If you don't have such a source for your particular product or service category, do some rough calculations yourself using information you know about your current accounts.

Using The Estimate

So, now you have an estimate of the prospect's potential—how do you use it? First, use it to shape your proposal. The estimate of total potential spending gives you a sense of the dollars you can go for, the value of the components you can build into your plan, even the length of contract to propose. You should also use the estimate to allocate your time to the prospect.

As I've said many times, I suggest you make a specific proposal on your first call on the client. The fact that you've invested your time into researching the prospect makes a great first impression—and the information you'll gain in response to your proposal will be accurate and highly applicable to meeting the client's needs on subsequent calls. You'll also be surprised at how often the prospect's response to your proposal will confirm your estimate of their spending potential.

One major point to keep in mind: don't go through your estimating methodology with the prospect! Your estimate is simply a tool for your use in preparing for the initial call on a new prospect. It's not a reason for them to give you an order. Focus your presentation on the benefits of your idea to the client—not on how you came up with the dollar amount of the proposal. Remember, the prospect is buying your proposal, not your methodology.

Preparing an estimate of the prospect's potential spending is homework that will pay off for you in the long run. You'll be working smarter, not harder, when you take the small amount of time necessary to estimate how much the prospect is worth before you start calling on them.

Chapter 7
Uncovering Prospect Needs

"Invest a few minutes in a one-person brainstorm."

But what about the idea part? How do you answer that other question, "How can the client use my product or service?" without first calling on them to find out? Now is the time to invest a few minutes in a one-person brainstorm. First organize the information you've gathered about the prospect's business—who their customers are, what areas do they serve, what's the competition like, and so on, into a series of about six subjects. As an example, here are the general topics I use when preparing a marketing proposal for a prospective client:

1. Who is their best customer?
2. What is the frequency of the best customer's buying cycle?
3. How complex is the buying decision?
4. Does the best customer have alternative sources for need satisfaction?
5. What is the market position of the prospect and each of the top three competitors?
6. What apparent special problems does the prospect face?

In this example, the service you are selling deals with the marketing of their business. Your product may involve a step in the manufacturing process or a service that improves their back office operations. Whatever your field, you can draw up a list of five or six typical subjects applicable to your product or service that are pertinent to almost all prospects. In the Creative

Selling System, you answer these questions yourself—as best you can—using the information gathered during your reconnaissance visits and research. You also apply a great deal of common sense and a little "mother-in-law research" as you go.

As a first step, let's assume you want to sell them a marketing plan and work through some answers to these questions for your garden supply store prospect.

1. Who is their best customer? Note that you're looking for your prospect's "best" customer, not their average one. As you know, the 80/20 rule is highly accurate in most businesses. You're interested in the 20 percent of the customer base who provides 80 percent of the retailer's sales. In the example, you would first say that the best customer is a homeowner, since apartment dwellers and renters seldom spend a lot on landscaping. You would also assume that a slight majority of those customers are women. This assumption may not be politically correct, but if you stand in a garden supply store for any length of time, you'll find that it's probably true. This woman homeowner is probably also a physically active person who enjoys the outdoors—attributes dictated by the type of product being sold. Since she's a homeowner, she's also probably age 30+, since that's when most American's buy their first home.

2. What is the frequency of the buying cycle? Again, common sense tells you that the nature of the products sold means heavy buying in the spring (with maybe weekly store visits) and a tapering off in the heat of the summer. There is probably also a slight up-tick in store traffic in the fall, when bulbs and trees traditionally get planted. Even the best customer probably doesn't spend much at the garden store in January. This is mostly common sense. You might be able to verify it, though, by a visit to a garden and nursery industry trade association web site or some other source.

3. How complex is the buying decision? Is the customer going to spend a lot of time shopping and making a series of decisions as in car buying, or make spur-of-the-moment decisions about where to buy like you do when you need milk for the kids? Your garden store's best customer is probably a picky customer who will shop around for quality, selection, and price (in that order) but will make plenty of impulsive point of sale purchases. Ask your friends or your Aunt Bertha how and where they shop for garden supplies if you're not a gardener yourself. This is what I call "mother-in-law" research and the answers will be accurate enough for your purposes.

4. Does the customer have other sources for need satisfaction? Mail order, whether generated by a catalog or a web site, is probably another way (besides shopping at a competing store) that the customer can get what they want and need. So is shopping at a big box discount store, many of which carry garden lines during the season. Watch the ads in your local paper to get this information.

5. What are the market positions of the prospect and the top three direct competitors? I won't go through a lengthy explanation of the full theory of positioning here, just suffice it to say that each competitor in a category occupies one marketing position in each consumer's mind. Positions are those qualities that influence the consumer's decision to choose one brand or store over another to satisfy a particular need. They are the consumer's perceptions of factors like price, selection, quality of merchandise, service, convenience, etc. Different factors are more or less important to different consumers, but the best customers I'm talking about generally will all put the same weight on one outstanding factor.

In the case of your garden shop, that one factor will probably be quality of merchandise, since the serious gardener knows that cheap plants are often inferior stock that won't yield the best results. Again, ask your Aunt Bertha. In this exercise, let's assume that Aunt Bertha tells you that your prospect is identified as the low-price leader in the category, with his top competitors occupying the selection, service, and quality positions respectively.

6. What apparent special problems or advantages does the prospect have? Location? Parking? Employee turnover? Has the business changed hands recently? This list can be endless but the basic question deals with factors that might influence the best customer's purchasing decision that aren't covered by the previous five questions. Yes, this is the "miscellaneous" category. And your source for the information is your own research and observations.

Identifying A Need

Now take the second step in your one-person brainstorm, identifying a need. Go back and take a look at the answers to each one of the six questions and ask yourself, "Does this information indicate a possible need or goal for the prospect that is related to my product?" You'll want to write down one goal for each question, which will give you six in total when you're finished.

Once again, let's continue with the garden shop example. Remember, you're selling a marketing program, so the goals you list will relate to that type of service.

1. Best customer: If the prospect's best customer is a physically active woman homeowner (see above for detail), one goal for the prospect's marketing plan would be to expand their market by attracting the husbands of those women. They may not be the decision makers, but they will be what I call a "decision influencer" in this purchasing decision. And if you can provide some sort of incentive for them to visit the prospect's garden shop, they'll likely bring their wives.

Possible Need: Attract husbands of best customers to shop.

2. *Buying cycle:* Peak season is spring, and you seldom want to try to substantially change consumer behavior of that sort. A goal might be to get the jump on the competition by bringing the best customer into the store in the pre-spring weeks, say in February and March. They'll then be more likely to come back to spend the big bucks at your prospect's store in April and May.

Possible Need: Build pre-spring store traffic.

3. *Buying decision complexity:* The best customer will shop several stores in search of the best quality plants and seeds, so a goal for your prospect would be to get on every best customer's list of must-visit destinations. With 14 different stores to choose from, the best customer probably won't go to all of them. You need to be sure your prospect's store isn't on the to-be-ignored list.

Possible Need: Become a must-visit for highest category spenders.

4. *Alternative need satisfaction:* Your prospect's best customer may spend a sizable portion of her gardening budget with mail order suppliers. This not only cuts into primary purchases, but reduces the number of impulse items that are sold in the store.

Possible Need: Attract mail-order customers to the store.

5. *Competitive positioning:* Your analysis led you to believe that your prospect's store owns the low-price position in the market—but the best customer is primarily concerned with quality of merchandise. One goal of your marketing proposal might then be to raise the perceived quality of your prospect's merchandise in the mind of the best customer.

Possible Need: Improve store's quality image.

6. *Miscellaneous factors:* Let's assume that your prospect's store is the most conveniently located in town. A goal for your marketing program might then be to exploit this competitive advantage and build store traffic.

Possible Need: Increase store visits by distant customers.

Using The Brainstorm Results

Now you have a list of six possible goals that the marketing service you're going to sell to the prospect might help accomplish. Note how the six goals you've outlined are not necessarily related to each other. In fact, they could be mutually exclusive. This is brainstorming, where each thought needs to be put on the table first and then explored on its own merits.

You'll also notice that these are pretty specific needs. The less generic they are, the stronger the statement they make when presented. Try to avoid buzz words and general benefits like "increase store traffic" or "slice manufacturing costs" when you're framing your goals. Specificity should be the rule. Try to make the needs more specific as in "increase store traffic from senior customers on Tuesdays" or "slice the 32-ounce widget component cost in half" instead.

Notice also how the needs aren't the idea. At this stage, you don't think in terms of a solution to the need, you simply want to clearly identify the need itself. There's a huge temptation to stop the process when an idea pops into your head, but I strongly suggest you go ahead and complete the list of six goals. You're going to use them later in your relationship with the prospect and the greatest value of any brainstorming process comes from the volume of thoughts produced. Make it a rule to have a minimum of six available to you at this stage of the creative selling process.

What do you do with the six needs? Pick one (and only one) which you feel would be most important to the prospect. You're going to be guessing here since you haven't even met them yet, but your guess is based on some strong research and much thought, so go with your instincts. As you'll see as we work through the rest of the process, you can't really pick a *wrong* goal, so choose the one you feel strongest about. That single prospect need will be the basis for the idea you're going to propose. You'll use the other five for subsequent proposals to the client if you need them, so don't throw away your notes!

Chapter 8
Ideas To Sell

"You'll never grow bored with your job because you'll be putting something new into it every day."

Now you're ready for the next step in the Creative Selling System. Step one was acquiring some knowledge about the client. Once you've learned about the basics of the client's business, you went on to step two, identifying a potential client need to be satisfied. The third step is when you come up with an idea that satisfies that need. I'm careful to point out the three separate steps because one of the biggest temptations you'll face as a creative seller is to come up with the idea first, then go pitch it. But if the idea is not connected to a need, you're going to be wrong a lot of the time. If you'll just do the first two steps—identify customer needs and come up with a goal—before you take the third step, you'll find that your ideas are a lot more accurate and much more attractive to the prospect.

This is the process of "ideation." Creative sellers have an endless requirement for ideas to sell. If you open your mind, you'll find lots of them. But most people don't consider themselves "creative" enough to come up with good ideas. Their minds seems to just stop working when someone asks them for an idea. It's sad how many people really believe that they have to get ideas from sources other than their own heads.

On the other hand, some people actually have lots of ideas, but are hesitant to use them because they're afraid they won't be good enough. They don't offer their ideas, so they never get any positive feedback about them, and since they don't get any feedback, they don't offer their ideas. The loop is closed.

The problem with that kind of thinking is that it puts the onus of judgment on the wrong person. The salesperson shouldn't judge the merits of an idea—leave that to the prospect. If the customer thinks it's good—it's good! Put the idea in front of them using the best presentation skills you have and let the prospect make the final judgment.

Stop worrying about being "wrong" and start taking a few chances in life. If one prospect doesn't like the idea, take the same idea to the next prospect. "Bad ideas" are just ideas that haven't been sold yet, so keep pitching them. Like any good matchmaker, you'll eventually put the right prospect with the right idea.

Continual Brainstorming

To come up with ideas to sell you need to practice continual brainstorming. You've probably been in brainstorming meetings with your management and other salespeople. The creative selling brainstorming techniques are the same ones you'd use in a group meeting but you use them on an individual level. It's great to participate in group sessions, but you can't rely on them alone to generate the large number of ideas you'll need as a creative seller.

The first step is to write down the need you picked from your research into the prospect's business. On the page below it, make a list of possible ways your company's products or services could help the prospect reach that goal. And follow these ground rules of successful brainstorming as you're writing down those ideas.

1. There's no such thing as a bad idea. Write it down even if it's impossible. Especially write it down if anyone in the room says "We've never done that before." Reserve judgment until later.

2. See how outrageous you can be. Free-associate and put it down on paper. The wilder the idea, the better. Crazy ideas spark more ideas—mundane ones are dead ends.

3. Fill the page—then start another one. Quantity is your goal because the more ideas you list, the better the odds of finding a good one.

4. Don't stop when you come to the "right" idea. There could well be a better one waiting to come out.

You don't have to have a group of people to brainstorm, either. You can do it by yourself if you just open your mind and let it create.

Step two is to review the ideas and combine or extend them, creating new ideas through the interplay of the elements of other ideas. Again, don't be judgmental. It's not yet time to throw out bad ideas. This combining and extending process should add ideas to your list of possibilities, not remove them. As you're doing it, you'll probably come up with some entirely new ideas, too.

There are several ways to stimulate your brainstorm production. Look internally to see if there are any company-generated solutions that could possibly apply. Many companies package their products or create bundles of services that are designed to meet the needs of certain categories of customers. You certainly don't want to ignore those. The only caution is to be sure the pre-packaged offering exactly fits your prospect's particular goal. You may need to "tweak" the package to make it work.

Another source is free association with non-related concepts. This is a fancy term for stealing the germ of an idea from someplace else. One of my associates who is in the marketing business will often monitor television commercials or thumb through magazine ads to see if there's a slogan or concept he can "borrow" to serve as the springboard for his own idea. He'll take a character like Kellogg's Tony the Tiger, for example, and see if he can create a version of it for his client. Maybe an animated cat named Karla the Kitten who purrs "You'rrre grrrand" when it's owner feeds it Brand X. Or he'll lay out a slogan like "You're in good hands with Allstate" and plug in his client's name and products to see if they fit. He may come up with, "You're in good form with Diet Rite." He's not exactly stealing the other person's idea, just using it to spark his own.

Another place to start this process is to examine past sales to like customers. Don't look at the dollars and cents or the unit volume. Look deeper and see if you can determine or surmise why the customer made that purchase. Talk to the salespeople who made the sale and pick their brains about the circumstances and events that led to it. The veterans in the sales department (and the managers, too) are usually full of stories about their many battles and victories. Next time you're subjected to a war story, see if you can detect the idea that sparked the battle instead of politely nodding through it. Sometimes a polite "Why?" will prompt the story teller to reveal it you.

Choose An Idea

You've come up with the possible ideas, now pick one and pitch it. That's right. Pick one—any one that opens a clear and direct path to satisfying the prospect's need. It doesn't matter which idea you choose as long as you know your company can deliver it when the prospect buys it. You can't choose one based on your knowledge of the customer's likes and dislikes because you haven't yet met the prospect. So just pick the one you feel most confident in presenting. Judge the idea strictly against its ability to achieve the desired goal, not by any non-relevant standards like whether it's ever been done before or whether the prospect has ever bought anything like this before. All you need to be concerned about is the idea's ability to accomplish the goal, your company's ability to execute the idea (deliver the product or service), and it's profitability to the prospect and your company.

There is one final reality check to make before you begin preparing your presentation. See if you can clearly express your idea in a sentence or two that you can say aloud without taking a breath. If you can't, re-examine the idea to see if it's too complicated to execute as well as to say. It also may be too confusing for the prospect to grasp at first sight. Remember, you're preparing for a first-call presentation where your goal is to make a strong and favorable first impression. In my experience, overwhelming a prospect with a mind-boggling proposal that you can't explain in simple terms is a sure way to get un-invited for a follow-up call.

Can you use this ideation process if you sell something less exciting like plumbing fixtures or insurance? Why not? Don't your prospective customers have needs related to growing sales, cutting costs, or employee morale? Of course they do, or your product or service line wouldn't exist in the first place. You just need to open your mind to the possibilities of selling creatively and try it.

The Secret Of The First Call

That's when you'll learn the real secret to creative selling. You see, your real goal on the first call is not necessarily to sell that first idea—it's to gather as much accurate information about the prospect as you can so subsequent ideas will hit the mark.

As you gather that information, though, you're also accomplishing several other things. You will make a strong first impression on the prospect by demonstrating your willingness to invest your time (not theirs) in a study of their needs. You will establish yourself as an idea resource for them. You will bring them something of value in return for their time so that they are likely to see you again. Above all, your idea will provoke a discussion about the prospect's needs, desires, goals, and opportunities. And it's through that discussion that you will learn what they will buy from you.

Stockpile Ideas

Remember all those "rejected" ideas you didn't choose? Just like the unused goals from the needs analysis step, save them for later. The presentation you're preparing is just the first of many that you'll be making to this prospect. The prospect may not buy your idea on the first call, so you'll need another one for the follow-up. Even if the sale does happen, you may want to have those ideas available for further development of the account through add-on sales or for contract extensions. Either way, you're going to need more ideas at a later date.

Another reason to keep all the unused needs and ideas on file is their value to you in working on other prospects. The creative selling process is very effort-intense. You'll invest a couple of hours of research and ideation in the proposal for a given prospect and it's much more profitable to amortize that investment over several prospects rather than just one. You probably have other potential customers who are in similar if not identical businesses as the first one. You'll find that their needs will be much the same, too. It's just one of the principles of good time management to get the most results from the amount of work expended.

Many sales departments have a central file of ideas that all the salespeople can use. The background research and needs analysis are available in that file, too. Every time an idea-based proposal is created, it goes into this file and the entire team can then draw on it (if it isn't bought by the first prospect). From the company's standpoint such a system creates a valuable asset for future growth. From the individual salesperson's perspective it saves them from duplicating efforts already made by others.

As you can imagine, there are plenty of methods for organizing and accessing this valuable resource. They can range from index cards to computerized databases. Even salespeople who work in relatively isolated territories can pool their ideas through cloud computing. No matter what form it takes, the keys to building this resource are volume and team work. Everyone has to pitch in or the major contributors will begin to feel unfairly treated and keep their research and ideas to themselves.

Your Motivation

Ideation has another benefit besides creating good customer relations. It keeps your job interesting. There's an old sales adage that says when you first start out, you're 90 percent enthusiasm and 10 percent knowledge. After you've sold for a while, it changes to 90 percent knowledge and 10 percent enthusiasm. That's because you do the same things over and over again, gaining the knowledge to do them better but losing enthusiasm for them through repetition over time.

If you're selling the same tank car load of the same solvent to the same customer at the same time year after year, it's hard for you to get very excited about the next sale (and can you even imagine the customer's excitement level?). But if you're constantly challenging yourself to come up with a new use for that solvent or a safer way to dispose of it or any other reason for the customer to buy more of it, your enthusiasm for both the product and the customer relationship is bound to go up. And so will the customer's.

Get out of the rut before the next truck comes along and grinds you down deeper into it. Become an idea seller. Learn the skills of ideation and practice them. You'll never grow bored with your job because you'll be putting something new into it every day.

Chapter 9
Price It In Writing

"Making a proposal too small is a common obstacle to sales success."

Now it's time to put your idea on paper. Yes, the sale will ultimately be made through an oral presentation, but expressing your idea in writing has a host of advantages. Writing a proposal is kind of like broccoli—you may not like it but you know it's good for you.

The very act of preparing a written presentation will help clarify the details of your concept in your mind. Many times the writing will reveal a hidden weakness in your idea that can be corrected before you pitch it to the prospect. Or it will change your thinking about which are the strongest points in your idea and lead you to re-order or re-structure the pitch to highlight them. In either case, the writing of the proposal serves as a form of rehearsal that will make you more familiar and comfortable with the idea you're going to be selling. This will increase your confidence in the idea and will result in a more forceful oral presentation.

The fact that you have prepared a written presentation can also in itself encourage the prospect to buy. One of my prospects said he knew which proposal to take seriously because those were the ones that came with a cover page. Writing takes time and effort, even in this day of word processing and presentation software. Most people hate to write almost as much as they dread speaking in front of groups—and your prospect will be no different. They'll recognize your investment in their proposal more readily when they see the written proof of the work you've put into it. The written presentation demonstrates to the prospect that you're willing to spend a great deal of your time and energy on their behalf. Also, as long as the presentation looks good, it will also convey the high level of your professionalism and your dedication to getting the details right. Incidentally, that's why you must go through the proofreading steps I'll be talking about later.

The written presentation will serve as the prospect's tangible reminder of your oral presentation after you leave. Very few of your prospects are going to give you a "yes" answer on your first call. They're going to want to "think about it" before they reach a decision. So, after you've tried all the tactics for overcoming a decision stall and leave, you want them to be able to refer to a persuasive outline of your proposal while they are doing their "thinking." That proposal needs to highlight the same things you'll be stressing in your oral presentation—the benefits of your idea.

During your oral pitch, your properly-structured written presentation will focus the prospect's thinking on the points you want them to see in the order in which you want them considered. The presentation will keep them from jumping to the price before they've seen the benefits. It will provide a visual link between the idea and the benefits of the idea. Above all, it will reinforce and lend greater credibility to the points you make orally. Many people still believe a written statement is more trustworthy than an oral one.

Finally, the written presentation serves as a script for you to follow during your oral presentation. You'll see how the two inter-relate when you get to the chapter on making the sales pitch, but suffice it to say that having that written presentation in front of you while you're talking will give you greater confidence and help you stay on track. It will free you from having to remember what comes next in your pitch. The written presentation will help you cover *all* the points you want to make. There are very few worse feelings in sales than remembering a key point you wanted to make—after the call is over and you're walking to your car.

Those are the advantages of developing a strong written presentation. So how do you go about it?

Presentation Elements

At the risk of sounding like your ninth grade English teacher, let's start by developing an outline of sorts. List the points you want to make in the presentation in the following format, which will make sure you persuade the prospect that 1) a need exists and 2) your proposal will satisfy it. As you might have guessed, the work you've already done in assessing needs and creating an idea are the beginning elements of the outline.

At the top of the page, put your prospect's name in nice, big letters. You should keep that in front of you at all times to insure you stay customer-focused.

The next item on the outline is the need you're trying to satisfy for the prospect. Once again, write it down in a sentence or two.

Next comes the idea you came up with to help the prospect achieve the goal. You've already done this step, so you're really just copying the work you did earlier.

Benefits vs. Features

Now list the benefits of the idea. In other words, if the prospect buys the proposal, what is it going to do for him? Here's a big hint: the first benefit will be to accomplish the prime goal you just wrote down. The rest of them will be related but lesser in importance. List three of these (okay, four if you've got them, but no more) in one sentence or sentence fragment each. These are bullet points, so they need to be concise yet self-explanatory.

Benefits are different from features, which is an important concept for every salesperson to keep in mind. A customer buys a product not to get the product itself, but to get the benefits that product provides. This holds true for everything you sell, whether it's a service like housekeeping (the customer doesn't hire your company, she hires the results—a clean home) or an intangible product such as life insurance (the client doesn't want a document full of legalese, he wants peace of mind). The same principle applies to retail selling as well. Unless the customer is a rather eccentric power tool collector, for example, he doesn't buy an electric drill just to have one, he buys it to get holes. To help determine whether an item on your list is a feature or a benefit, ask if it answers the question, "What's it going to do for me?"

Using the power drill buyer as an example, here are some phrases that demonstrate the difference:

(Feature) High horsepower motor - (Benefit) Drills faster with fewer binds.

(Feature) Large capacity chuck - (Benefit) Accepts larger bits to drill larger holes.

(Feature) Long battery life - (Benefit) Cuts work interruptions for battery change.

(Feature) Ergonomic design - (Benefit) Reduces fatigue and soreness.

A truly creative salesperson knows every feature of their product—but also what the customer gets from those features when they buy them. And that's what they talk about.

Critically read the benefits list you just made for your proposal. Are there any features on it? If so, you can turn them into benefits by asking, "What does this feature do for the customer?" You want to list the result, not the cause.

Now list the elements you need the prospect to buy in order to get these benefits. This is where you outline the package of products or services you're going to sell the prospect, along with any "behind the sale" actions that you or your company need to take to execute the idea. Think of this not just as a product description, but as a checklist for your use in delivering that product. If you're selling a marketing promotion that includes a contest, for example, some of the elements you'll need to execute the contest are entry blanks, prizes, and rules, as well as media to promote it, which entails ad production, media buying, and other similar items. If you're selling a piece of manufacturing software, you may need to provide an interface with the customer's computer system, training, manuals, installation, or other related items besides the software itself. Once again, these are just your notes, so make these bullet points rather than paragraphs. Just be sure you list *all* the potential elements you'll need.

Setting The Price

When you finish, it's time for the final element on the outline, which is the dollar value of your proposal. You'll obviously use the checklist of elements to price the package you're presenting using your company's prices for the various goods and services included. You'll also use whatever pricing latitude you have and follow whatever guidelines you normally use for negotiation, volume discounts, or special offers.

Now, here's where you use that estimate of customer potential you completed earlier. How does the price for your execution of the idea—including all the elements you just listed—compare with the customer potential estimate figure? If it exceeds it, you may have a problem. You'll need to rethink your idea to take it out of the realm of wishful thinking and put it back into the category of the possible. Remember, that's one of the main reasons for doing the estimate in the first place: to make sure you're presenting something the customer can afford.

But what if the price of the proposed idea is only a very small percentage of the total estimated potential? Same drill: rework or rethink the idea to bring it into line with the prospect's potential. My rule of thumb is to go for no less than 50 percent of the prospect's potential annual spending on your product or service category. In other words, build a proposal that's worth at least half of the dollars you came up with in the estimating stage.

You may want to propose a deal that's more or less than a year in length, of course, depending on the purchase cycle in your industry. Still, use the 50 percent goal as your base and adjust your proposal accordingly.

Many salespeople are inclined to back away from such an aggressive tactic, especially with a new prospect. They argue that they need a small proposal to "get my foot in the door," "give them a taste of what we can really do," or "let them get used to doing business with us." These answers are rationalizations of the worst sort. They make no logical business sense whatsoever. What these salespeople are really saying is that they don't have much faith in their product. They want to sell the prospect a sample because then the prospect won't be as unhappy if the product doesn't meet expectations.

Good creative salespeople have the courage of their convictions. If your widget is the ultimate answer to the prospect's most pressing need, why wait for them to try a sample before you let them have the full benefit of the product? Is delayed customer gratification a virtue of some sort? What kind of favor are you doing them by withholding the full benefit?

If you don't believe in your product, you'll never have a truly successful sales career. Not that you won't make a living—you may even make a good one. It's just that you won't get much satisfaction from your job. If you lack faith in what you sell, you're labeling yourself a liar every time you try to sell it and a fraud every time you complete a sale. That makes it pretty unpleasant to go to work every day. If you don't believe your product does what you claim, do yourself, your customers, and your company a favor and find another line of work.

Salespeople who undersell their product or service sometimes just don't believe that their customers could possibly have the potential they've estimated. This self-defeating attitude can be attributed to a general lack of knowledge. This is also the single biggest problem I'm asked to overcome in my consulting practice. It's shocking how many salespeople—even experienced ones—don't give their customers and prospects credit for running large successful businesses.

It's human nature to view prospects through the filter of your own experience. As successful salespeople, you make a good living—maybe well into six figures or even more. You know how hard you have to work, how much effort goes into producing that sum. You also know how much dollar volume you have to produce to create that living. So you sometimes find it hard to imagine someone else making many, many multiples of your income except in a theoretical sense. Unless you've run a business like your prospect's or otherwise gained an intimate first-hand knowledge of their financial statements, it's sometimes difficult to picture their reality.

This misperception of the real world leads some salespeople to internalize the buying decision. They try to put themselves in the customer's shoes and judge the proposal through the customer's eyes. This is normally a very good step to take, but it can lead to problems if you're not rationally objective. Unfortunately, it's easy to let your judgment be determined by the size of your own pocketbook, which you know intimately, rather than the real potential of the prospect's, which you're estimating. With many products or services, you may very well be proposing a sum in excess of your annual income, and it's easy to confuse your vision with your customer's.

Whatever the reason, making a proposal too small is a very common obstacle to sales success.

Big dollar volume proposals send the message that they are important. That means the important decision makers in the prospect's chain of command need to see them. Small proposals have the opposite effect—they get delegated to the lackeys and flak-catchers.

Big proposals have the potential for making major impacts on the prospect's business, so they get a much higher level of consideration than small ones, which are often seen as more trouble than they're worth. This is especially true when you're selling to major corporations. Think about what's necessary to "move the needle" on the sales of what is today considered a small company—one with $200 million in annual sales. A measly 5 percent gain is $10 million. If you're selling a product or service that's supposed to help increase your prospect's sales, you'd better be able to show that it can contribute to a significant part of that growth or your proposal won't get serious consideration.

Or maybe your product's main benefit is improved profitability. If that $200 million prospect has a 40 percent gross profit margin, the scale you're working on is $80 million. How far will your idea move *that* needle? Look at the numbers you worked up for your prospect's estimated annual revenues and ask yourself what impact your idea could have on them. That will tell you the importance of your idea to the prospect and how it will rank among others he might be considering.

Here's a good example of how large proposals are perceived. Have you ever tried to raise money for a new business? Banks, venture capitalists, even deep-pocket private investors don't even want to consider requests for amounts less than tens of millions of dollars. No matter how foolproof, secure, and ultimately profitable a mere six-figure loan or investment actually is, they won't even look at it because their cost of analyzing it is too high.

In addition, they can only properly investigate so many deals each year, and it takes just as long to look over a $100,000 application as it does to eyeball a $100 million one.

The same is true for your proposals. Do you want to get Mr. Big's attention? Ask him to spend a million dollars with you. His time is limited and he wants to spend it on those decisions that matter most to his business. Do you want to spend the rest of your life pitching the second assistant night co-manager of the West Fork branch office? Make a $1,000 proposal to Mr. Big. He'll send you packing off to West Fork in a heartbeat—and you'll probably never get another appointment with Mr. Big again.

Less is never more. This concept is crucial to the success of the Creative Selling System. If you're inclined to under-sell, overcome this problem by addressing it head-on: Prepare estimates of prospect potential and make your proposals significant within their context.

Chapter 10
Your Written Proposal

"The customer is the focus of the proposal."

It's time to turn your outline into the finished product, the pieces of paper you'll show the client. This is going to go very fast, because you've already done all the hard work. The standard proposal in the Creative Selling System has five pages. There may be other printed material used to supplement it, but the heart of the proposal has just five pages.

Page One

The first page is the cover page. It contains the things you would expect: the prospect's name, your company's name, and contact information for you such as address, phone, fax, email, and so on. Your company may well provide pre-printed cover pages for proposals complete with logos and pretty pictures. That's great. Just make sure that the largest item on the cover page of *your* proposal is the prospect's name. Larger than your company's logo. Larger than the picture of your product. Larger than anything else on the page. That's why I had you write the prospect's name at the top of your outline—to remind you that *the customer is the focus* of the proposal.

Page Two

The second page contains the benefits of the proposal. That's right, just copy the three (or four) benefits you wrote on the outline and list them as prominent bullet points. You might have a headline with the prospect's name, but that's the only other item. This page won't have much on it, but it's such a key part of the Creative Selling System that you're going to use it twice.

Page Three

The third page is the idea page. Here's where you explain what you're going to do for the prospect and how you're going to do it. The goal of the idea page is to convince the prospect that your idea will deliver the benefits you've promised on the preceding page. This page is free form, since every product or service has different ways of presenting itself. You may want to use paragraphs and full sentences, bullet points, or a combination. Just make sure that you cover all the elements of execution that you listed on the outline.

This page is where you present your selling points in persuasive language, weaving the prospect's name into the text as often as possible, and making the explanation as clear as you can. The idea page carries the reasons to make the prospect believe your idea will work. It also gives the "arguments" in favor of buying your product or service.

The idea page needs to be clear and simple to read. A good rule of thumb is that a layman (or first time buyer of your product) needs to be able to read this page unassisted and understand what's going to happen if they buy your idea. In fact, one of the best tests of whether you've accomplished this is to find someone—your spouse, a friend, or anyone who is not familiar with the intricacies of how your product works—to read this page and tell you what it says without any coaching from you.

And here's an absolute rule: the idea page can be no more than one page long. If you can't adequately explain what you're going to do for the prospect in one page or less, your idea is probably too complicated for your company to execute and it's way too complicated for the prospect to buy it without deep reservations and/or multiple misunderstandings. Great big complex proposals with lots of minor decisions and multitudinous options take a long time to be approved.

K.I.S.S. also stands for Keep It Sell-able, Stupid.

Page Four

The fourth page is the proposal page, which contains the answers to the dollars and cents questions about your idea. Nothing up to this point has included a price tag of any kind. Now you're going to lay it out in such a way that it actually lends credibility to your presentation. Don't look at price as an obstacle, but rather as an aid to closing the sale.

The first part of the page should specify the length of time the agreement covers, list all the elements you're including in the package, and provide all the other contractual elements such as delivery dates, quantities, qualities or grades, and other specifications of the product or service you're selling. This page should also have detail on which party is responsible for which actions if applicable. Who's going to install the software, for example, or purchase the prizes for the contest. It should contain all the information the prospect needs to know to say "yes" or "no" to the proposal.

There's one thing this page does not contain, however, and that is unit pricing. The prospect needs to know the total cost of the idea, of course, and you're going to give that to him in a minute. He doesn't need to know how much each element costs, however, because you're not asking him to buy it element by element. You've presented the prospect with an idea in a complete package to solve his problem or meet his need. Every element in the package is integral to the success of the idea. The idea is offered for sale as a whole, not piecemeal.

The only reason for the prospect to have unit prices is so that he or she can negotiate the individual items to arrive at a lower total price. Or to pick and choose the ones they want, perhaps substituting a competitor's item for one of yours. If the prospect insists on having that data, you can give it to them, but only after you've completed this presentation and secured agreement from them that the idea is something they want. You intentionally don't put unit prices in the proposal as a way to manage that process.

This tactic is also a way to keep the prospect focused on the merits of the idea. If they start examining the minutiae of unit pricing, they can very easily lose sight of the big picture—your idea. So only put those items you want to discuss on the agenda—and that does not include unit prices.

What about the total price? That will be readily available, of course. I suggest, however, that it be expressed in some other terms than the "Grand Total." Even billionaires are subject to sticker shock, so I like to present the price in smaller incremental terms. "Investment per month" or "budget per location" is usually an easier pill to swallow. That's the figure that's printed on your proposal, never the "Grand Total." When the prospect reaches for their calculator to multiply the budget by the number of locations, you step in and tell them what the total is. Just don't put it on the page. The total should be on your lips, not on your paper.

This serves another purpose, too. If you've ever watched a prospect's eyes when they are handed a proposal, you know that they immediately go to the bottom of each available page. They're instinctively looking for the price, of course, and when they find it they will keep that figure in the front of their minds the entire time you're going through the rest of the presentation. From that point on, everything you say will be heard in the context of the price. In fact, they may well spend the entire pitch mentally preparing to slam you with a price objection, ignoring or just slightly attending to the many brilliant points you're making in your presentation in the meantime.

By leaving this grand total off the page, you're denying the prospect this opportunity. We'll talk about other ways to deal with this problem later.

Page Five

The fifth and final page of the written proposal is the easiest of all—it's just a copy of the second page, the benefits page. That's right, you make two copies of this page and use one of them as the last page in the proposal. This is the piece of paper you want the prospect to be looking at when you ask them for the order. The page you don't want them fixed on is the proposal page, which has the price you're asking them to pay. So put the benefits page in front of them again at the end.

You want the prospect to say "yes" or "no" to acquiring the benefits you're offering, not to spending the money you're asking for. It's a subtle point, but one that's at the heart of all good selling. You use the written proposal as both your script and as your major visual aid during your oral presentation so it's easy to ask for the order while the prospect is reviewing the benefits of your idea.

Sample Proposal

On the following pages is a sample proposal in my five-page format to give you a visual idea of what I've been rambling on about. This particular proposal is designed to sell an advertising program to a hospital. You'll notice that it's pretty simple. The need-solving idea entails a year-long television advertising campaign, extensive video production, awards and giveaways, and many other details. Yet the idea is explained completely in one page and the proposal for $120,000 is outlined in another.

K.I.S.S.

<Sample Cover Page>

Creatively Marketing St. Luke's Hospital

a marketing plan from WSDA-TV

for further information, contact:
Dave Donelson
(999) 999-9999
fax (999) 999-9999
email dvd@WSDA.com

<Sample Benefits Page>

Here's an idea for St. Luke's Hospital that will…

- Maintain and enhance the caring image the hospital has earned throughout your service area
- Increase your inpatient occupancy rate
- Encourage and further raise the morale of the volunteers who serve the patients in St. Luke's Hospital

<Sample Idea Page>

The concept is simple. Each month, St. Luke's Hospital will select a volunteer group for special recognition. WSDA-TV will produce a 90-second video salute to the group, which will air followed by a 30-second commercial designed to promote one of St. Luke's units.

These messages will air as a two-minute block isolated from other commercials. This insures greater viewer attention to St. Luke's message.

Following is a suggested schedule of Volunteer Groups and Units

Jan - Methodist Church - Pediatric
Feb - Candy Stripers - Cardiac
Mar - Kiwanis - Long-Term
Apr - St. Luke's Auxiliary - OB/GYN
May - Sweet Adelines - Geriatrics
Jun - Rotary - Health Club
Jul - Baptist Church - Ontology
Aug - Community Theater - Emergency
Sep - Optimists - Outpatient Rehab
Oct - Lion's Club - Sports Medicine
Nov - Knights of Columbus - Hospice
Dec - Unitarian Church - Burn Care

At the end of the year, WSDA-TV will sponsor a banquet with St. Luke's to honor all volunteer groups at the hospital. A highlight of the banquet will be a showing of the 12 vignettes produced during the year. We will also provide each group with a copy of that video for use in their own fund-raising or other activities.

This program puts the full power of television's impact behind St. Luke's powerful message. It uses all of television's communications tools—sight, sound, motion, and the full range of human emotion—to spread the word that St. Luke's is the most sympathetic care-giver in the market. This year-long program will not only promote St. Luke's services, but will convey to the community that the hospital is the home of many caring, giving staff and volunteer members.

<Sample Expenditure Page>

St. Luke's Hospital

Proposed Annual WSDA TV Schedule

Day – Time	Program	Units/Week
M-F - 5-5:30 PM	First Edition News	2
M-F - 6-6:30 PM	WSDA Early News	1
M-S - 10-10:30 PM	WSDA Late News	1
M-F - 7-9 AM	Network This Morning	2
M-F - 3-4 PM	Talk Show of the Day	1
M-F - 4-5 PM	Famous People Program	1
M-F - 6:30-7 PM	Young Adult Sit-com	1
M-F - 10:30-11 PM	Older Appeal Sit-com	1

Your investment includes:

Total Messages 520 / Year

Video Production of 12 Volunteer Vignettes

Video Production of 12 Unit Commercials

Volunteer Banquet for 100

Monthly Investment - $9,965

This program begins January 1 and runs through December 31, 200X

<Sample Last Benefits Page>

Here's an idea for St. Luke's Hospital that will…

- Maintain and enhance the caring image the hospital has earned throughout your service area
- Increase your inpatient occupancy rate
- Promote the usage of outpatient services
- Encourage and further raise the morale of the volunteers who serve the patients in St. Luke's Hospital

<End Proposal>

The Final Step

There's one last step in preparing your written presentation. *Please* proofread it. Then *please* have another human being proofread it. These few pages will make a powerful impression on the prospect—but that impression could be a negative one if it's sloppy, has misspellings, or grammatical errors. The presentation will have a life after you leave, too, so make sure there are no mistakes in it. You should have a zero-tolerance policy when it comes to the quality of the impression you are making on your prospects.

Proofreading isn't accomplished by just reading over the material. You have to look at each word and sentence in isolation and check it against your mental dictionary (then against a real one if there's the slightest doubt) to make sure it's right. And don't rely on your computer's grammar or spell checker—they're notorious for missing simple mistakes. "You scan have this find produce reel cheep" has five typos that make the writer sound like an idiot—but it will pass through both the grammar and spell check program in most word processing software.

Write once, proofread twice, to put a spin on an old carpenter's adage.

Chapter 11
Alternative Proposals

"How can there be three *best* plans?"

This written proposal format contains the answers to the only two questions directly pertaining to the prospect's buying decision: 1) What's it going to do for me? and 2) How much does it cost? Anything else is superfluous to the prospect's decision-making process. In fact, cluttering up proposals with company histories, mission statements, maps of your worldwide plant locations, etc., can very easily distract the prospect from the job at hand: buying your idea. All of these things have their place in the selling process, but that place isn't on the prospect's desk while you're asking for the order.

The only other material you might want to have in addition to the basic five-page written proposal is a demonstration of some sort of the idea you are presenting. You can add something like a sample of the reports generated by your software or a storyboard of your television commercial. Just make sure that these items are customer specific—produced just for this prospect—so that they enhance rather than detract from your position as an expert working for the prospect's benefit rather than as a peddler trying to move some unsold inventory.

These support materials should not be a physical part of the written proposal. Keep them at hand and use them separately to keep from distracting the prospect from the meat of your proposal. You'll see why this is a small but important point when you read the section on delivering your presentation.

Alternative Proposals

An old sales theory says that you should offer the prospect three alternative proposals: one for more than you think they want to spend, one for much less, and one in the middle which you really expect them to buy. The reasoning behind this theory is that the prospect won't buy the little proposal because that will make them look cheap. They won't buy the biggest one because they can't, and they will buy the middle one because it looks like a bargain relative to the biggest one and it's the safest, middle-of-the-road choice.

This approach may be fine for some types of products or services, but I've always felt that using it seriously undermines your credibility. When you practice creative selling, you're really presenting yourself to the prospect as an expert in your field. You're sending the very clear message that you have studied their situation, analyzed their opportunities and problems, and used your expertise to come up with the optimum plan just for them. Your proposal is that optimum plan.

How can there be three *best* plans? When you give the prospect three different proposals, aren't you subconsciously saying that you're not sure enough of your own abilities to make a positive strong recommendation?

Another similar tactic is to give the prospect proposal "A" while keeping proposal "B" in your briefcase for use "just in case." Proposal "B" is always smaller, of course, and it's the one you whip out at the first sign of a price objection. This tactic sends *two* really bad signals to the prospect. The first one we've already covered: what kind of an "expert" is so unsure of himself that he can't decide which alternative is best? The second signal you're sending is a real killer, though. Having seen proposal "A" and then proposal "B," the prospect will be sure to think proposal "C" is waiting in the wings, and if they give the salesperson enough price resistance, it will appear as if by magic. Way to go! You just created your own price objection.

There's another big danger in using either of these methods to give the prospect alternative proposals to consider. Faced with choices, most humans delay making a decision. In fact, many people hate to make decisions so much that they will actually welcome choices that have to be made so they can use them as an excuse to delay giving you a final "yes" or "no."

Anyone who has been selling for more than about a week knows that the most frustrating customer isn't the one who says "no," it's the one who says "maybe." So why would you ever intentionally give the customer an excuse to "think it over?" Give them *one* proposal so they can give you *one* answer. It'll simplify your life tremendously and you'll be absolutely shocked at what it does for your time management.

A common excuse for offering alternative proposals is that the first proposal might be too expensive, so you should be ready with a fall-back position. I'm going to discuss ways to deal with proposals that are off the mark a little later in this book, but for now suffice it to say that there's nothing wrong—and many things right—with changing your proposal at the prospect's desk. After all, you're still on the first call on a new prospect and you've basing your proposal on some estimates you've prepared, not on hard data. It's unreasonable to expect that you're going to be right on target every time. You can make alterations in the proposal along with the prospect as part of your closing strategy.

Chapter 12
Demand Stage Selling

"The salesperson who carefully listens to their prospect avoids mistakes."

Wouldn't it be great if you could read your customers' minds? You know, get inside their heads and walk around a little bit? The very best salespeople seem to have that ability—it's as if they know what customers are going to say before they say it. They have a sixth sense about which objections a particular customer is most likely to raise. They know which ideas offer the specific benefits that really ring the prospect's bell.

Some of this clairvoyant ability comes from experience, of course. Even more of it comes from advanced listening skills. Top salespeople really listen when their prospect is talking and pick up small cues that many others miss. Many good salespeople are also students of human psychology. They make it a point to study human nature and learn a lot about their customer in the process. As we get ready to make the actual oral presentation, let's put it in context.

One important talent top salespeople have is the ability to recognize the prospect's state of mind and shape their presentations accordingly. They determine if the customer is getting ready to place an order or just starting to comparison shop. They can tell whether the prospect has already decided to buy the product and is negotiating for the best price or whether he or she is weighing other options. They understand that different things are important to the customer at each step in the buying process. They practice Demand Stage Selling.

Demand Stage Selling is a technique that identifies how far along in the buying process a customer has progressed. This tactic dictates that you deliver the type of presentation that appeals specifically to someone at each particular stage. Demand Stage Selling immediately helps block out irrelevant objections and tremendously improves your closing ratios.

Three Stages Of Demand

Prospective buyers go through several stages in the decision process—unconsciously, to them. First, they have to recognize a need and decide to buy something to fill that need. This decision creates primary demand. You can equate this stage to that little pang of hunger you get in the late afternoon. Your hunger is the need—the first stage of demand.

The prospect then has to decide on a *type* of product or service that will fill the need they've identified, which creates secondary demand. In our example, what are you hungry for? You have choices—a candy bar, a piece of fruit, or some microwave popcorn (which invariably creates more demand from everybody else within aroma range—but that's another story).

Finally, the customer must decide which service provider or product brand to buy. This is third-level demand. In our afternoon snack example, this is when you decide whether to buy the Snickers or the Milky Way. Your prospect decides whether to buy from you or from one of your competitors. In sales, this third level of demand is the one concentrated on most heavily.

Primary Demand Tactics

There are many different kinds of selling, each of which works best at different demand stages. There's transactional selling, which focuses on filling orders efficiently. There's negotiation, which concentrates on securing the greatest share of business at the most profitable price points. Both of these occur at the third level of demand. There's also missionary selling, which aims to create new primary or secondary demand through educating customers about the desirability of a particular type of product.

An exciting idea for a premium gift program, for example, can ignite primary demand by helping the prospect identify a need they may not have realized they have. The good salesperson who strongly presents the potential benefits of their product—building customer goodwill, creating loyalty, encouraging employee performance, and so on—will spark demand that didn't exist until they walked through the door to make their presentation. This is what should usually happen when you're making cold calls.

Unfortunately, most salespeople aren't trying to create primary demand when they cold call. They're really just making as many calls as possible hoping to stumble across a few prospects who have already made the primary demand-creating decision to buy something, but just haven't decided what to buy. Typical cold-callers then hard-sell the prospect who is already in the market, securing the sale instead of allowing a competitor to get it. This is fine, but, in the meantime, the salesperson wastes a great deal of time and effort making the wrong type of pitch to other prospects who aren't in the market at all.

Why do so many salespeople work this way? It's because persuading the prospect that they have a need is the most difficult hurdle to overcome. If I'm not hungry, it does little good to pitch me on a candy bar. But if you waved a little chocolate under my nose, it might stimulate new hunger. It's the same way with ideas. When you can show the prospect an idea, or a new way of looking at the possibilities for their business, they might recognize a need for what you sell they didn't see before.

Second and Third Stage Presentations

If the prospect called *you* for information or to get a bid, they're in at least the second or more probably the third demand stage. If they're in the second stage, it's important to narrowly identify the need they're trying to satisfy and concentrate your presentation on it. If they want to increase sales production, for example, they're going to be looking for a product with different qualities than if they need to reduce customer turnover. In the first instance, the solution has to be something that's flashy and exciting enough to inspire their own sales staff, which "top producer" plaques don't do but incentive trips to Bermuda certainly can. In the second, it may pay to point out that a rebate for repeat customers is fine, but a gift delivered to the desk of a volume buyer will make a much more lasting impression.

Pricing, by the way, is usually a purchase factor only in the third and final demand stage, when the prospect is choosing between competing providers. One of the biggest mistakes sales people make is to bring up pricing before the buyer is at that stage, which simply muddies the waters and diverts their attention away from the first- or second-stage decisions they need to make.

It's easy to confuse the different types of selling and expect the tools and techniques that apply to one to apply to another. It's also easy to incorrectly identify a customer's demand stage and take the wrong approach. The salesperson who carefully listens to their prospect avoids these mistakes.

There is only one way to influence all three stages of the demand creation process: Sell problem-solving ideas! When you sell ideas, you create primary demand by identifying the client's needs—it's part of the idea development process. You also create secondary demand by presenting an idea related to your type of need-satisfaction. You most certainly create third-level demand by selling ideas that your competitors can't offer.

Chapter 13
Getting Your Foot In The Door

**"There are many ways to skin a cat—
or to get an appointment."**

You've researched your prospect's needs, estimated his potential spending, and written a proposal that's worthy of a Pulitzer Prize. It's time to make the sale!

Right about here is where most new salespeople (and plenty of experienced ones, too), make a major mistake. They're eager to get the process started, they've got a lot of things to do, and their sales manager has been bugging them about all the time they've been spending in the office working on proposals. So they rush out and drop in on the prospect, saying something like, "I was in your neighborhood, so I thought I'd stop by and see if you wanted to buy something today."

This is not a great way to impress the prospect with the careful thought that went into your proposal.

Or they try to make an appointment by calling ahead with a pitch like, "Hello, Mr. Big. I'd like to show you our newest line of widgets. When can you see me?" Then they wonder why Mr. Big is too busy to fit them in. And why they always seem to get his voice mail when they call back.

At least the second salesperson made an attempt to demonstrate some professionalism by making an appointment. The first one apparently didn't place enough value on the prospect's time to reserve some of it in advance.

When you just "drop in" on a prospect, you and your proposal are placed in the same category as the other salespeople who work without appointments. These include people like political pamphleteers going door-to-door, cute little girls selling cookies, and route sales operators who fill up vending machines. All of these people serve perfectly respected functions in the grand scheme of our economy, but do you really want your $120,000 idea considered along with the proposal for a new gum-ball machine in the employee's lounge?

Making cold calls in this day of voice-mail-protected, work-overloaded executives isn't easy. It's about as much fun as changing a flat tire on the New Jersey turnpike during rush hour in the snow. Done correctly, though, it doesn't have to be a chore. It's also helpful to remember there are many ways to skin a cat—or to get an appointment.

"There are people who like the bizarre and the strange, and those are the people you do bizarre and strange things for." That's one of the marketing tips from Stewart Intagliata, Director of Operations, and owner of St. Louis-based Unispot, Inc. Like many (if not most) HVAC salespeople, Intagliata has faced his share of difficulties getting appointments to see prospective customers. It's the first hurdle in selling—the one popularized by the cartoon with the salesperson's foot stuck in the prospect's door. If you can't see them, you can't sell them.

Fortunately, not every prospect is stand-offish. Intagliata says there are big differences geographically. "If I'm in Mississippi, I can get in to see anybody I want. They might not do business with you, but they'll sit there and talk to you for an hour." New Yorkers tend to be more brusque; Californians less focused, in his opinion.

South of the border, though, there's another factor at work. Intagliata says you have to establish a friendship before you can do business. "I remember flying down to Mexico, my first time, and walking off the plane and the guy kissed me on the cheek. That was his way. What are you going to do? You just sort of stand there and say, 'I appreciate it.'"

Obstructions And Obstacles

Perversely, new "advances" in communications technology have made it harder than ever to make person-to-person contact. Bill Nowak, Vice President of Martin Walshin, Inc. in Hastings-on-Hudson, NY, says, "You have layers of firewalls before you can reach somebody that can make a decision these days."

Selby Seay, HVAC Division Sales Manager for Reliable Products in Geneva, AL, agrees, "Voice mail to me is a real headache," he says. "With cold calls, they don't call us back 90% of the time. We have to call them again. We also use the fax machine a lot."

Technology isn't the only roadblock, either, according to Steve Hill, Sales and Marketing Manager of Blender Products, Inc., of Denver, CO. He says, there's also "the business of engineers trying to run offices with minimal staff. As corporations have gotten bigger and marketing and sales strategies have become so much more elaborate, we find that engineers are just tired of having people in their face all the time."

Jerry Moechnig, Sales Representative for Architectural Energy Corp. in Boulder, CO., points out, "In this economy, more businesses are having fewer people do more work. That's just the reality that we have to live with."

Be Persistent Over And Over Again

That's why, according to Intagliata, you do what you have to do. "If a guy won't return your calls, just keep calling him," he advises. "Keep calling. Keep calling until you get him. Some guys are just that way."

Moechnig quantifies the process, saying, "I try to be patient. It takes anywhere from five to eight calls and messages for somebody to return your call."

Intagliata outlines some other methods he's used. "I've stayed outside of places and waited an hour, hour and a half, for people to come out so I can talk to them," he says. "Or you've got to know somebody. A wholesaler can get you in a lot of places you can't get into just by cold calling."

The machines may have made it more difficult, but they haven't taken over completely, according to Hill. He says Blender Products works on "Maintaining direct relationships with end-users, with specifying engineers, while at the same time maintaining a sales force to echo our message. The importance in this industry of continuing to have that face-to-face relationship, which only a local person can build, still holds a lot of weight."

Attention Can Be Bought

"Sometimes you have to put yourself outside of the box," according to Moechnig. "So many people get so many calls everyday, and people just don't have all the time they need to do all the work they have to do. Fresh baked cookies is probably the best door-opener that comes to mind."

There's general agreement that cookies—or other signs of appreciation—help establish customer relationships. Seay says, "What we like to do is attend customer appreciation days and give door prizes away to their customers."

"You grease the wheels," Intagliata says. "You send them a shirt, a handwritten note, news clippings. If it's handwritten, they'll open it. It's the soft things. It's the relationships." But there are limits.

"We haven't sent any hookers over to customers or anything like that," says Nowak.

Moechnig, too, follows a straighter path to get the customer's attention. In fact, he has a very systematic approach. "Typically, we'll do a mailing, then an emailing. Then we make an effort to call those individuals with whom we had prior contact." And what happens after numerous calls? Moechnig says he makes just one more. "When you reach that point when you're finally ready to throw in the towel," he says, "I find it very beneficial to leave one last message that reiterates what I'm trying to say, then tells them that this will be the last call I'll make to them. That gets a response 15 to 20% of the time."

It's Still About People

Establishing relations with a new customer isn't the only part of the sales game that can be problematic. Unfortunately, existing customers sometimes drift away and it can be even harder to get their attention than to get an appointment with someone that doesn't know you. After all, they know (or at least think they know) what you have to sell. As Intagliata explains, "I was one of those people. I wouldn't listen to anybody. How much can you tell me about a humidifier? You turn it on, you add water, and you're ready to go."

To get back on the past customer's radar screen, Moechnig recommends trying something different. "We did a mailing campaign to previous customers to re-intrigue them," he relates. "We went to an old record store and bought some cheap LP's. We brought them back to the office and broke them with a hammer and stuck them in an envelope with a mailing that said 'we hate to sound like a broken record....'"

It doesn't matter whether you're selling sheet metal, diagnostic software, or million-dollar multi-work-station cooling systems, you still have to get the customer's attention first. The best way is on the human level, because, despite a wide-spread opinion to the contrary, customers are people, too. You need to understand their foibles. As Intagliata says, "They're all crazy, but I like crazy people."

Chapter 14
Getting Past The Screeners

"As long as you're polite and conversational most people will give you a little information you can use."

Press one to speak to sales…two for service…three to hear this message again…or press four if you just like to hear little beeping sounds in your ear. Welcome to the voice mail battleground.

That is where small and larger business owners and managers fight to communicate with their customers, vendors, and even their own employees. Voice mail irritates many of us, but those salespeople who have learned to infiltrate it can improve their personal efficiency and sales effectiveness. These skills are growing more important every day. In a recent informal test, we found that 68% of our calls were transferred to a voice mail box, 24% required a message left with a live operator, and only 8% went through to the person we were calling! What's worse, less than a third of the message recipients returned the call!

How do you improve those odds? With preparation and attitude. Here are some tactics that help.

Start by trying to find a human. Incoming calls at most companies are handled either by a mostly-live operator or the dreaded "automated attendant." If possible, you want to speak to a human being first so you can get some information before you speak to your prospect, or, as is more likely, before you get their voice mailbox. So, even if the system doesn't give you that option, punch "0" in an attempt to reach a live operator. If you get one, don't just leave your name and number. Ask if they know when your target will be available. Do they have another number? A fax number? Find out if anyone else in that department can handle your call right now. If you are nice (and aren't you always nice?) an operator or receptionist may even give you valuable information about how and when the voice mail system is on, other voice mail addresses or extensions to call, or even how likely your prospect is to return your call. When you're infiltrating behind enemy lines, reconnaissance is key.

Read It—Don't Wing It

Sooner or later, of course, you are going to be transferred to your prospect's voice mailbox. YOU MUST BE PREPARED! Assume you're going to leave a message and jot down some notes (or better yet, a complete script) before you start dialing. This prevents overlooking something and helps you make the best possible impression. Think of your message as your first sales presentation to this prospect, where the first impression is often the only impression you will get a chance to make. Your message should contain the same elements as a sales presentation: a benefit the customer will receive by buying your product and an attempt to close the sale. In this case, the benefit is the reason you give them to return your call (the product) and the close asks them to do so.

Most people don't do either one of these things, by the way, which is why their calls don't get returned. They say something like. "Hi, this is Dave. Call me at 555-1234." Click. Now that is a voice mail message only your mother will return—maybe.

Your message doesn't need to be long (that's where writing it out beforehand helps). Briefly describe how happy your products or services have made people, or mention another company that buys from you. Say that the prospect can enjoy the same kind of success if they'll return your call. In other words, offer the recipient a reward for calling back. By the way, use this same method when you are leaving a message with a live operator! Ask them to put it on the message slip along with your name and number.

In the close of your call, let the recipient know how they can reach you and what you need from them. Tell them you'll be waiting for their call at a certain time—then be there to take it. If you're trying to set a meeting, leave two specific dates and times and ask the prospect to either choose one or suggest another. Or list the information you need and ask them to leave it on *your* voice mailbox. Avoid voice mail "tag" by keeping your messages specific.

Little Things That Count

There are a couple of other things you can do to improve your voice mail results. Always mention the date and time of your call even though most voice mail systems do this electronically. This will underscore your professionalism. Also at the beginning of the message, give both your first and last name (it's shocking how many other people are named Dave) and spell your name if it is difficult, unusual, or of foreign origin. Give your telephone number at the beginning, too. Repeat both your name and your number again at the end of the call so the prospect doesn't have to go back to get it if they like the message in the middle.

Attitude counts big time in a voice mail message. You want to sound like a winner, so speak energetically and confidently. That doesn't mean speaking fast! One of the worst things you can do is rattle off your message like you can't wait to finish—especially when it comes to leaving your phone number. Sit up straight or even stand while you are talking. Smile and use gestures—the prospect can't see them, but they most certainly can hear the energy they create. It really pays to rehearse your message out loud a few times before you leave it. Get rid of the "downgraders" in your speech. These are those little words that move your message to the bottom of the pile because they tell the prospect even you don't think it's important! "I'm *just* calling…" "*If* you have a chance…" "*Nothing* urgent, *just* a message about…" If you don't think you use these phrases or others like them, try listening to that message you just recorded!

Which brings up another good tactic. Before you hang up, try pressing the pound key ("#") to replay your message and re-record it if necessary. If there is any stumble, hesitation, or glitch—no matter how small—do it over! A poor message will make a negative first impression that you may never be able to overcome. Not all systems have this feature (or make it readily known), but it's worth the effort. You may also be given some other options like marking your message as "urgent" or transferring to another number or person.

Hello Again

What do you do if the prospect doesn't return your first call? Call again, of course. And unless there's some specific reason not to (like the prospect is on vacation), don't wait a week to do it—call within two or three days of the original message. If they haven't returned your first call by then, they're not going to. It's essential on the call back that you say nothing about your previous call! If you do, no matter how hard you try, it will sound like whining. Instead, put a slightly different spin on your first pitch or add some useful information that they can get by calling you back.

Call backs are also where you really use that information you got from the human operator. Try the other phone numbers the company may have—especially direct ones. Call during non-business hours. This can be particularly effective when using direct-dial numbers since many people will answer their own phone when the switchboard is closed.

Don't run from the voice mail battleground. With a little preparation and a positive attitude, you can win the battle!

The Human Screener

Even in those unusual companies where voice mail isn't used, it's a rare prospect who answers his own phone or takes calls from people he doesn't know. Despite the odds, though, you still need to make an appointment. So call and ask to speak to Mr. Big. You'll probably hear some variation of, "No, you can't talk to him now." Don't be offended. They say the same thing to everybody who calls for Mr. Big because those are his instructions. In fact, they treat you like you were Mr. Big's ex-wife's attorney calling. What do you do?

Stop right here and first make sure you're not sabotaging your call. It sounds crazy, but I've heard salespeople say thing like, "Is Mr. Big busy?" or even, "May I speak with Mr. Big—or is he doing something important right now?"

Openings like these reduce the screener's perception of your importance and your value to Mr. Big. You need to take just the opposite approach, and make it sound like a telephone conversation with you is the single most important thing Mr. Big can do today.

I like to put the value of the call right up front. In the Creative Selling System, you're always selling ideas, so use an offer of an idea as a reward for Mr. Big to return your call. Say something like this:

"Hi, this is Dave Donelson with SDA, and I've got a great marketing idea to give to Mr. Big. May I speak with him, please?"

Now, you're a giver of value, not just a consumer of time. So, state your request with confidence. Assume the close. Act as if you expect to be put through right away. Don't be snotty; just be confident.

After you make your offer and ask for Mr. Big, be quiet. Let the screener respond. Getting through a screener is a lot like making the sale—you need some information before you can close the deal. So encourage them to talk and see how much information you can get from them. When the screener asks you to leave a message, politely ask a few questions. For example:

"Oh, is he in today?"

"Is he out of the building?"

"What time do you expect the meeting to be over?"

"Do you expect him to go to his desk after the meeting?"

These queries will help you obtain information that will give you an edge in reaching the decision maker. As long as you're polite and conversational most people will give you a little information you can use.

Asking questions works because the screener isn't expecting it. Since he or she is giving you a standard brush-off, they expect to get a standard response from you. When you don't just give them your name and number (which is what they expect), you open the door to more informative communication. The best response to the screener brush-off is persistence. You have to show them that you will not just go away. In order to get rid of you, he or she is going to have to answer some questions.

You're still going to have to leave a message with the screener, so be polite. Watch your tone. And remember to stress in the message itself that you want to give something to Mr. Big—not just take his time.

Chapter 15
Getting A Cold Call Appointment

"Make it worthwhile for the prospect to spend some time with you."

Once you've navigated the voice mail system, dodged the screeners, and connected with Mr. Big, you'll want to make the most of your chance. If there were ever a time when the first impression really counts, this is it. But don't panic, there are five easy steps you can follow to get that first appointment.

Step One: Get Permission

One of the biggest fears about cold calling is that you'll be mistaken for those pesky salespeople who call at dinner time with the latest long distance calling plan for the phone company you've never heard of. These unfortunate folks are intruders into your life. To avoid being put in that category by your prospects, you need to first find out if this is a good time for the prospect to talk. It's an appreciated courtesy, and it makes sure you and your call get the respect and attention you deserve.

To get permission, just briefly ask if the prospect has about a minute to speak to you. Not to buy anything or make any decision, just a moment to make an appointment for a short meeting in person. Try several phrases until you find one you like, then use it on all your calls. You might try "Is this a good time to talk?" or "May I have about a minute?" as starters until you strike a phrase that works for you. My personal favorite is "I know you're busy, so I'll only take a minute."

Step Two: Share Your Enthusiasm

Your next step is to share your enthusiasm. We think of communication as an exchange of information between two people and, in a limited sense, it is. But truly persuasive communication—as in sales—requires sharing enthusiasm, not just information. That's never more true than when you're on the telephone.

There are a couple of simple tricks I learned when I worked as a radio announcer that will help you in all of your telephone work. First, stand up and move around when you're talking on the phone. When you're standing, you're more energetic because your legs are more active and they're increasing your circulation. You also breathe more deeply, which puts more power in your voice.

Secondly, smile. Imagine that the prospect is standing right in front of you and you're greeting him for the first time. You'd be smiling, wouldn't you? You don't know it, but that smile on your face comes through on the telephone, too. It will make you sound less threatening and more friendly, which makes the prospect more receptive to your message.

If you want proof that these two techniques work, try recording yourself sitting and talking on the phone as you normally do and then record the same message standing and smiling. You'll hear the difference. Of course, your office mates may think you've slipped over the edge when they see you standing with the phone in your hand and a smile on your face, but that's their problem.

Don't be distracted from the purpose of this call. It's not to sell your company or product, it's to sell the value to the client of spending some of his or her time with you. It's your enthusiasm that will make that sale happen. Enthusiasm is infectious. The more excited and enthusiastic you are, the more the prospect will want to see you. By the way, if you always assume that the prospect will want to see you, they will.

Step Three: Promise A Reward

Make it worthwhile for the prospect to spend some time with you, and I don't mean by promising them a set of steak knives. Off them a unique reward: the need-satisfying *idea* that you've developed especially for them. When you offer to give the prospect something of value—an idea for improving their business—you're essentially paying them for their time.

Remember, though, if you give the idea away over the phone, there's no longer any reason for an appointment—so you've squandered your payment without getting anything in return. You have to tell the prospect that the purpose of your call is to arrange a meeting so you can show them your idea without giving it away over the phone. This serves two purposes: 1) you establish in their minds a reason to meet with you, and 2) you appeal to their natural curiosity!

If they press you for details, just keep politely pointing out that the telephone won't let you show them the concept you've designed for their company. You'd like to, but that's just not physically possible. We're a visual society. Television, movies, billboards, and magazines communicate mostly with pictures, not sound. The prospect will subconsciously understand what you mean by "showing" her your idea.

It's a good practice to talk about the benefits of your product or service, but never the full description (or price) of the concept itself. If the prospect absolutely insists, give him or her a morsel of detail, but nothing they can say "no" to. It's a good idea to plan for this contingency by deciding which tidbit to use as bait *before* you make the call.

What about the prospect who absolutely refuses to see you unless you give him all the details over the phone? Express your regrets, promise to contact him again, and hang up! That's right—say "good bye" and hang up. We both know—and so does the prospect—that the only reason he wants to hear about the idea now is to say "no" and avoid a meeting. So why should you pay for something (the appointment) that you're not going to receive?

There's no point in getting into a tug-of-war with the prospect. You can't possibly win it and the longer it goes on, the more likely the prospect is to get aggravated. So cut your losses and move on. I'm not suggesting that you give up on the prospect, by the way, just that you end today's call and try again in a day or two when he will, hopefully, be in a more receptive mood. These kinds of prospects are in the minority. Almost everyone else will give you a few minutes if you follow the rules we're talking about. Remember: keep that enthusiasm up!

Step Four: Guarantee No Obligation

Your prospect has seen far too many movie scenes where the salesman literally sticks his foot in the door to keep the hapless housewife from shutting off his sales pitch. So remove that kind of fear and guarantee that giving you an appointment doesn't obligate him or her to make a purchase. Make it clear that all you ask is to be heard. Remove the threat and give your prospect the opportunity to let natural curiosity take over.

Step Five: Close Your Sale

Now close the sale for the appointment by directly and specifically asking for fifteen minutes of the prospect's time. Fifteen minutes is a small price to pay for an idea that they can use. And fifteen minutes is an easily managed quantity of time. The prospect can slip it in between other appointments and meetings. It's only half the time of a typical TV sitcom. Fifteen minutes is a coffee break. Anything longer, though, and most busy prospects imagine their day eaten away by you and your presentation. Remember, the prospect's time is very valuable and so is yours. Don't worry that you won't have enough time to make the sale once you get there. You'll see that you can easily complete your presentation of a standard Creative Selling System proposal in fifteen minutes.

Next, name an exact date and time to meet, generally no less than two days or more than a week after your call. If the prospect can't accept your first date, offer two others to choose from. Just be sure to always name the exact date and time *yourself*. By the second or third specific date you offer, they'll offer one themselves if one of yours doesn't work.

Absolutely never just ask them, "when can we get together?" For one thing, it sounds like your time isn't important enough to be scheduled. Or that there's so little demand for your service that your calendar is empty and you don't have any other customers. The other problem with posing the question this way is that it makes it much easier for the prospect to say they'll get back to you—which they probably won't. Control the call by asking for a specific date and time.

Script Your Call

Those are the five points to keep in mind as you're making your appointment telephone calls. Because each of them is important and there are several subtleties to them that aren't necessarily second nature to many salespeople, I think it's a good idea to prepare a script for the calls in advance. You don't want to sound like a slick salesman working out of a boiler room, but you also don't want to stumble around looking for the right words to use. And you don't want to forget an important point. Just write down (in your own words) the key points you want to make during the call:

- Is this a good time to talk?
- I have an idea to give you.
- It'll only take 15 minutes to explain.
- Can we meet at…? Name the specific time and date.

With a simple outline in front of you, you don't have to exert effort to remember what you're going to say. The better you know your material, the more strongly you can focus on sharing your enthusiasm.

Rehearse The Call

It also doesn't hurt to rehearse the call a few times before you make it! Rehearse *out loud.* That witty phrase you've had spinning in your mind may not sound quite so impressive when you hear it coming out of your mouth. Or you may have accidentally put a tongue twister into your script. The words look fine on paper but they get stuck behind your teeth when you try to say them. More than anything, though, rehearsing out loud gives you confidence—the real key to making telephone appointments.

In a well-executed call, the prospect gets two chances to talk. The first one is when you ask if this is a good time to talk. The second one shouldn't be until you ask your closing question. When you rehearse, try to deliver the four points without pausing for the prospect to respond (except after the permission question). Don't be impolite or rude, but try to smoothly get from the idea offer to the closing question without pausing for an answer. You want the prospect to say yes or no to the appointment date, not to the idea, so make sure that's what you ask for when you give them their second turn to talk.

Your call should go something like this:

You: "Hello, Mr. Big. This is Dave Donelson with SDA. I know you're busy, so I'll just take a minute of your time. Is that okay?"

Mr. Big: "Yeah, but make it quick."

You: "I'd like to set up a time when we could meet to discuss a powerful idea that we've developed just for you, Mr. Big. If you could spare 15 minutes just to see it, I'll show you how this idea can make you lots of money. Would Wednesday at 10 be convenient for you?"

It's short and to the point—a 30-second phone call asking for a 15 minute meeting. And Mr. Big doesn't have to exert himself at all, just say "yes" or "no."

Making cold call appointments isn't anybody's idea of a good time, but, if you remember that you're offering to bring the prospect something valuable—your need-satisfying ideas—you'll find it easier to pick up the phone with enthusiasm.

Chapter 16
Persistence Counts

"Where there's a will there's a way."

There's one overriding key to getting appointments. Polite persistence. It really, really counts. Your prospects are busy people. They have many demands on their time. They don't always return calls in the time frame you want them to. Sometimes they "forget" to return calls. Don't get mad—and don't get even, either. Get focused. If they don't return your first call, wait an appropriate amount of time (anywhere from two hours to a day) and call again. If they don't return your second call, same drill. Same for the third and fourth calls.

But always be polite, especially to the poor folks (including the screener) who have to repeatedly take your messages. It's not their fault Mr. Big's so busy. The same goes for the messages you leave on his voice mail. Above all, never, ever complain to anybody about the difficulty of getting through to the prospect. If you even convey the impressions that you want to say, "It's about time you returned my call," their response will be "Who the —— do you think you are?"

If you take non-returned calls personally, you're doomed to live your life in a perpetual rage. Just relax and keep smilin' and dialin'. There's no magic number of messages to leave before you intensify your effort with other tactics, but don't drag the process out too long or you'll lose your enthusiasm. Very generally speaking, if I've left five messages over a two week period without getting a return call, I don't quit, I just call in the heavy artillery.

Increasing Pressure

But what do you do when the prospect just won't see you? You've called and called, left countless voice mail messages, even "dropped by" unannounced to try to set an appointment for a presentation, but the S.O.B. won't give you the time of day. The door is firmly closed. Do you give it up and move on to greener pastures?

Actually, that's a serious option. But before you do, consider the relative value of this prospect and what turning him into a customer could mean to your income and your company's revenues. If you're following the Creative Selling System, every prospect you're working on has big potential. You will have confirmed that fact during your research on the prospect's business. I assume you wouldn't even be calling for an appointment if the prospect weren't potentially a big customer. So retreating just because the guy won't answer the phone isn't an attractive option.

The truly creative seller will embrace the situation as a challenge to be overcome. And believe me, where there's a will there's a way. Let's review some of the obvious (but sometimes forgotten) methods of getting your message to the prospect.

What's your goal? You're trying to get an appointment, right? Telephone calls haven't worked because he doesn't answer his own phone. He also doesn't return phone calls—at least not yours. Have you tried other communication media? How about a fax, email, registered letter or telegram? Sometimes the unusual delivery method is enough to break the barrier down. When was the last time Mr. Big got a telegram?

Or what about asking someone else to make the phone call? Maybe Mr. Big will return your sales manager's call, or your company president's.

Or check to see if one of your company's directors is a member of Mr. Big's country club. Don't let internal politics or your own fears of admitting failure stop you from using these resources. Most of your superiors will view your request as a sign of persistence and a willingness to go the extra mile, not as a sign of weakness on your part. And as far as career politics go, it never hurts to flatter the boss by asking him or her to exhibit those powerful skills that raised them above the masses in the first place.

Still no luck? The door is still closed? Raise the ante a little bit and see if that gets their attention. Don't just send a fax—send flowers. Still no response? Don't send more flowers—send a brick wrapped up in a note that says you have a "solid idea" for Mr. Big. What? Still getting the Sphinx treatment? Don't send a brick this time—send a singing telegram delivered by a guy in an ape suit. When you're a creative seller, this can go on and on.

You have to look on this entire process as a campaign that will take time. Have some fun with it. Pretend you're laying siege to a castle. Every once in a while you launch a couple of stones against the walls with your catapult, but that's mostly just to remind the inhabitants that you're not going to go away until they deal with you. It's the same thing with Mr. Big. Wear him down by lobbing a few stones at a time.

Chapter 17
The Brochure Brush-Off

"The first step is to fight off your own desire to take the easy way out."

"Just send me sumpthin' and I'll look at it."

We've all heard that brilliant brush-off when calling a new prospect. Unfortunately, many of us take it as a sincere expression of interest and jump at the chance to spend our valuable time writing a compelling cover letter, stuffing several dollars' worth of glossy brochures with four-color pictures of every award-winning product our company ever created into an expensive overnight envelope, and waiting breathlessly by the phone expecting an order. Or, being realists who have been stung before, we say, "sure" and hang up, knowing that the chances of our literature ever being read are somewhere between slim and none. That's a shame, because there is a third alternative that can help you sell more products.

Before we get to that, though, it's helpful to understand why the brochure brush-off works so well. It's due mainly to the fact that, as human beings, we all want to escape from potential conflict or stressful situations without physical or mental injury. That's why salespeople so readily accept the answer "I'll think about it" when they ask for the order. It's not "no" and it allows them to leave the prospect's office without being turned down (they think). "Send me some literature" is the same kind of answer. It gives us a convenient excuse to relieve the stress that builds up while we're trying to make a sale. So, the first step in dealing with the brochure brush-off is to fight off your own desire to take the easy way out.

Then recognize the ploy for what it is: an opportunity! When the prospect says, "send me something," you're getting the perfect chance to *get* more information. And information, whether it is about his or her needs and wants, decision-making procedures, potential budget, or whatever, is powerful fuel for the selling machine. Seize that opportunity and ask a few questions:

- "I'll be happy to send you some material. So I can highlight some things for you, can you give me an idea of what you might be looking for?"
- "I'd hate to overload you with all of our literature, so perhaps you'd tell me a little bit about your business so I can filter it for you."
- "What kind of questions do you expect to be answered by our material?"

Delivered in a non-threatening tone, these kinds of questions can get the prospect talking about why they might become interested in your products or service in the first place or why they're not interested at all at the present moment. Try to keep the conversation going and listen carefully to the answers. You should also try to get some more specifics:

- "Is there anyone else in your company that should get copies of the material? How about other departments?"
- "Do you have literature from our competitors?"
- "When will you have had a chance to look at our material so we can speak again?"
- And, if you get far enough along in the conversation and the time seems right, it doesn't hurt to turn up the heat a notch:

- "If you like what I send you, then what will happen?"
- "If you like what you see, will you be buying?"
- "So, can I assume you want the material because you're definitely interested in making a purchase?"

Always keep in mind that the purpose of your call in the first place is to arrange a face-to-face meeting with the prospect. With that goal in mind, offer to deliver the material in person. If you need to, even promise to just "drop it off" in the interests of saving the prospect some time. This may seem very time-consuming and inefficient, but it actually accomplishes several things, including showing the prospect how much you want his or her business. It also demonstrates your company's dedication to personal service, something sorely lacking in today's impersonal, call-screening world that will help you stand out from the crowd.

Just as an aside, there's another way to provide information about your products and services to potential clients: use the Internet. One way, of course, is to offer to email your materials to the client instead of depending on the good old US Postal Service. You can attach files containing your brochures along with digital pictures of special products, or even put them into the body of the email itself. That approach saves you a lot of time (not to mention money for printing) while getting you a valuable piece of information you can use for future selling, the prospect's email address.

If you have a website, you can direct the prospect to it instead of, or in addition to, sending them expensive printed brochures. But don't just tell them to look you up on the web; ask for the prospect's email address so you can send him or her the link to your site. If you want to take it a very effective step further, put a "private web page" up on your server that has a specific message for that prospect with some pictures of products you think would be particularly appropriate. Email the prospect a link to *that* page, and it's as if you've designed a brochure just for them, which, in effect, you have!

Follow-Up Call

Next comes the key step, following up on the material. Far too many salespeople mail the brochure, wait a couple of days, then call and say something like, "I sent you some stuff, didja get it?" Instead, you should start by reviewing some of the details of your last call, particularly the needs and wants the prospect hopefully expressed at that time, then ask if the material you sent addressed them. If so, you may be able to ask for and get an order right over the phone! If not, ask for a personal face-to-face meeting where you can better learn about the prospect's needs.

By the way, you should follow these same steps with someone who calls *you* and asks for a brochure or a price quote as a result of your company's advertising or other marketing. Don't just send it to them; get some information first! Take advantage of the circumstances surrounding their request by asking why they made it. Was there something in your ad that caught their eye? Did someone refer them to you? Do they have a special problem they're trying to solve? In other words, find out if they have a need you can satisfy or if they are just collecting literature. If your company has someone (like the receptionist) who typically fulfills such requests—stop! Have a salesperson respond to them, even if it means calling the prospect back.

The brochure brush-off is an old standby for prospects who are assailed by salespeople all day long. It works most of the time, because so many salespeople respond by hanging up the phone so they can hurry up and get an over-stuffed packet to the post office. The next time you're tempted to do that, ask yourself when was the last time an envelope full of brochures produced anything except bulging muscles for the mailman? Then start asking the prospect some questions.

Chapter 18
Essential Presentation Skills

"Your task is to constantly bring their attention back to your pitch."

Some people say that the ability to speak is what separates man from beast. I don't know about that, but I do believe it's the salesperson's ability and willingness to communicate persuasively that separates him or her from mere mortals.

Willingness is just as important—maybe even more so—than the ability to communicate. There are plenty of people who can construct a strong legal argument or write a powerful piece of advertising copy. But selling requires a crucial disposition to put your self-respect, personal income, and some other sensitive items on the line time after time every day in face-to-face persuasion.

Your success as a salesperson depends in no small degree on your ability to persuasively communicate one-on-one with your prospects. I'm sure that's not a major revelation. What you may not realize, however, is that many of the same skills you were exposed to in Public Speaking 101 are the same ones you will use in selling. The techniques your seventh grade English teacher made you use to deliver that stirring oration "Rally Round The Flag" are much the same ones you'll use to make that almost equally stirring speech about "Acme Widgets: the Finest Made."

But there's one skill you probably weren't taught in Public Speaking 101 that's crucial to selling. That's not talking, it's *listening*.

Listening

In my consulting practice, I never talk about the salesperson's speaking ability—I always refer to their communication skills. Communication is a two-party, two-action process. In sales communication as in other types of inter-personal communication, each person takes turns speaking and listening. Person A talks and Person B listens to what they say. Then Person B replies and Person A listens to their answer. There is a completed communications loop—hopefully.

Unfortunately, it doesn't happen that way much of the time. In fact, I'm sure you can probably identify plenty of instances where the communications loop isn't completed. Your spouse is talking to you about the necessity of squeezing the toothpaste tube strictly from the bottom, but your mind is on what your best customer was complaining about today, so you don't "hear" a word that's being said. The sound physically strikes your ear drums. Your neural system transmits it to your brain, but it doesn't register because your brain is busy with something else. And so you have the same "conversation" the next morning.

Or your sales manager is going over (for at least the tenth time) the pricing strategies for your fall line but you're busy mentally calculating the effects of the new pricing on the sales incentive payouts and, besides, you've heard this spiel nine times already. He's talking and you're hearing, but you are not *listening*. There's a big difference.

It happens all the time. One of my favorite examples occurs when you use that automatic conversation opener, "How are you?" Most of the time, you'll get an automatic answer like, "I'm fine. How are you?"

Every once in a while, though, the answer is far from automatic: "I'm terrible, my dog died yesterday and I'm just heartbroken about it." But you're still in auto-answer mode, so you come back with, "I'm just great, too. I know you're busy, so let's get right into the presentation." I've done it and I bet you've heard it happen, too. You *think* you're paying strict attention—but you're not *listening* to the other person.

Most people think that a salesperson's job is to talk. Even worse, many salespeople think that. And salespeople who believe that their job is to *talk* the prospect into submission then fail to complete the feedback loop by listening to what their prospect is saying. And they wonder why their closing ratio is so low.

I won't belabor the point. Just remember that more sales are made with your ears (and what's between them) than your mouth.

Selling Across The Desk

There are many kinds of sales calls and presentations. One-on-one across the desk in a private office. Or in a cubicle with a dozen unseen eavesdroppers on the other sides of the dividers. Or on the factory floor with machines clanking in the background. Pitches to a group of decision-influencers sitting around a conference table. Or listening in on a conference call. Or with your sales manager on a double-team call. There are specific variations on your techniques that you'll develop to use in each situation, but for now let's work through the most basic scenario: you're solo in Mr. Big's office face to face across his desk.

Our goal is to equip you to make your very first sales call, so bear with me if you've been selling for a while. If you're a new salesperson, or have ever had to learn to sell a new line of products or represent a new company, you know that one of the most difficult things in sales is figuring out what to say on your first few calls. Most salespeople eventually develop their own "patter" through trial and error. But the new situation can still be frustrating. If you follow these techniques though, you'll find you can make very effective sales presentations right away.

Meeting The Right Needs

The Creative Selling System is based on meeting customer needs. As you would expect, the creative sales pitch is no different. You start by talking about the prospect's needs, then you listen to what they say about their needs, and finally you offer your product or service as the solution to their needs.

It's as simple as that. Except in real life, of course, nothing's ever simple. You may have the best intentions in the world, but while you're sitting there separated from Mr. Big by that acre of mahogany he uses as a desk, you're going to be thinking about the huge commission you've got on the line, about whether your company can really deliver all the things you're promising, about whether this sale will win you the trip to Las Vegas in the latest sales contest for your region. In other words, it's human nature to be thinking not about his needs but about your need to make the sale.

Prospect Language

The language you use reflects which set of needs you're talking about. Your vocabulary reveals your knowledge of your industry or your company's products and services, but its specialized terms may not be in the same language spoken by Mr. Big. Every industry has its own argot, or set of words, acronyms, and code phrases that serve as a verbal shorthand for insiders. Some of this jargon has become fairly well-known in the general version of English we all speak—but most of it hasn't.

For example, most people know that a "spot" on television means a short commercial message. But how many know what a "donut" means in TV-language? (It's a commercial message where the beginning and end remain the same from showing to showing but the middle—the hole in the donut—is changed frequently.) Your industry has its own jargon, too.

It's important that you identify the specialized terms you use in your presentations and make sure they are ones that Mr. Big will understand. Be especially careful of acronyms—those collections of initials that are taking over our language.

"We are offering you only Bb+ rated or better NYC GO's, Mr. Big, so your 1099 will be very simple."

This may be perfectly clear to a stockbroker or an accountant, but what does it mean to simple folk like you and me—or Mr. Big?

One of the biggest dangers of using specialized terms is that not only are they not understood, they can make the prospect feel ignorant. And few people enjoy that feeling or appreciate the person who gives it to them. Most of the time, the prospect will never let you know that he doesn't understand what you're talking about. After all, who likes to admit their ignorance? In the worst case scenario, you'll lose the sale and never really know it's because Mr. Big didn't comprehend just exactly what it was you were trying to sell him.

The specialized language you do need to know, though, is the prospect's. Sprinkling a few well-chosen (and correctly used) phrases from Mr. Big's line of business into your presentation will help you gain credibility. If you're selling to a car dealer, you should know what an "up" is. Furniture stores carry "case goods" and appliance stores sell "white goods" and sometimes "brown goods." Almost all retailers keep track of their "SKU's." If you're going to sell to prospects in these categories, you need to know their language. Just make sure you use the terms correctly—and don't overdo it.

You'll pick up a lot of your prospects' jargon when you do your research. You can also learn a lot by reading the trade publications from their industries and browsing the web sites of their trade associations. Many of them offer a glossary of industry terms that you'll find particularly useful.

If you suspect that your prospect doesn't understand something, by the way, there's nothing wrong with pausing in your presentation to clear up the confusion. This holds true whether it's because of your use of an unfamiliar term or any other cause of lack of clarity. When the prospect gets that quizzical look, stop the pitch and offer to clear up the misunderstanding. Just make sure you blame yourself for the problem by saying something to the effect, "I sense that I've failed to make something clear. You look like you have a question." Then give them time and space to ask their question.

Communication that is not *received* can't be understood, so it doesn't occur. I don't know if a tree that falls in the forest when no one is there makes a sound—but I can guarantee that no one is going to buy the lumber. Sales don't happen if the prospect doesn't receive the message.

Attention And Interest

Another factor essential to the completion of sales communication is holding the prospect's attention throughout the pitch. That's harder than it sounds, as anyone who has done any public speaking can attest. Holding the listener's attention is one of the hardest tasks a communicator faces for several reasons.

For one thing, the human brain is programmed to check for distractions—to actually seek them out—while it's listening to you. This involuntary reflex probably dates back to the early days of prehistory when our ancestral prospect's knuckles dragged the ground. As our proto-prospect walked across the savanna he was in constant danger from predators. He had to check out every sound, movement, or scent that came along, just like the deer that raises its head between every bite of grass.

When you're making your pitch, your prospects are constantly tuning in and out of your sales presentation to check for other "dangers" lurking about the room. Unlike the deer, though, your prospects have a lot of other things on their minds. These subjects pop into their consciousness every time they momentarily stop listening to you. They may be staring right at your face, apparently hanging on your every word. In their heads though, there's a monologue going on about what their spouse said last night at the dinner table, what they're going to have for dinner tonight, how much traffic they can expect to encounter on the commute home, whether their car needs a tune-up, how large the balance on their credit card has become, and on and on. They tune in and out of your presentation while they're also tuning in and out of that monologue in their head.

Your task is to constantly bring their attention back to your pitch. You have to continually recapture and hold their interest. Your presentation skills can help you do that.

Change is the key to holding interest. The mind attends to stimuli that change. The deer perks its ears up when a twig snaps in the background or the wind sweeps from another direction. Your prospect will tune back into your presentation when something—anything—in your delivery changes.

Work on varying the volume, pitch, and tone of your voice. We've all sat through presentations delivered in a monotone and know how deadly boring even the most interesting subject can be if it's delivered in a consistent, constant drone. To avoid a monotone delivery, vary your volume, pitch, and tone.

Speak louder and softer, emphasizing different points in your presentation with different vocal volumes.

Practice speaking in higher and lower pitches—which convey excitement and intimacy among other emotions.

Work on different tones for different places in your presentation—authoritative, humorous, decisive, inquisitive.

Every time you change one of these factors, you get the prospect's attention back on your pitch.

You can also vary the rate, intensity, and spacing of your speech. Some people seem to speak at machine-gun rate all the time. They wear their listeners out from trying to keep up. Believe it or not, it's almost impossible to speak too *slowly*. The sentence that sounds to you like it's never going to end will probably sound just fine to the listener.

Remember that the adrenaline pumping through your veins while you're making a pitch will speed you up unless you make a strong conscious effort to control it. The intensity of your presentation can range from conversational to table-pounding, as long as it's appropriate to the points you're trying to emphasize.

And don't forget to pause. An intentional silence will bring a listener back to you every time. It will also heavily underscore the point that precedes it.

Use your body appropriately. It's almost impossible to stay enthusiastic and keep a high energy level while you're slouched in a chair. If you can, stand for some or all of your presentation. Moving about the room, even if it's just a few feet, will help keep the prospect focused on you and what you're saying. If you have to sit down while you're making your pitch (and you do, most of the time), sit on the middle of the seat and don't let your body touch the back of the chair. Keep your arms away from the armrests so you don't slouch to one side. The very act of sitting erect will make you more energetic and interesting.

Good posture, whether sitting or standing, gives you better breath control, too. This puts more energy into your voice and helps you speak more clearly.

You should make lots of gestures whether you're sitting, pacing, or standing still. Gestures re-capture interest and provide strong non-verbal emphasis to important points. To help free your hands for use during the pitch, don't fold them in your lap or on the desk. And don't put a pen or other object in your fingers automatically. You'll have a tendency to "fidget" with it if you're not using it, so put it back in your pocket when you're done with it.

Ask Questions

All of these techniques will help hold the prospect's interest during your presentation. The best technique of all, though, is to ask questions. I'm not talking about closing questions or agreement questions or quizzing the prospect about your pitch. I'm referring to questions about the prospect's business and its needs as they relate to your idea. That's how you learn what they want to buy.

When you ask the prospect a question, their attention is immediately brought back into your presentation. Questions demonstrate your focus on the prospect and their needs. Also, you must ask questions to accomplish the purpose of the call, which is to learn as much about the prospect as you can in order to shape your current and future proposals to them accordingly.

Salespeople who don't ask questions are almost always those who have a canned pitch they use on everybody—and prospects can sense that. Very few people will invest much effort in listening to a canned presentation. After all, the salesperson doesn't care enough about them to present a custom idea, so why should the prospect care enough to listen? They know it's not about *them,* so they don't have much interest.

Questions are so important that I format the entire Creative Selling presentation, both written and oral, around them. The five-page written presentation, in fact, is designed to prompt you to ask a question at the end of four of the five pages. You're encouraged to ask more than that, of course, but if you at least remember to ask a question before you turn every page, you'll keep both the prospect and yourself involved in the pitch in a positive way.

Chapter 19
Your Creative Presentation Script

"If you won't shut up and let them talk—
they can't give you an order."

Here's where it all comes together. Let's go through the written presentation page by page and outline a presentation script for you to follow. You may want to refer to the sample written proposal for St. Luke's Hospital as you go along. You'll notice that the script includes some specific stage directions, too. That's because what you do and what the prospect sees are just as important as the words you use.

Opening The Sale

Page One (the cover): As you're chatting about the weather and thanking the prospect for seeing your and making other small talk, take one copy of the presentation out of your briefcase. Don't hand it to the prospect. Before they see it, you need to very briefly cover three items and ask a question. This is the introduction to your presentation, but keep it as conversational as possible.

In the first sentence, you "set up" the need. In the second one you promise to meet the need, which is the prime benefit of your proposed idea. In the third one you describe the idea. And, finally, you ask the prospect a general question to get them used to talking during your pitch.

If you use the St. Luke's Hospital presentation as your example, your opening statements would go something like this:

"We've been studying the health care market, Mr. Big, and have observed that St. Luke's is a great institution with a lot of competition. *(That's the problem.)*

To help St. Luke's stand out from that competition *(that's the benefit.)*, we've developed a year-long marketing plan for your consideration.

What we're going to recommend is a series of television messages that highlight the caring nature of St. Luke's as exemplified by the many fine volunteer organizations that help you. *(That's the idea.)*

Does that sound interesting?" *(That's the question.)*

Read that sequence out loud and time yourself. You'll notice that it takes much less than 30 seconds to say all four of those sentences and accomplish those tasks. If the introduction to your presentation takes longer than that, you're spending too much time on it.

What you're trying to accomplish with this introduction is to tell the prospect what's coming in the presentation so he or she can better absorb it. This is very important because people need repetition of key points to truly understand them so they can act on them. One of the best ways to do this is to practice one of the first rules from Public Speaking 101:

Tell them what you're going to tell them. Tell them. Then tell them what you told them.

Physical control of the written presentation also comes into play here. Assuming you're sitting across the desk from Mr. Big (and not in a conference room addressing a group), this is accomplished by the simple tactic of producing only one copy and holding it yourself. Don't hand it to the prospect! If he or she reaches for it, politely tell them that you'll leave them a copy but you need this one at the moment. Then use the written presentation as a visual aid.

The reason for this is simple, of course. You don't want the prospect grabbing the presentation and immediately turning the pages looking for the price while you're trying to explain the benefits. You want to control the pace and timing of as many elements of the call as you can.

If you have access to a laptop and good presentation software, or can comfortably use one of the many small desktop presentation easels available, these help you accomplish the same thing. They're not necessary, though, and have some drawbacks of their own. I once flew halfway across the country to make a pitch to a prospective client. I was ready with my laptop and a really snazzy PowerPoint presentation on it. Then the little gremlin that lives inside all computers decided that the presentation wasn't going to run (after three tries in front of the squirming prospect). I had to deliver the pitch *a cappella*, so to speak. Have you ever known a computer to work exactly how you want it to when you want it to?

I generally prefer the simple tactic of holding a single copy of the written presentation so the prospect can see it without grasping and controlling it himself. I've also practiced my upside-down reading skills until they're second nature.

Selling the Benefits

Page 2 (the benefits): This page has three short bullet points summarizing the benefits your idea will bring to the prospect. Your commentary should cover each of the benefits, rephrasing and repeating each one three times before you move on to the next one. The last thing you do before you turn the page is—you guessed it—ask a question.

Going back to the St. Luke's example, the first bullet point on the benefits page is,

"Maintain and enhance the caring image the hospital has earned throughout your service area."

While you are showing this page to the prospect, here's what you say about the first bullet point. The lines are numbered just to show you how we've covered the same benefit with different words three times:

1. "Our program is designed to maintain and enhance the caring image you folks have developed in your market."

2. "It's taken years of hard work for you to build a reputation for delivering warm, responsive care and we want to spread that word to every corner of the market."

3. "St. Luke's is known as the best, and we can demonstrate that very clearly on television."

Remember, repetition sells. After you've presented the other two benefits in the same way, it's time for another question, which might be something like, "Are these goals consistent with your goals?" or "Have we identified some goals you'd like to accomplish?" If the answer to your question is "yes," you'll go on with the presentation.

But what if you ask a question and the answer is "no?" What if all your research and brainstorming have pinpointed a need that the prospect can't or won't perceive? If that's the case, take the presentation off the table and start asking questions. Just like in jujitsu, you use the prospect's own momentum to move them in the direction you want them to go.

Keep in mind that you're there to learn as much as you are to sell—it's the first call—so keep the door open for your next presentation by switching on your prime selling apparatus—your ears. Here are some learning questions to ask:

- "That's interesting. Could you elaborate on the goals you want to achieve?"
- "I appreciate your candor. Could you tell me more?"

- "Let's not waste any of your time on this particular idea, then, since it's designed to reach these specific goals. Tell me what you'd like to accomplish so I can give some thought to another idea."

You need to be prepared for this contingency, but you'll be surprised at how seldom it happens. If you're a conscientious creative seller and do your homework on the prospect before your meeting, your benefits are going to be pretty close to their needs most of the time. Besides, if the prospect has let you get this far, he wants to hear your idea before he passes final judgment.

Selling the Idea

Page 3 (the idea): Once the benefit question is answered, turn to the idea page and explain how it will work. Try to go step by step through the elements of your plan and make sure the prospect comprehends each one before you move to the next one. Here's where you'll usually start to get some questions, so take your time and explain everything in detail.

This is also the place where your talent as a artist in words will shine. The very best salespeople have a wonderful ability to describe their idea so vividly that the prospect can "see" it happening. Your enthusiasm can't be too high during this section. You've brought in an exciting idea and you want the prospect to get excited about it. Take them to the top of the mountain and show them what you're offering. Make them taste it, feel it, smell it. You want Mr. Big to hear the bells ringing and the cheers rising as the world recognizes the brilliant decision he made to buy your idea. Sell it to him!

And then ask another question before you turn the page.

The prospect knows you're getting ready to ask for the order, so let them off the hook by saying something like "I know you're wondering how much this is going to cost, and I'm getting to that next. But first, do you like the idea?" or "No obligation—would you like to do this?"

You have to get a positive response, or there's no point in going on to the proposal page. If the prospect likes the idea, the price hurdle is pretty much the only one left to overcome. If the prospect doesn't like the idea, the price doesn't matter, does it? So why even talk about the price if that's the case? If the answer is "no," it's time to take the proposal off the table and ask some more questions:

- "What bothers you about it?"
- "Is there something else you have in mind?"
- "How can we change this to make it work for you?"

Before I go on, let me point out that you're not asking these question in order to identify and answer objections. That shouldn't be your attitude at this (or any other) point in the presentation. You're simply asking questions to get a more clear understanding of how you can be of better service to the prospect. You're not asking questions so you can argue with the prospect. If you do, you'll blow the entire budding relationship.

Selling the Investment

Page 4 (the proposal): This is the only page where you don't ask a question at the end. What you *are* going to do, though, is carefully review the specifics of what you're selling the prospect.

Think of this as a way to anticipate the "why" questions and to answer them before they get asked. Why you chose this exact selection of widgets. Why you're scheduling these particular commercial announcements. Why you're asking the prospect to buy these three special services instead of those other three. In short, you're exhibiting your expertise in helping the prospect make best use of your company's products or services.

You'll also want to point out as often as possible how a particular product or feature in your plan delivers one of the specific benefits you're selling. Your goal at this point isn't to justify your price, it's to demonstrate that you can produce the elements that make the plan work for the prospect.

This is an important time to keep your ears open. If you've gotten this far, the prospect has some strong interest in doing business with you. The comments and observations he or she has made about the specific offerings in your proposal will tell you worlds of information about the prospect's likes and dislikes, hot buttons and turn-offs. You'll need that information to close this sale or open the door to the next one, so *listen.*

The Moment Of Truth

Now, there it is. Right at the bottom of the page. Staring the prospect in the face. Jumping off the paper and burning right into his brain. The *PRICE*. You know he sees it. He knows you know he sees it. He also knows you're getting ready to ask for the order. So do it.

In one fluid sentence,

1. State the price,
2. Turn the page,
3. Restate the prime benefit and
4. Ask for the order.

Don't skip any of these four actions and do them in this exact sequence. You must turn the page so that the prospect is looking at the benefits, not the price, when you ask for the order. It's a small but vital step. Prospects are much more likely to say "yes" to buying benefits than they are to spending money. You want them to envision the satisfaction of their needs rather than the effect on their bank account.

The fifth page (the one you turn to) is a copy of the second page—the benefits page. That's so you don't have to physically fumble around looking for it when you're going through this sequence.

Do not pause at any step in this process, even for breath. This encourages the prospect to comment on the price. When two people converse, they basically take turns talking and listening. When one person stops talking, it send a signal to the other person that's it's their turn to start. The second person (the prospect) almost always starts talking about the last item mentioned, which will be the price in this case. In my experience, what they say about the price is never "Gee, that's not very expensive at all."

It's all too easy to cue the prospect to raise a price objection unless you're prepared to avoid it. You've been encouraging the prospect to talk throughout the pitch. You've solicited their opinion on everything you've said. It's only natural to do the same with the price. But that's the one time you don't want the prospect's opinion.

Besides, you probably won't have to ask for it. Most prospects will offer their opinion on your price whether you want it or not. Let's not make it any easier for them. We'll get into handling price (and other) objections in subsequent chapters. For now, just concentrate on managing your presentation so that the prospect is looking at the benefits page (the last one) when you ask for the order.

And please, please, please make sure you explicitly ask for the order. You'd be surprised at how seldom salespeople do that. They think they're asking for the order lots of times, but they're really not. You need to say words that mean exactly one thing: "Do you want to buy this today?" In fact, that's not a bad phrase to use! I'll cover some other closing techniques later, too, but be forewarned that I recommend you just ask for the order in plain English most of the time.

The closing sequence for St. Luke's would go something like this:

"Your investment in this program is less than $10,000 per month *(turn to the last page)*, Mr. Big, and for that investment you'll have a television marketing program that will even further enhance St. Luke's stellar reputation. Would you like to make that investment?"

Read these two sentences out loud without taking a breath. Be especially careful not to pause as you're turning the page. That's the end of your presentation.

It's not the end of the call, of course, because now it's time to shut up and really listen.

Listen Hard

There are three reasons to keep your mouth shut and your ears open. First, you don't want to miss it if the prospect says "yes." Second, you need to hear what questions, modifications, and concerns the prospect has in mind. Finally, you don't want to talk yourself out of the sale.

The sales truism that says "He who talks first, loses," is generally true but not for the reason most people think. You're not engaged in a power struggle with the prospect, which is what this adage implies. The salesperson is likely to "lose" the sale if they talk first simply because they're not giving the prospect a chance to say "yes." Shut up and give the prospect a chance to express their judgment before you jump in with more information for them to consider. If you won't shut up and let them talk—they can't give you an order.

While you're "listening" to what they are saying, be sure you really listen—so that the words they're saying are registering in your brain. It's an easy time to get distracted. You've been singularly focused on making your presentation up until this point, but now your mind has a chance to seek other stimulus. Don't let it. *Listen* to the comments Mr. Big is making about your idea.

Your silence also keeps you from talking yourself out of the order. It's a tremendous temptation to offer just one more tidbit of information, one more reason the prospect should buy, one more point. But don't do it. You're just as likely to bring up a new objection as you are to present a new reason to buy.

Chapter 20
Honing Your Presentation Skills

"Stage fright is your friend
—all you have to do is control it."

So, are you ready to go out there and sell? Not just yet. First you need to work on your stagecraft a little. Making a sales presentation is a lot like being in front of an audience. You have lines to deliver and stage directions to execute. You have a script to follow which will, if you are a good actor, convey the emotions you are communicating to the audience, your prospect. But you can't do any of these things if you don't know your role. That's why you need to rehearse.

There are lots of ways to effectively rehearse. You can get a friend or coworker to play the prospect. If you can get past the side issues, you can even ask your sales manager to help out.

If you want to work alone, pitch yourself. Just sit in front of a mirror while you make your presentation. If you have access to a video camera or webcam on your computer (or even just a voice tape recorder), use those tools as well.

Just make sure that you make every practice session a *dress* rehearsal. Do it "for real." Out loud. With props. In costume. Silently running through your lines can't help you work on the variety of tone, speech rate, intensity, gestures and other techniques that will make your performance an award-winner.

The goal of rehearsal is to make you more confident of yourself. If you know your lines, you can concentrate on your delivery instead of what you're supposed to say next. If you've rehearsed asking questions, they won't sound forced or artificial—and you'll be able to listen to the answers instead of worrying about your presentation.

The repetition of your idea will also make you more confident of its value to the prospect. Your enthusiasm will increase with each practice session until you'll be a dynamo in front of Mr. Big. Remember, enthusiasm is contagious—and you want your prospect to catch it from you.

There are two parts of your presentation script that I suggest you memorize word for word. That is the opening sequence and the closing, the lines I asked you to read out loud in the previous chapter. It's important at both of these points to sound confident, to be in total control, and to get through the lines smoothly. The best way I know how to do that is to actually memorize the lines.

Stage Fright

Do you suffer from stage fright? I hope so! You'll be a more effective seller if you do.

I've done thousands of sales presentations, speeches, seminars, and live radio and television appearances—and I get that little flutter in my stomach, sweat on the palms, and shortness of breath every time. Every good speaker I know has similar reactions.

Most speakers welcome them, because they are signs that our energy level is going to be high. In fact, if I don't have an attack of stage fright before I speak, I know I'm not focused on my presentation. The same is true before every sales presentation—I *want* the extra energy that comes from an attack of stage fright.

Stage fright is your friend—all you have to do is control it. The first step is to recognize the symptoms for what they are, which is a small rush of adrenaline which prompts a "fight or flee" response to a perceived danger. The next step is to make a conscious choice to "fight" rather than "flee," which is usually not an option anyway. You'll know you've made that choice when your concentration turns away from yourself and how you feel and toward the reactions and feedback you're getting from your prospect. In other words, you replace your inner fear with intense concentration on your audience.

This change in focus allows you to energize your presentation—using the adrenal rush to your best advantage.

There is a little secret to controlling the intensity of your stage fright symptoms. As you're waiting in the lobby before your presentation or just before you get out of your car to see Mr. Big, take the physical edge off by doing some simple isometric exercises. Press your palms together—hard—for 30 seconds. Grip your steering wheel or the arms of your chair as hard as you can for another half minute. This will burn off some of that excess adrenaline in your system while leaving you the energy you need to convey enthusiasm.

Now take a couple of deep, long breaths, using your diaphragm to fill your lungs completely. Let each breath out slowly to a count of 10. This will steady your voice and make you ready for a powerful opening statement.

Your stage fright has now become a reservoir of energy that you can tap into when you need it. You'll find that you're better focused on your prospect and your presentation is much more intense and powerful. You've made stage fright your friend.

Mirror, Mirror, On The Wall

While I'm in this "do's and don'ts" mode, a brief word about appearance and conduct for sales calls. Chewing gum, tobacco products, and anything else that goes in your mouth shouldn't be there during a sales call. They not only interfere with your ability to speak clearly, they make you look highly unprofessional. And there's always the distressing possibility that your wad of gum might pop out of your mouth and land on the prospect's desk.

If you're offered coffee or a cold drink, have one if the prospect is having one. Sharing sustenance is a primeval-level bonding experience, so take advantage of the opportunity when it arises. If the prospect isn't partaking, though, you're better off without as well. You don't have to drink it, by the way, and you actually shouldn't try to juggle a cup of hot coffee with your proposal while you're trying to talk. Just accept it, take a sip, then set the container to one side—preferably someplace where it will be impossible to spill.

You should dress appropriately, which means in the same manner or *slightly* better than your prospects. If you're not sure, check out how their staff dresses by making a reconnaissance visit to the account. If they wear ties and jackets, you wear ties and jackets. If they wear open collars you can too, but it's also fine to wear a tie. Just don't show up in a three-piece suit if they're in blue jeans and T-shirts.

The same basic rule applies for women. You want your attire to seem perfectly natural to the prospect without drawing attention to itself. It should go without saying that hemlines and necklines should not be a distraction. The goal is to keep the prospect focused on your presentation, not on your physical attributes.

Chapter 21
Fear Of Closing

"Closing is more of a process than an event."

Fear of flying. Fear of snakes. Fear of heights. They are all based on your conviction that a bad thing is going to happen to you if you get on that airplane, touch that snake, or climb that ladder. Fear of closing the sale stems from the same conviction that something bad is going to happen to you if you ask for the order: the prospect is going to say "no." My intuition tells me that more salespeople suffer from fear of closing than all other phobias combined.

Yet it shouldn't be that way. Closing the sale is the most misunderstood of all the various selling skills. It's probably also the most over-rated. Regardless, there's no question that closing causes the most sales-related antacid consumption.

There is no mystery behind closing. It's not a hard skill to learn or to practice. If you are concerned about it, just keep in mind that the goal of every sales call is to leave a happy customer behind. If you concentrate on that instead of how badly you want to make the sale, you'll both be happier at the end of the call.

Closing Mythology

There's a big misperception about closing. It relates to the traditional view of the salesperson as a silver-tongued devil who weaves a trap of words around his unwary prey, snapping it closed with clever ruses and mental manipulation. This view characterizes the prospect as a dolt who can't make up his own mind until tricked into buying by the "closing techniques" so assiduously studied by the salesperson. Nothing could be further from the truth.

I've never sold to any dolts, have you? Most of my prospects—and I'm sure most of yours—are pretty smart people or they wouldn't be in the decision-making positions they're in. They are good buyers who consider all the options and the pros and cons before they make a decision, then they negotiate hard until they get a deal they can live with. Not a dolt among them. There have been a few customers whose sanity and/or parentage I may have questioned, but I've never found a prospect stupid enough to be tricked into buying something by my fancy closing tactics.

Short And Long Term Relationships

A familiar sales adage says you should close early and close often. That's a clever way of defining the salesperson's job as getting the order at all costs. The problem with this concentration of effort on closing skills is that it shifts the emphasis away from developing long-term customer relationships and onto writing orders today. One mark of a manager with this attitude is how much they boast about their team's high closing ratio.

These sales managers believe that the actions that form long term relationships—researching the prospect, making multiple proposals and revisions, focusing on meeting the customer needs—consume too much time. They divert the salesperson's attention from the real job at hand, which is generating orders. "Let the long-term relationships take care of themselves," they say. "I've got to make this month's quota." To them, long-term customer relationships are fine, but what really matters is the order brought in the door today. And if enough orders are written each day, long-term relationships don't matter.

That's true as far as it goes. Where that shortsighted philosophy doesn't go is into the realm of profit margins. The long-term customer is almost always the most profitable one as well.

This short term philosophy is also the exact opposite of the Creative Selling System, where one of the major goals is the creation of long term customer relationships. You should approach the act of closing the sale with the idea in mind that every sales call should give the customer yet another reason to do business with you—again. It's a pro-active, pro-customer way to look at your job.

Complex Sales

Another reason salespeople sometimes develop a fear of asking for the order is that they vastly overrate the importance of the step. Closing gets a lot more credit for its place in the sales process than it deserves. Those who practice the Creative Selling System for preparing and making presentations often learn that they never even get a chance to close because the client buys right away. My seat-of-the-pants estimate is that about half of all successful sales calls end this way. You don't close the sale—it just happens.

This is particularly true for products and services that require a complex sell, or one in which several decisions and decision-makers and decision-influencers are involved. A complex sale doesn't occur in one sales call—or even two or three. It may take weeks or months of presentations, revisions, and proposal "tweaking" before the prospect becomes a customer by giving you the order.

In complex sales a classic closing opportunity may never even arise. Instead, word comes down from one of the many people involved in the decision that your relationship with them has now evolved into a partnership with your proposal at the center of it. What "closes" that sale isn't any clever technique, but rather the tenacious effort you put into the proposal and working through the client's decision-making process.

The salesperson who pushes and pushes and pushes to close a complex sale can blow the whole opportunity by selling too hard. It's one thing to be aggressive and keep pursuing the proposal. It's quite another to back the prospect into a mental corner and try to force their hand. This sends the message that you are less interested in becoming an ally than you are in making the sale, which is a major turn-off for many prospects.

Closing Made Simple

But if half of your sales "just happen," that means that the other half don't—and half don't feed the bulldog. It's this *other* half of the time that closing skills come in handy.

In these situations, for one reason or another the prospect won't say "yes" until you ask him to. Maybe he lacks the self-confidence to make a decision and announce it. Maybe he's reluctant to make the first move. Maybe he's waiting for a better offer from you and you need a closing question to signal that negotiations are over. Or maybe the prospect is a salesperson as well, and is just waiting to see if you are professional enough to close the sale.

If you get to the end of the sales presentation without a voluntary "yes" from the prospect, you know you are going to have to make a closing move. Welcome it. Embrace the opportunity. Remember, if you *never* needed to ask for the order, you wouldn't have a job.

Just don't fret about it. There's no reason for closing to cause as much anxiety as it does. All you have to do is ask a simple little question: "Do you want to buy this now?" And it's all over but the shouting. Take a page from George Carlin's book and say that sentence out loud a hundred times. A thousand times. It becomes less threatening the more times you say it, doesn't it?

I'm convinced that salespeople get up-tight and nervous about closing because they make too much out of it. They spend so much time figuring out which maneuver to use, which set of magic words will trick the prospect into saying "yes" that they overwhelm themselves. They build go-carts with four-cycle engines and three-speed transmissions when a soap box on wheels will get them there just as fast.

The Almost Close

I learned a lot about sales behavior when I started videotaping role-played sales calls. So did my training clients. One of the most interesting things I learned was how many times a salesperson would think they had asked a closing question when in fact they had not. Call it wishful thinking or delusional behavior, but many, many salespeople would swear that they had tried to close when I asked them about it after the role playing exercise. And they wouldn't believe they hadn't until they saw themselves on tape during the playback and critique.

A form of that is the bobble head close. In this particular maneuver, the salesperson won't ask a closing question verbally, but when a natural closing opportunity arises (like naming the price of the proposal), the salesperson vigorously nods his head up and down. They look a lot like bobble head dolls.

I've considered many explanations for this behavior, including some pretty exotic psycho-medical phenomena. I have finally concluded that the salespeople who practice this move are hoping that the prospect will start nodding in rhythm with them, thus signaling that they are buying what the salesperson is selling. As you can imagine, the bobble head close doesn't work very well.

It's so much more effective to just ask for the order.

Closing Is A Process

Ultimately, you'll find that closing is more of a process than an event. It will often occur over several calls, not just within the context of one presentation. As a rule of thumb, the larger your proposal in dollars or length of commitment, the longer the prospect will take to make a final decision. Again, if you're practicing the Creative Selling System correctly, you're focusing your efforts on large proposals to large potential accounts, so you should not expect to close the sale on the first call.

What you should try to do, however, is mark some progress on each successive call on a particular prospect. Think of your relationship with the prospect as a journey you're making together. Sometimes you travel through known territory at a fast clip, other times you'll both go more slowly because the road is a little slippery. Sometimes the two of you will make detours to avoid major obstacles. Along the way, though, you'll mark your progress toward your ultimate destination, which is where you amicably agree on a plan of action to exchange your goods and services for some of the prospect's money. Try to make some measurable progress on every call.

And never give up! One of the biggest mistakes salespeople make is to let their enthusiasm flag after three or four calls on one prospect without an order. It seems like the prospect is just toying with them, wasting more and more time as the decision-making process drags on and on. Keep in mind that the single most effective closing technique is to keep trying. To keep pitching new ideas, learning about the prospect's needs, and pitching more ideas. That's the way to finally close the sale. And remember that not every journey ends at the original destination.

Chapter 22
Buying Signals

"The most important part of the close is not the clever way you phrase the question, it's the amount of attention you give to the answer."

The best way to learn a new skill or improve your current ones is to break the process down into simple, non-threatening steps and master them one at a time. A good place to start building your closing skills is with an understanding of buying signals.

We often think of closing the sale as something that happens at the end of the sales pitch. In fact, the Creative Selling Presentation format is set up that way. But keep in mind that you don't have to wait until the end to ask for the order. There's no law that says the customer can't buy until you're finished with your presentation. In fact, there's a lot to be said for seizing the moment and speeding up the decision-making process by asking for the order when you receive a strong buying signal.

Sales Skill Number One: Listening

A buying signal is an action the prospect takes that tells you they are ready to say "yes" to a direct question. These actions are sort of like the "tells" that a professional poker player watches for. When you see or hear a buying signal, it's time to pop the question.

That's why listening is such an important selling skill. If all you're hearing is the sound of your own voice, you'll probably miss any buying signals the prospect sends out. If you're listening, though, the prospect will tell you when he wants to buy. That's why I consider listening the single most important closing skill. Let's take a look at some of those buying signals you should be listening for.

Buying signals are generally pretty obvious—as long as you know what to look for. Tune in to the prospect's behavior during your presentation. One buying signal you'll see is when the prospect starts paying extra close attention to something you're saying. They may have silently nodded through the first five minutes of your presentation and grunted noncommittally when you asked them a question. But if they sit up straight and come alive when you start covering a certain point—that's a buying signal. That's likely to happen when you get to the idea page of the presentation and start enumerating the contents and explaining how your idea will work. If they perk up at a particular point, it's time to ask if they'd like to make a purchase.

Another buying signal is voluntary agreement with your points. What we're talking about here is a prospect who says "yes, I agree with that" without being asked. That's voluntary agreement. The prospect has become so wrapped up with the presentation and so enamored of the idea that he forgets he's being sold. This buying signal often precedes a sale that "just happens" without a closing question. Don't count on it, though, and remember that you have nothing to lose by asking a closing question at this point.

When prospects ask "how" questions, they are sending very strong buying signals. "How" questions generally mean that the prospect has mentally moved beyond the "should we" phase of consideration to the "how can we" phase. The prospect is now offering you the opportunity to remove the "can't" obstacle so they can give you the go ahead. This is a good sign because "can't" comes after "won't" in the logical sequence of buyer's decision making.

Green Light Means Ask For The Order

So the lights are flashing green, master control is completing the countdown, all systems are go…what do you do now?

When you hear or see a buying signal, go with the flow. If it's appropriate, review the point that sparked the buying signal and ask for the order. "I can tell you appreciate this unique design, Mr. Big. Would you like to order a dozen now?" This type of closing question will either give you a "yes" or prompt the prospect into telling you what he really wants. Either way, you've come out ahead in the exchange of information.

But what if this is one of those prospects who won't be rushed? What if this is a complex sale that's not going to happen on this call? Are you harming your future chances for a sale by asking for the order? Only if you're trying to close without receiving a buying signal first. And if that's the case, you'll have plenty of opportunities to change direction and recover lost ground if you practice the first rule of selling—listen!

When you ask for the order, shut up and listen. You've heard it before and I'll say it again and again: You make more sales with your ears and what's between them than with what comes out of your mouth. The most important part of the close is not the clever way you phrase the question, it's the amount of attention you give to the answer. Good closers aren't fast talkers, they're fast and effective listeners, ready at all times to hear what the prospect has to say.

Trial Closing

Much has been written about trial closing, which is where you ask a closing question early in the pitch without any real expectation of getting an order at that point in time. I like this technique because it prompts the prospect to talk, which is almost never a bad idea. It there's a buying signal coming from the prospect, especially early in the presentation, your closing question is really just a trial. In fact, if you look closely at the format for the Creative Selling System presentation, what you're really doing is a series of trial closes when you ask a question at the end of every page. You're asking the prospect to "buy" the benefits, then the idea, and finally the proposal.

Every one of these trial closes generates feedback that tells you which direction to take next. But you'll receive that feedback only when you *listen* for it.

Chapter 23
Closing Techniques

"Use only positive action words."

There are many different closing techniques that will make the sale a positive experience for both you and your prospects. I've covered some of them in various guises in other chapters, but let's spend a little time now on an examination of some of the most common ones in greater detail.

The Direct Question Close

My personal favorite closing technique is also the simplest. It's the direct question. It's my favorite because I'm a pretty direct person who likes to say things clearly. I also believe most prospects appreciate this type of close because it's the most honest. It doesn't try to sneak up on them and it gives them credit for being mature, responsible business people able to reach a quick, firm decision. The direct question also eliminates much prior thought about technique on my part, which allows me to concentrate on what the prospect is saying rather than on what my next lines are going to be.

My favorite direct question is, "Would you like to make this investment today?" Since I'm usually selling a fairly expensive consulting service proposal that will pay off in the long run for my clients, the term "investment" suits the offering very well.

I also use the imperative "today" because I'm trying to get a commitment from the prospect now—not later. That word serves as a signal to them that it's "yes or no" time. If you want to use the direct question method, find words of your own that fit your product or service line.

Some other direct questions you might try are

- Would you like to do business today?
- Can I order this for you now?
- Do you want this plan?
- Are we in agreement on the deal?

The direct question needs to be short, sweet, and to the point. It should not have any "wiggle room" in it for the prospect to use to back out of the commitment. It should be strictly a "yes or no" proposition. If the prospect wants to say "maybe" to a "yes or no" question, they have to work at it.

It's important that the words you choose for the direct question close be *your* words. They have to seem natural to you when you say them and natural to the prospect when they're coming out of your mouth. If you seldom use twenty-dollar words in normal conversation, don't stick any into your closing question. If you're a distinguished-looking professional man or woman, stay away from an MTV vocabulary.

You should write down your closing question (and a few variations) and read them out loud to see how they sound. You'll probably be able to tell pretty quickly if those words belong in your mouth.

The Benefit Review Close

The direct question is my favorite closing technique, but I certainly recognize and use others that may be equally effective. In fact, another closing technique, the benefit review, is basically the one we use in the Creative Selling System presentation. As I hope you recall, once you've named the price of your proposed idea, you turn the page, review the prime benefit, and ask for the order.

This technique is grounded very firmly in the fact that your prospect actually buys the benefits you're offering, not the product or service you're selling. He buys the holes, not the drill. She buys the romance, not the perfume. That's why the benefit review strikes closest to the heart of the buying decision.

I like the benefit review method also because it encourages the prospect to talk about their needs and wants. If you're not getting anywhere by reviewing just the prime benefit, go over the others as well, pausing after each one to ask the prospect how he or she feels about it. Each time you get a particularly positive response, ask for the order.

If you get a negative or neutral answer, don't try to counter it or argue; probe for more information. You'll accomplish your goal—moving the closing process along—either way.

The Minor Decision Close

Closely related to the benefit review is the minor decision close. The difference is that you ask the prospect to make an intermediate decision about the product or service before making the final big decision to buy your proposal.

When done properly, the string of minor decisions takes away the obstacles the prospect has in mind one by one until there is no real reason not to make the final one. It also builds a positive team-decision attitude into the presentation as you and the prospect shape the proposal to best suit his or her needs.

When using the minor decision method, try to project an attitude of "*if* you were to buy my proposal, would you prefer option A or B?" so that the prospect doesn't feel any sense of obligation or commitment by making the intermediate decisions. When you do this, it makes the minor decision method a good one to use on prospects who seem to have a hard time making up their minds out of fear of making the wrong big move. Making the minor decisions with your help gives them confidence to make the final big decision.

On the other hand, you sure don't want to use the minor decision close on a prospect who can't seem to make a decision! People like this fear making both large and small decisions. But they are especially hesitant to make quick decisions, so your request for a series of intermediate decisions on the spot could slow the sale to a snail's pace. You'll encounter enough of that problem without causing it yourself.

The minor decision close allows you to test the waters before you plunge into the big question. If you're getting a lot of resistance to the little things, you don't want to shut down the opportunity by pressing for a final decision. You may want to probe their thinking a little bit to see if there are any obstacles lurking under the surface. It's much easier to do this before you ask for the order than afterwards.

The Deal Maker Close

Yet another closing technique is one that requires equal amounts of finesse and brute strength of will. It's the deal maker close. The deal maker is essentially a form of quick, hard negotiation. It's particularly effective when used after an objection or when struggling to modify a proposal to fit the prospect's needs. The exchange goes something like this:

The prospect says, "I'm not sure I like this feature of your proposal."

So you reply, "If I take it out, can I have your order today?"

As you can see, it's put up or shut up time for the prospect. Done correctly, though, it's not as dangerous as it might seem for the salesperson. If the answer is "yes," you obviously have the order. If the answer is "no," you have a natural opening to ask "why" and learn more about the prospect's needs by carefully listening to the answer. You'll also find out if there are other objections that are intentionally hidden or otherwise haven't surfaced yet.

The two dangers in the deal maker close lie in the words that are used and the authority the salesperson has to modify the proposal.

If the salesperson doesn't phrase the deal offer correctly, the prospect can say "yes" without placing an order. This happens when the salesperson says something like, "If I make the change, will you *consider* the deal?" The prospect can easily agree to consider the deal without buying it, so the salesperson hasn't really advanced his sale very far in this example. It's that positive word thing again.

The second problem with the deal maker close rears its ugly head when the salesperson makes a deal without authority to do so. More times than not, the price of the proposal is involved. If the salesperson can't adjust prices on his or her own authority, the deal maker close based on pricing should not be used. What are you going to do if you've shaken hands on a "deal" only to have it rejected by your sales manager when you get back to the office?

Some salespeople will try to work around this problem by making an offer contingent on approval by a higher authority. I don't care for this, since it reeks of the old used car salesman's game of "let me see if I can sell this deal to the big boss" routine. Everybody knows he just goes into the back room with the "big boss" to smoke a cigarette and tell a couple of jokes, then comes back out like he's done you a big favor to close the deal. Either way it works out, the prospect is left wondering if the salesperson can be trusted—and that's no way to start a relationship with a new customer.

But if you can make adjustments in your proposal and you have the brass to make a "put up or shut up" offer, the deal maker close is a highly effective technique to master.

The Alternative Close

Then there's every sales manager's favorite close, the alternatives method. In this technique, you let the prospect choose between two alternative courses of action, either one of which means he has agreed to buy. You don't list "no sale" as one of the options, forcing the prospect to actively tell you if he doesn't want to buy.

The alternatives close is the ultimate assumed close. It assumes that the prospect has already decided to buy even though the words have not been uttered, so all he has to do is to confirm that fact by making a choice.

This method is probably as popular as it is because it is actually a little charade both the salesperson and the prospect can play, avoiding that sometimes ugly, tension-filled moment when the salesperson asks a direct question and the prospect has to give a direct answer.

As you might guess, I've always found this method a little too manipulative and denigrating to the prospect. It's as if you're saying, "I don't think you're smart enough to see through this." But that's just my opinion based on my reactions when someone tries to use the alternatives close on me.

The biggest problem with the alternatives close is that it opens the door to delays by the prospect. And the delayed decision is the salesperson's most dangerous enemy. The problem is, once you've laid the alternatives out on the table, you have no place to go if the prospect says, "Gee, I don't know which one I prefer. Let me sleep on it." After all, you brought up the options. Now are you going to make them rush the decision?

Danger Words

As you're trying out various closing techniques, watch out for a few words and phrases that I generally avoid.

A big one is "commitment," which has a scary, no-turning-back sound to it. People don't make commitments lightly—they think about them, review them, sleep on them before they make them. Commitments are final. Commitments last a long, long time. It's not just men who are reluctant to make commitments, either.

Another touchy phrase is "sign up" as in "Can I sign you up for this program?" People sign contracts, but only after they've read them thoroughly and had them studied by their lawyers. And whenever you get a lawyer involved in a decision, it will take three times as long and be six times as complicated as necessary. Even if the prospect doesn't consult a lawyer, he'll wonder if he should, which gives him another reason to delay making a decision. If you need a signed document, ask the prospect to "okay the order" on the dotted line.

No matter how you phrase your personal closing question, make sure to use only positive action words. "Do you think you might like to maybe make this investment someday?" sure doesn't carry the same persuasive force of "Would you like to make this investment today?"

Take a look at your list of closing phrases. Did you use "might" or "maybe" anywhere? Strike those two words from your vocabulary along with "I think" as in, "I think this is the best plan for you." That says this is your opinion—and you are admitting that someone else (like the prospect) could have another opinion!

These are a small semi-psychological points, but these little things add up to the prospect's total impression of you and your offerings. You want the prospect to see you as a person with total positive confidence in your products and yourself.

Chapter 24
Objections In Four Steps

"The first step in handling an objection is to *listen* to the prospect."

Among people not in sales, the misperception persists that a salesperson makes a living by glibly making presentations, overcoming objections with snappy comebacks, and closing sales with slick, smooth verbal maneuvers. That may be the way you sell aluminum siding to the dimwitted, but it's not the way you sell anything to an even minimally intelligent businessperson or today's educated, wary consumer.

But the image persists, perpetuated by books and training programs constructed around *Sure-fire Answers to Every Objection* and *Make Objections Disappear in Three Easy Steps.* I confess that my sales training programs—just like this book—devote a section to handling objections. That perception of the salesperson as an objection-fighter is so pervasive I couldn't sell them without one.

But my approach to managing objections is very different from the traditional one. That's because I don't believe you win sales by winning arguments with your customers. And that's what "overcoming objections" really is—trying to win an argument.

What Is An Objection?

In the broadest sense, an objection is any obstacle that prevents the prospect from buying your proposal. It can be a totally irrational reason to not buy that the prospect believes to be absolutely true. He may believe your product is inferior to your competitor's, for example, or that he doesn't need what you are selling. The reality may be different, but the prospect's perception is what matters.

It may also be a maneuver that the prospect is using to satisfy an internal need. He may tell you the price is too high or that your proposal includes some feature that he doesn't want. The purpose of the maneuver is to get you to change your proposal in some way to better fit his perceived needs.

Many, many times, a prospect will object—or throw up an obstacle to buying—simply because that's his job. Prospects in business-to-business sales are professional buyers, even if their title isn't "purchasing manager." It's part of their function as decision makers in their companies to purchase goods and services under the most advantageous terms. And part of a good buyer's job is to throw up obstacles in order to test the product and the salesperson's ability to deliver it. They will also, of course, want to test the bottom of your pricing and the top of your proposal's value. It's a little game they play.

Some of these obstacles are real and some are not. What you need is a way to identify which are which and a strategy to deal with each kind of obstacle.

Your Attitude

The Creative Selling System way to deal with objections is to adopt the attitude that you are going to be an ally to your customers, not their adversary. You're not going to prove them wrong for refusing to buy your product, you're going to create a way that they *can* buy it. You're not going to demonstrate their ignorance, you're going to educate them so they can make better-informed decisions. You're not going to overcome their objections, you're going to answer their questions. Above all, you're not going to win the argument, you're going to win the sale. It's a different attitude.

This Creative Selling attitude is designed to build solid, long-term customer relationships, not make an individual sale. There's a lot less testosterone involved, but a lot more income received over the long run. And you'll be surprised how many individual sales occur when you adopt this attitude.

Are you negative or positive? Do you believe that the prospect will buy if you remove all objections? If you do, you're actually a negative seller. Salespeople who approach their prospects with the conviction that objections are the reason the sale doesn't occur are starting from the position that the prospect will buy only if they can just remove all the obstacles. It's basically a negative outlook.

It's also pretty short-sighted. I've seen plenty of prospects still refuse to buy after all their objections have been answered and all obstacles removed. Why? Because they don't have a positive reason to want to buy. People don't buy just because they can, they buy because they want to. If you want to be a positive seller—a true Creative Seller—approach each prospect with the attitude that you're going to keep adding reasons to buy until the sale occurs. You'll find your closing ratio will go up tremendously.

My preferred method for dealing with objections is to step around them. Don't fight the objection, ignore it. The second is to use the objection to close the sale. It's sort of a jujitsu approach to dealing with objections—you use their own weight and momentum to further your goals.

Step One: Listen

What a surprise. The first step in handling an objection is to *listen* to the prospect. Listen to what he says and how he says it. Give him time to talk and get it all out of his system. Make sure you hear what the prospect is saying—and react accordingly.

You need to *really listen*. The next time you encounter an objection, step back and observe yourself in action. When the prospect is talking, are you processing the information they are sending to you, or are you preparing your reply? Are you listening or getting ready to talk? These are two mutually exclusive mental activities. You cannot do one while simultaneously doing the other.

One of the most helpful learning techniques (or tortures) I use in training is videotaped role-playing. In one of my basic courses, I have the person playing the prospect make a comment designed to catch the salesperson who isn't listening and trap them into answering an objection that doesn't exist. It's kind of sneaky, but it teaches the lesson very well.

In my little drama, the "prospect" waits until the salesperson asks for the order, then makes the comment, "Gee, this is a lot of money." That's all. No explanation or other comments. Just those words. You'll notice that the prospect doesn't say, "it's too much money," or "I'm not going to pay this," or anything else judgmental or argumentative. They simply make an observation.

Invariably, the salesperson will launch into their favorite answer to the ever-popular price objection. They'll deftly demonstrate the relationship between price and value. They'll reduce their price to absurdity by calculating the cost-per-hour of their annual contract. They'll calculate return on investment. They'll start bad-mouthing their competitor's product, service, management, and ancestry. In short, they'll raise all sorts of issues that the prospect never even mentioned.

Believe it or not, salespeople in my training sessions have been known to do this even when they've been forewarned that it was going to happen! When I play back the tape for the critique, the salesperson often has to watch it two or three times before they actually *hear* what the prospect says. The urge to argue is real, real strong in some people.

Salespeople who "overcome objections" are invariably preparing their comeback while the prospect is talking. They practice what every good adversary practices—they are prepared. When the prospect starts throwing that punch at them, they strike back. They truly believe that in sales, the best defense is a good offense. It's the old "Ready—Fire—Aim."

This is one of the most common causes of failure to close. More often than not, the salesperson who's not truly listening to the prospect will answer an objection that doesn't exist! And, what's worse, this salesperson not only doesn't manage the real obstacle to the prospect's satisfaction, he may easily plant some new ones of his own.

I've seen it happen thousands of times in the field and even repeatedly captured it on videotape in my training seminars. Don't let it happen to you. Make sure you listen to what the prospect is saying before you start dealing with the objection—you might just learn that you don't have to deal with anything at all.

Step Two: Restate

Just to make sure you're hearing what the prospect is really saying (and for a couple of other pretty good reasons), restate the objection after the prospect stops talking.

You accomplish several things when you restate the objection. First, you make sure you've got it right—that you understand what the prospect is saying. It also gives the prospect a chance to correct your understanding before you do any damage by answering the wrong objection.

Secondly, it gives you a little time to think about what your next action should be. Is this a question or an objection? Is it sincere or a smoke screen? Is it a misperception you can correct? Is there some information that the prospect missed or that you forgot to provide? You need some mental processing time to consider these things, and re-stating the objection gives you that time.

It also gives the prospect time to reconsider the objection. Have you ever made a statement, then realized how wrong it was when someone repeated it back to you? Your prospect may have the same reaction when he hears his own words. He may even withdraw the statement and remove the obstacle. It happens often enough to make it worth trying.

But the biggest reason for restating the objection is that you get a chance to soften it—to put it into your own words so you can deal with it on your own terms.

Any salesperson with some experience will tell you that they encounter the same objections over and over. This is both a blessing and a curse. The curse is that you learn to give the same answers over and over—and that you start giving those answers as soon as you think you hear the prospect raise one of the common objections. That's what happens in my videotaped exercise.

The blessing is that you have an opportunity to prepare your answers in advance, since you generally know what objections you're going to hear. I suggest that, in addition to coming up with stock arguments for stock objections, you develop some standard restatements of those objections. That will make the softening process much easier—and your management of the objections go more smoothly.

It's not a bad idea to confirm your restatement, depending on the flow of the conversation. This can be as simple as saying, "is that what you mean?" or, "did I understand you correctly?" along with the restatement. This buys you a little more time and really helps keep the tone of the exchange non-argumentative.

That's what this is all about. Restating the objection reinforces your position as the prospect's ally, not his adversary. You're not only listening to what he says, you're making sure you understand it by confirming it with him. It sets a tone of agreement instead of a tone of argument.

Step Three: Agree

The next step expands the good feelings because you essentially agree with the objection!

This makes the prospect feel *really good*. You've told them how perceptive they are to have found this little weakness in your idea. You've congratulated them on seeing through to the heart of the matter. You've praised them for helping you analyze the situation correctly. And you do all this by saying anything but "you're wrong," which is the attitude underlying the "overcome objections" method. Of course, agreeing with the objection doesn't mean that you give up and walk out now, it just means you are getting ready to deal with the substance of the objection in a non-confrontational manner.

There are several alternative routes you can take at this point. Your first choice should always be to just ignore the objection and go on with your presentation. You've listened to and acknowledged the prospect's perception, so get on with your pitch.

This isn't as crazy as it sounds, because it's the best way I know to find out if the objection is "real" or just a smoke screen. If it's a real obstacle to the prospect buying your proposal, it will come up again when you ask for the order. If it's not, it'll just go away—and this happens more often than not. Either way, you haven't lost any ground.

If you've listened carefully, though, you may learn that you're dealing with a lack of information or a misperception rather than an objection. Obviously, you don't want to ignore these. Clear them up right away with a short statement of the facts. Apologize for confusing the point in question, then correct the error.

Remember, you're doing this not because the prospect is too stupid to understand you but because you're too excited about the proposal to get everything out clearly. It's an attitude thing.

Once you've agreed with the prospect, you have to get back into the flow of your presentation. The best way to jump start the pitch is to go back to the benefits page of the proposal. It never hurts to repeat them, and they're good neutral ground to revisit since the prospect has already agreed with them. Just touch on them lightly and then get on with the other points you're making.

This technique—going back to the benefits—is also a good one to use with other types of interruptions, such as a phone call the prospect takes in the middle of your meeting.

Step Four: Close

As soon as you can, take the final step in managing an objection—close the sale. This may seem a little aggressive, but it's actually a natural extension of the conversation you're having with the prospect. You've just completed the final step in the closing process, which is reviewing the benefits. You've agreed on some issues, right? So why not extend that agreement to the proposal itself?

About the only time you can't close the sale on an objection is if you haven't yet covered the price of the proposal. Even then, though, you can "close in principle" by phrasing your question conditionally: "Assuming we can agree on the size of your investment, would you like to execute this plan?" You'll have to judge whether and how to do this based on the content of your discussion with the prospect up to this point, but if there's the slightest doubt about where to go next or what to do, ask for the order.

Consider the downside of this strategy. The worst thing that can happen is that the prospect says "no." Which gives you a perfectly natural reason to ask "why?" and find out what other objections or obstacles might be lying in wait. The bane of every salesperson's existence is the hidden objection—that obstacle to making the purchase that the prospect doesn't tell you about. These are just plain obstacles, either a reason the prospect doesn't like your proposal or a situation which prevents him from buying it, like the necessity of getting approval for the decision from someone else. In any case, the hidden objection generally doesn't come out until it's forced out.

Another possibility, of course, is that your brilliant answer to the original objection wasn't accepted by the prospect in the first place, in which case he'll tell you so when you try to close. In any case, your tactics will be the same: start over with the four steps to handling an objection and handle this one.

There is no silver bullet to kill every objection. It takes a calm, controlled, persistent effort to listen attentively, restate carefully, agree amicably, and ask for the order over and over and over.

You're not there to bludgeon the prospect into submission. Your purpose in making the proposal is to use it as a framework for finding a solution to the prospect's needs. You and the prospect are supposed to work together as a team. And teamwork requires the positive give and take of information and ideas, which starts with the objection.

Remember the videotaped role play? Let's rewind the tape and start over from the point where the prospect baits the trap. You'll see how the four steps work.

The prospect says, "Gee, this is a lot of money."

The wary salesperson waits a beat to see if there's more to come out of the prospect's mouth. That's the listening step.

Then comes the restatement and close: "Yes, this is a substantial investment. Would you like to make it today?"

It's simple. It's non-argumentative. You're both saying the same thing, only *your* words sounds so much more positive. You've told the prospect he's a genius for recognizing the size of the purchase. And now that you've cleared up the little matter of the price, you ask for the order.

Chapter 25
Four Non-Price Objections

**"Don't try to win the argument—
just walk around it."**

Managing objections is a lot like surviving a marriage; one of the keys to success is to see the other person's point of view. You don't have to give in to it, just know what it is. Keep that thought in mind as we go over some of the specific obstacles you'll be likely to run into in one form or another on every call. Some of them you can cut off at the pass. Others you'll just have to grin and bear. In either case, it's important to understand what's going on in the prospect's mind.

You also have to have a pretty thick skin (just like in some marriages). Some people will intentionally say some downright mean and hurtful things to you when you're trying to sell them something. Fortunately, they are very much in the minority. A great many others, though not mean-spirited, will toss out comments like hand grenades just to see how you deal with them. And just like with a live hand grenade—you better deal with them or your presentation will find itself in pieces.

We'll talk about price objections at length in another chapter or two, but here are four common objections that you'll face in all types of sales.

I'm Not Interested

We anticipated this obstacle in the discussion about making cold call appointment telephone calls. You can encounter it again, though, when you show up to make your presentation. But you shouldn't let it stand in your way; you've already overcome it once, haven't you? Be encouraged—it's easier to manage this problem in person that it is on the phone.

The prospect who sees you but then tells you he's not interested in what you have to sell is contradicting himself. He's playing poker with you and you know he's bluffing. But before you call his bluff, you have to determine whether he's saying he has lost interest in your presentation, is not interested in this specific proposal, or has no interest in your type of product or service. Those are three different problems.

If he's not interested in your presentation, you may not hear it in words—but you'll see it in the way they act during your pitch. While you're talking, the prospect sits and stares at you without changing expression. They look out the window. You know you're in trouble when they pick up a paper from their desk and start reading it—and it's not your presentation. They play the great poker face.

The best way to get the prospect interested is to ask a lot of questions. "Don't you think so?" "Doesn't that make sense to you?" "Does that match your experience?" These are all the kinds of questions you can throw in almost at will—and the more of them the better when you're dealing with the Great Poker Face.

Just don't be put off by one-word answers. This prospect is playing hard to get or trying to ruffle you. Either way, you can play the game by keeping control of the situation. If you respond to a one-word answer by looking flustered or exasperated, you've let them take control of your presentation. Be strong. Keep peppering them with questions and make them respond to you. This is a game of wills.

Declining Attention

If the disinterest is related to your proposal, you need to do some probing. Make the subject of your questions Mr. Big's business and the way it relates to your proposal and try to make them topically specific. "Does this investment fit in your existing budget?" "Have you ever done anything like this before?" "How do you think your employees will respond to this?" If you ask these kinds of questions you still may not make the sale but you will learn something of value about Mr. Big's needs that you can use in subsequent proposals.

As a last resort when dealing with either type of disinterest, you can always ask that nasty open-ended question, "Why?" Be polite about it and say something like, "Your mind seems to be on something else, Mr. Big. May I ask why?" or "You seem to have lost interest in our idea since the time I spoke to you on the phone. May I ask what's changed?"

But remember, "why" is a dangerous question. When you ask "why," you have to be prepared for almost any kind of answer. The good thing about asking "why" is that it doesn't allow for a "yes" or "no" reply. The bad thing is that you never know what you're going to get instead. Here are some of the responses to "why aren't you interested?" that I've heard over the years:

"We tried that two years ago and it cost us a lot of money. If I'd known that was your big mysterious idea, I'd never have agreed to meet with you in the first place."

"When you called I thought you said you were with TME, our biggest customer—not TNA., which I've never heard of."

"My lawyer called just before you arrived to tell me we're being sued by the EPA."

"My bookkeeper didn't show at the office today. I just found out he ran away with my wife after I left for work this morning."

I must admit these answers threw me at the time, but at least I learned something about the prospect in each one

The third variation on this theme is the prospect who really contradicts himself by saying he's not interested in your type of product or service. If he wasn't interested, why did he agree to the appointment? This is generally a smoke screen of the first order. All the prospect is doing is trying to make you earn your commission by putting on a good dog and pony show for him. This problem is actually one of the easiest to deal with because you *know* it's a bluff.

Accept the challenge and put on a great show. Use the bluff as inspiration for a great performance and make the pitch of your life. Combine maniacal enthusiasm with persistent questioning and add one more element—blatant salesmanship. It seems that many of the prospects who use this ploy are in direct sales businesses or have a sales background themselves. At the very least they can recognize and admire a well-executed sales tactic when they see one. So give them what they want and use some of the less subtle techniques from the Creative Selling System.

Even if you don't make this sale, you'll establish a position for yourself in the prospect's mind as a sales professional who won't be put off by a little gamesmanship. That reputation will get you in the door much more easily the next time.

I Don't Need It

Of course not. If the prospect knew he needed your product *he'd* have called *you*, right?

Let's not let this little bit of prospect nonsense get in the way of a good sale.

Actually, this isn't an objection at all. It's nothing more than a brush off to get rid of the pesky salesperson. It works pretty well, too, because there is no "answer" for it. The salesperson may have some cute comebacks to this one, but they're probably going to backfire because they all rely on calling the prospect a liar in one way or another.

You encounter this obstacle in several forms, often depending on the type of product or service you sell. People whose product benefit is an increase in revenues for the prospect (like advertising, for example) will hear "I've got more business than I can handle." Those who promise improved profits may be told "That just means more taxes." Another variation is the prospect who says "I'm perfectly happy with my present supplier." How can you argue with these statements?

You can't, of course. And the prospect knows that, which is why he throws them in front of you in the first place.

So don't try to win the argument—just walk around it. When you encounter a statement like this, ignore it! Just say something to the effect of "That's interesting. Now, as I was saying…" and get back to your pitch. When you do, you'll probably discover that the prospect forgets all about this "objection" and considers your idea anyway.

This is such a common smokescreen that it pays to treat it this way every time. You don't have much to lose, because the worst thing that can happen is that the prospect brings it up again, signaling that he meant it the first time.

This is true of every objection, of course, and it doesn't mean the end of the call. It just means you have to dig deeper into the prospect's needs with some probing questions. If he doesn't need what you are proposing, what does he need? When you get the answer to that question, you're rounding third on your way to home, as they say in baseball.

I Don't Have Time

This usually signals a flaw in your proposal or at least in your presentation that can take a couple of different forms. When you hear this objection, it can mean that the prospect likes your idea, but doesn't want to take on the task of executing it. It may also mean that the prospect doesn't have time to *consider* your idea, which is just as bad if not worse. Let's consider the first variation.

Business managers and owners are busy people. We've talked about the many things they have to face every day—personnel, customers, taxes, inventory, and on and on. It's not unusual for a decision-maker to like your idea but feel that he or she has too many other things to do every day to make it happen effectively.

In one way, that's a complement to your presentation. You've probably built up the value of the idea so much that it seems like more than it is. You've painted a great word picture and the prospect sees Buckingham Palace when what you're selling is a three bedroom ranch on a quarter-acre lot. Maybe you should examine your pitch and see if there are any exaggerations in it.

You should also closely examine the elements of execution of your idea. Are you asking the prospect to do something himself to make the proposal work? Does his company have to provide additional training for its staff? Does he have to invest in another piece of equipment from another vendor to use your product? If so, re-work your proposal to include these items in it. Offer to provide them yourself if at all possible. It may mean subcontracting a service or purchasing some equipment, but you're removing an obstacle to the sale when you do. Charge for them (with markup), of course, but just don't make it the prospect's responsibility to make your idea work.

The second variation, where the prospect feels he doesn't even have time to consider your proposal, is a real problem. In this day of reengineered and downsized corporations, more and more managers simply have too much to do. They are paid for their ability to make decisions, but they are given too many decisions to make. As a consequence, they try to limit the number of decisions they have to make by not considering new ideas. Or, they think embracing the status quo is one way of insuring they won't make a wrong decision.

So make the decision-making process itself as simple as possible. Promise them that if they say "yes," to your idea, they won't have to deal with any of the details later because you and your company will handle them.

And above all, limit the number of choices and decisions the prospect has to make in order to say "yes." I've seen a lot of proposals that ask the prospect to choose sizes, colors, dates, quantities, even models of equipment as part of the buying process. These choices have to be made, of course, but they should have been made *before* the presentation by the *salesperson*!

If you've done your homework before the call, you'll have eliminated all the minor decisions. The worst thing that can happen is that you chose wrong. If that's the case, make the change on the spot and ask for the order.

Make your solution as "turnkey" as possible. This reinforces your position as an ally and resource. If the prospect wants to provide some of the elements, that's fine, but don't make it mandatory. And since you will have built in a cost for all those elements when you structured the proposal, you may even be able to use their exclusion as a negotiating tool.

Look at your idea critically for both of these problems.

I Don't Think It Will Work

This objection is a cry for help. The prospect is telling you that he likes the benefits you are offering, but doesn't see how your idea can deliver them. You need to better explain the connection between the benefits and the idea.

Repeat, clarify, and above all listen. What makes Mr. Big think the idea won't work? Has he tried it before? Is there some basic flaw in your underlying assumptions about his business? Any of these things can lead to a lack of belief in the idea's ability to deliver the benefits. Now is the time to probe and question—and listen carefully to the answers.

There are several avenues around this obstacle. If you can, cite examples of other clients who have used a similar idea successfully. Carry testimonials from them with you. (To get a testimonial, by the way, write it yourself then ask the testifier to put it on their letterhead for you. Don't expect them to take the time to actually compose it for you).

The one caution about testimonials is that they have to be specific and verifiable to be believed. Too many salespeople have gone before you raving about "everybody" and "lots of people" using their products. If you want your testimonial to carry some weight with Mr. Big, you must make it verifiable. Don't even think about making one up. Testimonials are just like references on a resume. If even one of them turns out to be a figment of your imagination, you're blacklisted.

Another way to prove that your idea will work is a demonstration. This tactic was fairly easy when salespeople sold tangible products—you just brought along a sample (unless you were a locomotive salesman). But what do you do if you sell services? You make them tangible in some way.

I know a very successful TV ad salesperson who produced a videotape containing commercials from many of the campaigns she created. She used it to show prospects the quality of the work she produced. Remember Matt, the engineer-salesman? He always carried a few copies of the detailed reports his firm prepared for his customers. If you examine your service, you will probably find a way to make it tangible.

When To Modify Your Proposal

There's another type of workability problem, though. That's when the prospect just can't swallow some part of your proposal. You may have proposed training programs for their clerks that take place after the store closes on Tuesday evenings, for example. The prospect tells you that plan won't work because it would generate over-time expense. If that's the only obstacle to the sale, go around it. Can you switch them to lunchtime? Or provide the training in smaller groups during store hours? How about putting the training on tape and sending it home with them? There's always a way if you keep your mind open to the possibilities.

Unfortunately, the first inclination of many salespeople will be to say, "Let me work on that and I'll get back to you." And that is about the worst thing you can do.

The prospect was sending you a very strong signal that he wants to buy your idea. He's mentally committed to it, but is crying out for help with this obstacle. Telling him you'll get back to him is like telling a drowning man you'll be back as soon as you find a rope—he may not wait. The prospect may not wait for you either, or at least his enthusiasm may well have subsided by the time you get back with your revised proposal.

Salespeople are particularly inclined to take this route when there is money involved. Let's put the reason for that into context. Remember, you're pitching a new prospective customer for the first time. As part of your preparation, you've estimated his potential spending and you've based the size of your proposal on that estimate. Have you built a skyscraper on a bed of sand? That's your fear.

So, when the prospect says "I like your idea but I'm not sure I can afford it," you get a grip on your fear long enough to reply, "What figure can you afford?" When he gives you a number, you jump up joyfully and promise to come back next week with a revised proposal for that amount. Then you rush out the door congratulating yourself on a sale made. The problem is, of course, that you haven't made a sale, all you've made is an appointment for next week. Lots and lots of things can happen before next week rolls around.

So why not just modify the proposal on the spot? You have a calculator, you know your product line and pricing, and you know the cost factors built into your proposal. You also have the prospect there to work with you on the revision, which will give you some great closing opportunities. So just take a few minutes and revise the proposal right there. You'll improve your closing ratio immediately.

Chapter 26
The Path Around Price Objections

"Find out what kind of price objection you're dealing with, then answer it appropriately."

Every one of your customers wants a lower price—or at least they say they do. For some, the price is really a deal-breaker. For others, it's just part of a game they play to test your limits. How do you tell the difference? Does it matter?

The way you handle price objections certainly does matter because it affects your relationship with your customer in several ways. If you arrogantly refuse to even discuss the price, they can easily jump to the conclusion that you don't care if they do business with you or not. On the other extreme, if you immediately cave in and offer a lower price, they may wonder if you were trying to screw them with the first one. Obviously, you need to find a middle ground.

That's not as hard as it sounds. The key is to use a decision tree to determine the best answer. Think of it as following a road with several forks. Every time you come to one, you choose which fork to follow based on the signals the customer sends you. Eventually, you'll get to the place where you and the customer reach agreement.

The first fork in the road is where you make sure they mean it when they say the price is too high. You want to know, is the price really more than they can or are willing to pay, or are they simply negotiating? One way to find out is to acknowledge their objection ("I hear what you're saying") then change the subject ("Did I tell you this system doesn't need any additional components?") and ask for the order again ("When do you want us to install it?"). Listen carefully to the way they bring up the price again—if they do.

If their answer is something like "I'll take it if you give me a better deal," you know you're selling to a negotiator so you can play the game the way you feel most comfortable. You can stonewall them nicely: "I'm sorry, but this is the price I've got to have, so do you still want it?" Or you can make some minor concessions like taking two percent off if they pay cash instead of using a credit card. Or you can go into full-blown rug-merchant mode and haggle back and forth until you're both equally unsatisfied with the final price.

Can't Pay or Won't Pay?

If you believe they are not negotiating, however, you are at another fork in the road. You need to probe to find out if it's a matter of not being able to pay your price (their eyes were bigger than their budget) or if the price itself, in their opinion, is too high. In other words, they can pay it, but they don't feel they're getting enough value for their money. The way they answer questions like "What's stopping you from saying 'yes' today?" will tell you which fork to take.

If the price is beyond their means, you may want to remove some components to make the total package smaller. Or, depending on the product you're selling, you may be able to install one component at a time, building up to the full system as your customer's bank account allows. You can also try to work out some payment terms, if your company finances allow carrying the customer on your books. These tactics can also be used when you're dealing with a negotiator, of course.

Then there's always the option of cutting the price by forgoing some of your profit, too, although there's a hidden cost to that: if your shop is busy doing this low-margin job, you may have to delay taking on a full-profit one, since there are only so many hours in the day, technicians on the staff, and facilities in the shop. Putting the full-profit job off until later has a cost, too, in terms of that customer's satisfaction.

If the problem is an imbalance between the price and the value in the customer's mind, you can either build up the perceived value, decrease the perceived cost, or both. To build perceived value, talk up the benefits of what you're selling; how much faster it will solve the customer's problem, how much more power it will provide to his application, how many more of his competitors will be eating his dust. Sell the sizzle along with the plain facts to get the customer excited about what they're buying and what it's going to do for them.

You've probably already listed all the advantages your product offers for the customer, but don't hesitate to repeat them at this point. Open your presentation to the idea page, put it between you and the customer and point to each feature as you talk about it. As you highlight each one, ask the customer an open-ended agreement question ("What do you think of that?" or "How do you think that would work for you?") to keep them talking about the value of the product instead of its price. A small tactic like that makes the product benefits more tangible and increases their perceived value.

You can also use the bandwagon effect. Talk about how many top performers are using the equipment he's considering or the product's record in other markets. The point you're trying to make, of course, is that he can be as good as them if he has the same equipment. You're not selling a product or service, you are giving him membership in the exclusive club that meets in the winner's circle.

To deflate the perceived cost, quantify it differently. How many times a year does the customer use it? If the life of the product is three years and the customer will use it ten times a year, divide the cost by thirty, and point out that it's only costing him X dollars per use. Lead him to the conclusion that it's a small price to pay for success.

Another option is to talk up the value your product or service adds to his company. Point out that he's making an investment in an asset, not buying some transient gratification. Those widgets you're selling will be in his production line for a long time. Someday, he'll want to sell his business. He'll be able to recoup at least part of the cost of your product at that time in terms of a higher price for the business he's selling.

As you can see, the key to handling price objections isn't just to give a standard reply and hope for the best. You have to find out what kind of price objection you're dealing with, then answer it appropriately. Engage the customer; talk to them; above all, listen to what they're saying about your product and your price. They'll tell you which fork in the road leads to a sale.

Chapter 27
The Maybe Challenge

"Actively helping the customer make a purchase decision is part of the service."

The four deadliest words in sales are, "I'll think about it." You've spent what seems like hours with the customer, answered all their questions, and repeatedly asked for the order. Maybe you've hauled in a box of samples or even put together a trial offer based on special research. You've invested a lot of your time in them, but the customer stalls just at the point of making a decision. It's doggone discouraging.

Why do otherwise nice people torture us like this? There are plenty of reasons, but many times, the prospect who says "maybe" is just too darned nice to say "no." They don't want to hurt your feelings by rejecting you, or they just can't think of a good reason to not buy, so they inadvertently torment you instead by saying "I'll think about it." Then there are people who are actually afraid of making a decision—any decision—especially on the spot. Maintaining the status quo is safe, so they choose to preserve it by avoiding decisions. Fortunately, of course, some really do want to buy but just need some time to decide. There are customers who won't buy anything costing over $100 until they've literally slept on it. Some want more information or have another decision-maker they want to consult.

It's a major problem that every salesperson faces. Bob Adler, General Manager of Adco Paper and Packaging in Brooklyn, NY, says, "It happens with new business more often than you would like. Repeat customers aren't so bad. They know what they need and will give you a yes or no." Short of holding a gun to their heads, how do you deal with the fence-sitter?

Decision Qualifying

The process—and making a sale *is* a process, not an event—starts with qualifying the customer in a way that will help you anticipate some of the potential delays. With a new prospect, you may not be able to determine whether they are psychologically decision-averse, but you can find out if there are other people involved in the decision. There's also nothing wrong with asking if they have a buying policy you should know about—like never making a decision the day of the presentation.

A big part of qualifying, of course, is also judging how much business potential the customer has. This helps set the "maybe" strategy. As Adler says, "First of all, you have to determine if the sale is worth extraordinary pursuit."

Steve Shockey, President of the W. Evans Company in Kansas City, Mo., agrees and adds that his salespeople qualify prospects in yet another way—their willingness to make a decision. "We spend a lot of time with a customer doing research, providing samples, conducting trials, and it's imperative that we know that time's not going to be wasted," he says. "We try to get a commitment as early as possible. That may not be an immediate order, but it lets us know the investment of our time will be rewarded."

But this isn't high pressure. High pressure is an attempt to *force* the customer to do something they don't want to do. The high pressure seller typically tries to mentally push the customer into a corner that they can only escape by making a purchase—which is a great way to generate a few sales and a lot of resentment. The high pressure seller may get an order, but it will probably be the last one from that buyer. What's more, professional buyers are immune to such tactics and will most likely cut the seller off immediately.

"Some salespeople are more comfortable than others asking early. They do their homework earlier, too, and often ask for the commitment on the first call," according to Shockey. "We ask upfront, 'If we can solve your problem, will you buy?'"

It's easy to go too far in the other direction, of course. Some salespeople fear offending the customer so much that they hesitate to ever ask for the order, much less apply pressure to get a decision. They don't realize that actively helping the customer make a purchase decision is part of the service their company offers. Selling is not bad—it's simply focusing the customer's attention on doing something that's good for their business. Even those customers who have a valid reason for "thinking about it" can save time and bother if the salesperson helps them reach a conclusion.

Test Questions

Once past the qualification stage, the effective salesperson will anticipate the "maybe" problem and try to eliminate it by testing the customer's feelings throughout the presentation. They ask open-ended questions to learn more about the buyer's needs and wants and to see if they are nearing a decision point. The best questions are like these. They can't be answered with a "yes" or "no."

- "How would this fit your process?"
- "What do you think of the material?"
- "How does this compare with what you're currently using?"
- "What kind of response do you think this would bring from your staff?"
- "Where would this fit into your product mix?"

Timing, as someone said, is everything. A high-pressure salesperson will start asking for the order right away. The more professional approach is to use positive answers to the open-ended questions to lead into some test questions. These can be answered "yes" or "no" without making the customer feel cornered because they don't demand an order. Their purpose is to uncover any hidden objections and remove excuses to delay the decision.

- "Do you like it?"
- "Would this work for you?"
- "It works well, doesn't it?"
- "Is there a place for this in your operation?"
- "Do you have any questions?"

A "no" or a qualified "yes" answer to the test questions calls for further probing, but a flat "yes" means it's time to ask for the order.

Once you've asked the question, be quiet and wait for an answer! Don't break the silence; give the customer time to think. Talking after asking for the order comes across as pressure—even if you're trying to be helpful. It also opens the door to other questions or objections—some of which the customer may not even have considered. Finally, it doesn't give the customer a chance to say "yes." It's tough to stand there waiting for the customer to respond to your question, but you have everything to lose and nothing to gain by giving in to the urge to fill the silence.

Columbo and Ben Franklin

Even after all this, though, some customers will still refuse to give up their seat on the fence. When they tell you they still want to think about it, it's time for a flanking approach. One method is the Columbo close, based on the TV detective played years ago by Peter Falk. Columbo's trademark move was to suddenly "remember" another question he wanted to ask just as he's walking away from the suspect. When you use this maneuver to overcome a decision stall, you play the same game. As you're preparing to leave the customer's office after a long tussle without getting a decision, you say, "I just remembered an important point for you to consider while you're thinking about this purchase. Can I have just another moment of your time?"

When you pretended to accept "maybe" and the customer thought you were headed for the door, the pressure on them to make a decision disappeared. So when you launch into your pitch again, the customer's defenses are down and you can follow up one more reason to buy with a good hard closing question. You may not catch a crook, but you may be able to snag a firm "yes" or "no."

And there's always the famous Ben Franklin close. The customer says he or she needs time to think about it and you say, "That's a good idea. Let's list some points to ponder while you're making your decision." Then you figuratively draw a line down the middle of a piece of paper and begin by asking the customer to list the reasons not to buy today. Then list all the reasons he or she should buy, asking for agreement as you go. At every point, of course, you have the opportunity to either overcome an objection or to ask for the order again, or both. And that's the purpose of the exercise; to keep the possibility of getting a "yes" alive. The longer the customer stays with the process, the more likely they are to buy.

Sometimes, what you say to help the customer decide may not be as important as what you do. Sales on approval, trial purchases, and other similar tactics all work to reduce pressure on the customer and help them make a decision. Adler says, "We may offer a baker's dozen or a special sweetener like that to move the buyer off the fence."

Many, many buyers know this happens, of course, and use "maybe" as a very effective negotiating tool. Consequently, the seller has to respond in kind by making the special offer contingent on getting a decision—now.

As in all aspects of selling, helping the customer satisfy their needs is the best way to move the customer from "maybe" to "yes." Consciously taking an active role in that process isn't high-pressure selling; it's simply giving assistance to the decision-impaired.

Chapter 28
Successful Call-Backs

"Time is money, and time spent waiting for a decision is money spent on nothing."

Here's the situation: You made a great sales pitch, the prospect seemed to like your proposal, and he asked you to give him a few days to think about it. You have to leave, but what should you do next?

There are five steps to closing the sale when you call back on the prospect who has been sleeping on your proposal. The single most important principle to keep in mind is that time is money, and time spent waiting for a decision is money spent on nothing. These five steps, from the time the prospect says "come back later" to the moment you see them again, should be designed to eliminate that wasted time.

Step One

Assuming you've exhausted all the alternatives for making a sale today, set a deadline for yourself and the customer. Immediately make an appointment to get an answer by suggesting an exact date and time to meet again. Be specific about it. Don't let the customer wiggle out of a decision by saying something vague like, "Call me next week." Nail the appointment down today. And if the customer says "Don't call me, I'll call you," go immediately to Step Five (see below).

Give the customer a few days—no more than a week—to say yes or no. You're probably not selling multi-phase inter-galactic transportation devices (this ain't rocket science!), so the customer shouldn't need to perform any in-depth analysis of the pros and cons of your proposal. It's understandable to require a couple of days to check budgets or get a second opinion, but anything longer than that is a sure sign that you're not getting a "maybe," you're just getting a classic brush off.

Insist on an in-person appointment to get the answer. Don't ever plan to just call back by telephone and say "have you thought about it yet?" Telephone calls are easy to avoid, as anyone who has dealt with voice mail knows, and the customer who insists on one may well be looking for a way to hide from you. Keep in mind, too, that your next contact won't be just a quick "tell me yes or no" conversation. It's going to entail a sales pitch probably as long as the first one (see step two), and you can't make an enthusiastic, energetic presentation on the telephone as well as you can in person.

Step Two

Even when you get an appointment, assume the answer is going to be "no." This is important for several reasons. Mentally, if you spend the next week building up your hopes, you're likely to be devastated by a negative answer, which will increase your reluctance to make another proposal to the same prospect. Since one of the keys to sales success is the frequency with which you pitch a given prospect, it's important to not let any mental barriers rise up to prevent you from doing that.

In addition, you need to prepare another new proposal (or be ready with a modified version of the current one) based on what you learned during the last pitch. The sooner you do that, the fresher the customer's feedback will be in your mind. As soon as you walk out of the prospect's office, review what he said, good and bad, about your proposal. What did you learn about his needs? Jot these thoughts down and review them as you prepare for your call-back meeting.

Step Three

Bring another copy of the proposal and do your pitch all over again just as if you were giving it to a brand new customer! You might want to start with a comment like, "I'd like to review some of the pertinent points we discussed last time to see if you have any questions," but basically, your goal is to review the benefits of your proposal and close the sale now that there aren't any more reasons to delay a decision. You have nothing to lose by doing this, and it's always good to grab the chance to reinforce the reasons the customer should say "yes," especially when it's decision time.

Above all, don't just show up and say, "have you thought about it yet?" For one thing, the prospect probably hasn't given the proposal much thought since you left his office last week—he or she has other things to do. In all likelihood, he hasn't even looked at your proposal in the meantime. Asking that question also puts the prospect in control of the meeting, which can be disastrous if his answer is "No, I need a few more days to think about it."

Step Four

Regardless of what the prospect says, accept no more delays. He doesn't really need any more time, he just doesn't want to say "no" for one reason or another. If he hasn't thought about it for the last week, why will he do so in the week ahead? Above all, you have to avoid an endless chain of no-decision call-backs, which wastes your time and energy and teaches the customer that you're an easy put-off. By the way, those are much easier to give over the telephone, which is another reason to insist on meeting face to face. If you can push him to say "no," you can find out why and move on to step five.

Step Five

Make another proposal—on the spot. Have an alternative in reserve that you'll only bring up when the first one is dead. Don't start the call-back presentation with the alternative—you'll only confuse the prospect and invite further decision delays—but have it ready to go for the moment the prospect says "no" to your original proposal. All you need is a simple segue like, "I took the liberty of preparing another plan after our last meeting."

The idea is to cut out the interval between a rejection and the next proposal. If you believe that time is money (and what salesperson doesn't?), you have to think of the time spent waiting for the prospect to make a decision as money poured down the drain. Anything you can do to eliminate it is going to make you a more productive seller.

If you just say "thanks, I'll see you later" and walk out of the prospect's office to start the process all over again, you'll add weeks to the sales process. First you wait a week (or more) to call to get an appointment to present another proposal. Then, if you're lucky, you get one for a week later. If, when you make your second presentation, the prospect asks for a week to think about that one too, you've shot three weeks before you get another answer—and heaven forbid it turns out to be "maybe." When you're ready to make your second proposal immediately after the prospect turns down the first one, you've put money (time) in the bank.

The Ultimate Call-Back

I once led a sales team working to get a contract with a particularly attractive prospect. They heard the pitch and variations on it several times over a period of nearly two years. But they wouldn't give us a "yes" or a "no."

We had to do something to break through their ennui. We sent gifts, tried president-to-president meetings, pitched revolutionary mixes of services. But nothing provoked a definitive response. This was a multi-million-dollar prospect, so it wasn't something we wanted to just walk away from. Finally, in yet another internal review, someone remarked that the decision makers were all big football fans of the major university located in their town. A little research indicated that most of them would be in the stadium on a particular game day.

So I hired a skywriter to fly over the stadium, streaming the message "Prospect Company belongs with Our Company." The plane circled the stadium for an hour and the decision makers couldn't very well avoid it.

Monday morning, a call came in from the decision-maker. He said that we had made a great impression on them and they were ready to switch their account as soon as their current contract with our competitor expired. That was the good news. The bad news was that their contract had just automatically extended for another two years. Before that time expired, I left that company to start my consulting business. This prospect became one of my first clients—mainly because the door had been opened and kept open for more than two years through the persistent presentation of attention-getting ideas.

Chapter 29
Managing A Complex Sale

"Develop a set of tools and tactics to reach and persuade the multiple decision influencers in your prospect's company."

Selling the way it's usually described is a pretty simple affair. You find the prospect, research their needs and develop a proposed idea, pitch the decision maker, manage the objections, and close the sale. Straight forward, isn't it? Nice and linear.

But selling in the real world isn't quite that simple. The "normal" sale is about as linear as a basket of eels. You may be able to find something that looks like a beginning, but which of the squirming bodies leads you to the other end? We all operate in the world of the complex sale.

The complex sale is easy to identify but hard to complete. You know you are in the middle of one when Mr. Big says, "I really like this idea, but I have to run it by my boss." And then his boss, Mr. Bigger, says, "Good idea. What does production have to say about it?" And then production says, "Interesting. Can we change these widgets into woudgets—if the new assembly line we're installing next year calls for it? Better check with the vendor." So the vendor of the new assembly line says, "We'll set it up any way they want. Besides, what's a widget?" Get the picture?

There is a decision maker, but there are also multiple decision influencers. There is ultimately a "yes" or "no" decision, but there are also multiple interim decisions to be made before that point is reached. Multiple decision influencers making multiple decisions. It's a recipe for mass confusion.

The dollar size of the buying decision doesn't necessarily dictate the number of decision influencers involved. One of the more interesting sales I ever made was a multi-million dollar communications tower to a company in Saudi Arabia. The situation had all the hallmarks of a complex sale. The purchasing company was a joint venture operated by two other companies, one French and one Saudi, and the item I was selling was a very high priced component in a much larger complete system to be operated by a ministry of the Saudi government. The construction manager was an Egyptian subcontractor to the Saudi/French joint venture.

Even the payment wasn't linear. The customer's funds were coming from an insurance settlement that was still in dispute. The payment to us was to be made in the form of an Irrevocable Letter of Credit, which had to be approved by the Saudi bank, our bank, and a transmitting bank in Switzerland.

There was an endless chain of meetings, referrals, studies, and opinions offered, countered, and negotiated by phone, fax, and snail mail that went on for six months and involved engineers, bankers, and various functionaries on three continents. Finally, the sale was closed after a single 90-minute meeting I held with the president of the joint venture and his construction manager. That meeting was basically a formality, however, since all the details had been ironed out in the months before.

On the other hand, I once sold a small-market television advertising package worth $300 that required four weeks of study and deliberation by an advertising agency's media planner, buyer, and account supervisor, their client's store manager, regional manager, and advertising director, and the co-operative advertising manager of one of the store's vendors. The Federal

Express and long-distance telephone bills were greater than our profit on that sale!

Watch out, a complex sale could be lurking anywhere out there.

Successfully completing a complex sale requires tremendous patience and perseverance, two qualities often in short supply among salespeople, who often chose sales as a career in the first place because they like the instant gratification of closing a deal. If the reason you get up and go to work each morning is to see how many sales you can make that day, I suggest you find something simple to sell—like Girl Scout cookies—and a simple market to sell it in—like sole proprietorships with fewer than two employees. Selling just about anything else to larger organizations requires the ability to navigate through a complex sale.

Decision Influencers

Have you ever heard this sales adage: Never take "no" from someone who can't say "yes?" There's more than a kernel of wisdom in it, but this truism undoubtedly pre-dates the age of virtual corporations with horizontal organization charts describing the functions of an empowered workforce. In most complex selling situations, the first hurdle to overcome isn't "no," it's identifying all the various players with something to say about the decision.

When it comes to identifying the people involved, I refer to decision "influencers" as well as decision "makers." That's because there are many people in the modern business structure who don't have the authority to say either "yes" or "no" but whose opinions are solicited by the final decision makers. Even seemingly simple decisions often go through the influencer mill. This happens for a variety of reasons.

For one, a large number of executives today practice consensual management. The old autocratic "buck stops here" decision maker is out of sync with the latest in management theory. These modern executives believe (and rightly so) that involving more people in a decision improves the ultimate acceptance of that decision. If you've ever sold consulting services, for example, you know that the client staff members who are going to be affected by the project can destroy it if they don't "buy in" early in the decision-making process.

There's also a widespread belief that the more people involved in a decision, the better that decision will be. It's a safety procedure practiced by decision makers who prefer to spread the risk among a larger group. Of course, decision making by committee has its downside, too. It tends to produce "safe" decisions because a group tends to grind all ideas down to the most acceptable level.

Group decisions may be safe, but they're certainly not necessarily better. Each member of the group has his or her own agenda and will act to carry it out within the group with varying degrees of success. I'm sure you've heard the story of the committee charged with designing a horse. Every member added the features they wanted. One suggested the beast have four legs and another made them long and added large, flat feet for traction on soft surfaces. Another insisted on a tail to shoo away flies while yet someone else modified it to not be bushy so maintenance would be lower. And so the process went through meeting after meeting until the committee to design a horse produced instead a camel.

Here's a scary number: 27. That's the number of "yes or no" interim decisions that need to be made in a situation where a committee of just three people is deciding whether to buy an item with three specifications (like size, color, and quantity) and where each person has to consider and agree/disagree with each of the others on each possible combination of specified features. And what's really scary about that number is that it does not include the final yes or no buying decision! Unfortunately, sound management practice or not, decision-making committees are often part of the complex sale.

That's one reason I suggest eliminating as many of the interim decisions as possible when you put your proposal together. If you give the committee just one decision to make (buy or don't buy), you've eliminated all of the interim decisions they have to debate.

And then there's the modern management mantra, "empowerment," which supposedly pushes decision-making further down the chain of command. Companies who empower their employees will proudly tell you that you don't have to pitch your product to Mr. Big because any number of subordinates can make the final decision. Mr. Big will go along with anything they decide. Did you notice that Mr. Big still has the final word? To me, just saying that he will go along implies that he also has the option to not go along.

Unfortunately, at least in my experience, many of the employees who have been empowered don't want the responsibility that goes along with the territory. Some people subconsciously feel threatened by the responsibility that comes with decision-making. They may even believe that upper management is copping out on their responsibilities by pushing decisions down in the organization. They're much more inclined to say "no" than "yes" because keeping the status quo is almost always felt to be the safer decision. And a great deal of second guessing goes on, too, especially among those who live to please upper management and as such are mostly concerned about what Mr. Big really wants them to decide. There's a tendency to push the decision back up the corporate ladder—or worse, not make any decision at all—if they can.

It's not a pretty picture, but it's one that you have to deal with constantly.

The biggest reason you'll constantly be involved in complex sales is that the fabric and structure of many industries have become more complex. The Mom and Pop grocery store has given way to the hypermart. The independent local realtor is now a franchisee of a national financial conglomerate. The local lumber yard has been replaced by a big box store and the neighborhood hardware store is under siege. Waves of consolidation have swept through every industry from toy stores to funeral homes.

And with size almost always comes complexity. The management of a nationwide chain of service stations has a vastly more complicated structure than the one running your local two-pump corner gas station. There are local managers reporting to regional managers reporting to division managers who draw on the resources of the corporate marketing, finance, legal, engineering, and administrative staffs. The decision to buy a new digital sign, for example, may have to be approved by a dozen individuals. At the local sole-proprietor gas station, one person—the owner/operator—will make that decision alone.

Since creative sellers focus on the larger potential accounts, they almost by definition pursue the national organizations rather than the mom and pops in their industry. You must develop a set of tools and tactics to reach and persuade the multiple decision influencers in your prospect's company.

The Decision Process

As you work on complex accounts you'll have to learn to be patient, because you're in for a long ride. Multiple decisions made by multiple decision influencers means multiple calls, meetings, and proposals. Sometimes you'll be fortunate enough to get everyone involved in a decision into one room at the same time—but that will be the very rare exception rather than the rule. For the most part, you have to count on individual pitches delivered over a period of weeks or even months.

And, because there are so many cooks involved in flavoring the broth, you'll have to count on making numerous modifications to your proposal as you go. Just about every time you make a change, you have to take the newly modified proposal back to the people you've already pitched! It will seem like an endless process but the ultimate size of the order will hopefully be worth it.

One of your first steps should be to identify all the decision influencers, which can be difficult at best. Figuring out which ones are important and which ones aren't is even harder.

Keep careful notes of each meeting with each person, because you'll never remember every individual's input weeks after the call. Try to determine who reports to whom and indicate that data on your notes, too.

Gatekeepers, Flak Catchers, and Other Obstacles

Many times you'll have to fight your way through an army of flak catchers to get your proposal in front of the people who matter. Flak catchers, by the way, are those people noted author and social commentator Tom Wolfe identified as the ones sitting in the outer office whose job it is to intercept incoming shrapnel, complaints, and sales pitches to protect the real decision makers inside.

There's a great temptation to try to blow right by the flak catchers and get to Mr. Big. The problem with this tactic is that it backfires too often. You never know just what the relationship between the two may be. Many a busy executive will take cues from an administrative assistant because they work so closely together day after day. And the assistant will know just how much power they have, too, and not hesitate to use it if they feel slighted in any way. Remember how much trouble Marie Antoinette got into because she brushed off the concerns of the little people.

You have to be careful, too, about job titles. Does the Senior Vice President of Marketing make the final advertising budget decisions? Does the Operations Manager buy the production line equipment—or does that job belong to the Purchasing Manager? Maybe. Maybe not. It all depends on the company and their practices. You obviously need to do your homework and ask lots of questions as you're working your way through the maze.

The decision influencer that will really drive you crazy is the invisible one. I don't know how many times I've worked for months on a prospect, making endless presentations to person after person only to get a final "no" because there was an unidentified decision influencer I missed along the way. You just never know and unfortunately you can't count on the prospect to offer you all the guidance you'd like to have. Ask, ask, ask.

Another source of sales insanity is the self-appointed expert. Every prospect seems to have someone on staff whose main job responsibility is to pass negative judgment on every sales proposal. They always seem to be hardest on those proposals that didn't start in their office, too, which is an interesting coincidence.

Some product and service lines draw these experts worse than others. More than two-thirds of American homes have computers, so you can count on at least half the prospect's employees having an opinion on your product if you sell information systems. Everybody is an expert on advertising too, of course, since everybody is exposed to it every day.

The strategy I've adopted to deal with all these contingencies is to make the presentation to anybody who will listen to it, whether I think they're directly involved in the decision or not. With a complex sale, you can never be sure who's doing what or who has the stroke, so cover them all. Since a complex sale can take time (weeks, months, or even years) to complete, it's not unheard of for someone you've pitched to get promoted, transferred, or terminated before the final decision is made. So cover all your bases and make the presentation to anybody you can corner long enough to hear it.

That goes for various associated procurement services, too. Advertising agencies, merchandise buying cooperatives, consulting firms and other concerns of that type heavily influence the buying decisions of many prospects. In fact, they often perform much of the "heavy lifting" when it comes to routine buying decisions, taking the mundane administrative burden off the shoulders of the actual buyer. And they earn their keep by generally being such efficient buyers that they will pay for their services in savings for the prospect.

You absolutely cannot go around these people—they'll get you in the end if you do. You must, however, make sure that your proposal doesn't stop on their desk. If you follow the guidelines in this chapter, you can be sure your idea gets beyond these dead ends.

Other Roadblocks and Detours

Another element adding to the complexity of the selling process today is the sale of services and product systems rather than items. You probably don't sell a line of widgets; you sell "widget-based interior manufacturing process solutions." You don't sell a bookkeeping service; you sell "digital financial management decision and accounting information systems."

The more complicated the product, the more "experts" required to make a decision about buying it. And the greater the number of incremental or interim decisions that have to be made before the final order is placed.

One of the many pitfalls in a complex sale is the "whisper down the lane" problem. You've probably played that parlor game where one person whispers a phrase to the next, who repeats it in the ear of another person until "Mary is going down to see Phil" becomes "Mary's gong rang on Sea Hill."

This is going to happen to you and your proposal when a flak catcher says to you, "Mr. Big is too busy to see you now, but I'll explain your proposal to him for you." This is not a good thing.

Not only is the flak catcher unlikely to get your proposal right, it's a given that he or she won't deliver it with the same enthusiasm and positive energy as you would. In fact, he's very likely to start his pitch of your idea with, "I don't know if you'll like this, but...." and go downhill from there. Remember, it's the flak catcher's job to say "no" to proposals, so he has to at least imply that answer to Mr. Big.

That's if he takes your proposal into the inner sanctum at all, of course. Most of the time, he's giving you that routine for the same reason a prospect says, "I'll think about it" rather than giving you a simple "no." It's a convenient, low-risk way to get rid of you for a while. In fact, when you call back to see how Mr. Big liked the idea, the flak catcher can tell you "no sale" and blame it on Mr. Big. And you have no way of knowing for sure whether Mr. Big actually saw it or not.

This same problem is magnified when you're forced to deal with a buying agent of some sort. They really have a vested interest in keeping Mr. Big in the dark about your proposals. And they will go to great lengths to make sure you don't even think about going around them.

The Complex Sale Campaign

When you're faced with this problem, approach it carefully but aggressively, following the steps I recommend in their exact order. If you try to jump ahead, you'll suffer the consequences.

Step One: First, establish contact with Mr. Big. Contact doesn't have to mean a face-to-face meeting. In fact, in this stage you don't really want a face-to-face. Put Mr. Big on your company's direct mail list. Make sure he gets your newsletter, press releases, and new product announcements addressed to him personally and with a brief "FYI" note signed by you.

Step Two: When you present a proposal to the flak catcher or buying agency, follow it up with a "thank you" letter and carbon Mr. Big. Make sure the letter praises the flak catcher for their perception and professionalism during your meeting. Do the same if they give you an order. Lay it on real thick. It'll make them look good to Mr. Big—and how can they object to that? That letter, of course, will also put your name in front of Mr. Big, establishing a human contact in your company he can call if he wants to.

It's also a good idea to send an actual, physical snail mail letter; they're not only classier than email, but much less likely to get lost in Mr. Big's spam folder.

These steps can't be rushed. Together, they'll probably take at least four to six weeks. You have to judge the time you need according to each situation, of course, but remember that the relationship has to evolve over a little time—weeks, not days—and work like water dripping steadily on rock. After enough drops have struck the surface, a hole will appear in the rock. It takes a lot of drops for that to happen.

Step Three: After you've laid the foundation, start to build the relationship. This step will probably require at least another four weeks. Now is the time to get some face-to-face contact with Mr. Big. Invite him (and the flak catcher) to any of your company functions where customers are welcome. If you don't have any, think about staging one. Maybe you can throw a cocktail party to announce a new product or a buffet lunch in appreciation of past business.

If your company gives away any goodies—coffee mugs, T-shirts, caps with your logo—be sure to give one to the flak catcher and one to Mr. Big. Hand-deliver them if at all possible. Your goal is to put your face with that name Mr. Big has been seeing on correspondence for the last eight weeks. If you have to leave Mr. Big's gift at the front desk, put a hand-written note with it.

Get your management involved, too. If your boss invites Mr. Big to dinner, the flak catcher can't take it out on you, especially if the dinner is a purely social affair, which it should be at this point. Most top management recognizes the importance of these occasions and considers it part of their job.

Step Four: After you've established a pattern of contact with Mr. Big, he's seen your name and face a few times and has been exposed to your company and its products, it's time for the next step, which is to pitch an idea to him.

Send a letter to Mr. Big much like your cold call telephone appointment pitch—promise him an idea and ask for 15 minutes of his time. Send a copy of the letter to the flak catcher. Then call the flak catcher and ask him if he's available for that meeting assuming it happens. Don't ask his permission—assume the close and invite him to the meeting. Then call Mr. Big to set the date and time.

The worst thing that can happen is that the flak catcher gets irritated by your end run. But what's he going to do? Tell Mr. Big that he shouldn't meet with that nice person who gave him all those gifts, invited him to dinner, and sent him that wonderful letter praising the flak catcher's performance? It's pretty hard for him to do that without sounding petty and defensive.

Is he going to tell you not to call Mr. Big? He can try, but if you remind him that you're not going behind his back, in fact you're inviting him to the meeting because you know how much Mr. Big values his opinion, he'll have a tough time justifying his demand.

Step Four Alternative: But what if Mr. Big still won't take your call? There's always Plan Two, which is your fallback strategy when you can't get in to see someone. Put your pitch on videotape or DVD and send it to them. The only difference here is that you send a copy to the flak catcher or buying agency as well.

In fact, having a video presentation is a very good way to avoid "whisper down the lane" problems and the general difficulty of making multiple presentations to multiple decision influencers. This is particularly true if they are spread out all over the globe, as is often the case. It may not be as much fun but it's a lot cheaper to send a video tape to the regional manager in San Francisco than to fly out there for a meeting.

What do you do when the buying agency forbids you to contact Mr. Big? Don't go into that battle without reinforcements. Go directly to your manager and give him or her a complete run-down of the events to date. Be prepared with a thorough analysis of the buying agency's past purchases from you for Mr. Big's company and any others they may represent. What's the worst case scenario? How much current business could you lose if the buying agency carries out its threat? How much future business? These aren't rhetorical questions; you need the data because some tough decisions are going to be made.

If you decide to enter the battle, go all out. This is no time to be tentative. Call on your other customers who do business through the buying agency to reinforce your relationship with them. Visit Mr. Big and ask him directly if he wants to be denied your ideas. Then go see the buying agency management and see if they're willing to soften their position. If they won't relent, cut them out of the loop and deal only with Mr. Big directly. When you're battling the forces of evil at the end of the world, you need to be strong.

Sell Actionable Ideas

Regardless of how you deliver the presentation to Mr. Big, it's paramount that you present an idea he can buy, not a list of product features. Mr. Big hired the flak catcher and the buying agency in the first place because he doesn't have time to make routine decisions like which brand of widgets to buy. He's usually the "big picture" guy, who is paid the big bucks because he makes the big decisions. So give him a big idea to make a big decision about.

As long as you are an idea seller, Mr. Big will see you—even if he doesn't buy your first idea. He'll admit you to the inner sanctum as long as you have the price of admission—an idea he can use. But he'll relegate you to the lobby with the rest of the peddlers if all you have to sell is a bag of product.

A problem-solving idea is the engine that drives the sale through many layers of complexity. If you are selling an idea, all the decision influencers will be interested in hearing about it. If your idea is strong enough, it won't be changed by everyone in the decision-making hierarchy.

Ideas sell, especially in the face of complexity.

Chapter 30
Opening Closed Doors

"If you're going to be a creative seller, you've got to take chances."

Every once in a while, you discover a great prospect, someone who has a real need for your product or service plus has the financial wherewithal to become a really big client, but they absolutely won't give you the time of day, much less an appointment. Their door is closed. You can't get your foot in it because the prospect won't open it even a crack. Your phone calls are never returned. Your singing telegrams are heard by a secretary. You've tried all the methods you've read about for getting appointments, but this door is closed, locked, and sealed tighter than a submarine. How do you get your presentation in front of someone who just won't see you?

Have no fear. There's a tactic that I guarantee will work every time you use it. This technique will require some extra work on your part, but it's a foolproof way to compel Mr. Big to listen to your presentation. It's a little sneaky, but I wouldn't ask you to do anything illegal or even remotely unethical.

I guarantee that Mr. Big will view your presentation if you record it on an unlabeled DVD, put it in a plain brown wrapper, and send it addressed to him personally at his home. Note the most important detail: Neither the DVD nor the package reveals anything about the contents. If Mr. Big is human, curiosity will drive him to see what's on the disc. It's human nature—that old curiosity works every time.

I stumbled on this tactic when trying to work around a problem with one of my clients. When I saw the results the first time, I knew we had found a powerful tool. Subsequent trials proved it.

My client had a simple problem. She wanted to pitch an advertising campaign for a local store to a prospect with headquarters several hundred miles away, but her travel budget for the year was exhausted. And her not-so-far-sighted boss wouldn't approve any more travel expense because the prospect wasn't a current customer. In the manager's defense, all the other salespeople in the company had failed to sell this prospect, so why spend all that travel money on a lost cause?

So my client borrowed a home video camera from a friend and put her pitch on videotape. The presentation wasn't anything fancy, just the same pitch she would make if she were sitting across the desk from Mr. Big. She sent it to the president of the prospect company. You guessed it—the phone rang about a week later and she got the order. Without ever meeting the actual decision-maker face-to-face.

Why does this technique work? I think one reason is because it's so different from what the great crowd of "normal" salespeople do. The prospect is besieged by salespeople, all clamoring for a few minutes of his time. When he can't seem them all, they send presentation folders and brochures and personal letters with proposals. Those that he does see are often armed with laptops and identical presentation software. They all tend to look and sound alike.

Your video is just another selling medium—the difference is that your version has obviously been prepared just for this particular prospect at some considerable effort. It demonstrates the creative seller's willingness to work hard for the business.

Another reason is that the medium itself, video, is the next best thing to a personal sales presentation. The prospect can see the steadiness in the seller's gaze, hear the sincerity in their voice, and get caught up in their enthusiasm for the idea. You just can't do those things in a letter.

When you use this technique, be sure to execute the entire plan exactly as I presented it. Don't send a cover letter. Don't even have a return address on the package or a label on the DVD. And under no circumstances send a copy of your written proposal along with it. You can send these things under separate cover to arrive a few days after the DVD if you need to. The full impact of the curiosity factor will be lost if the prospect even suspects what the video is about.

The video needs to be playable on a dedicated DVD player, by the way, not just a computer. In fact, DVD is preferable since many people are justifiably reluctant to stick unlabeled media into their computers from fear of viruses. The same is true for storing the video online and emailing Mr. Big an anonymous link. I wouldn't click on that, would you? The home DVD player is generally isolated, though, so your DVD can be seen without concern.

And send the tape to the prospect's home if you possibly can—in that plain brown wrapper. It will receive a heck of a lot more attention there than if it lands in his office in-box with the daily junk mail. Besides, Mr. Big is much more likely to have a DVD player at home than he is at work. To get the prospect's home address, start with the telephone book white pages. If you can't find it there, ask the screener (you never know until you try). If you can't find his home address, go ahead and send it to the office.

The Equipment

So how do you go about this? Using the mystery video tactic does require some extra preparation and work on your part, but it's not as complicated as it sounds. The key is to keep it simple.

If you don't have a computer with a webcam, beg, borrow, or rent a camera with a built-in microphone and light. You'll also need a tripod to produce a shake-free picture, even if you have someone else operate the camera. You're not producing a major motion picture, but you don't want it to look like the video of your kid's birthday party, either. You'll also need access to a computer with a DVD burner.

Now write your script—which should duplicate the presentation you'd make in person. If you feel comfortable enough to ad-lib the pitch (like you would on a face-to-face call), that's fine. You can even work from notes or the written presentation itself if you are confident of your presentation skills. Doing it this way makes it more natural and therefore more effective.

If you are a little camera shy, you can handle the script much the way television news anchors do. You probably won't have access to a teleprompter, but you can hand print "idiot cards" that a friend can hold for you out of camera view.

The "set" for your little production should be as simple as possible. In fact, all you really need is a quiet place with a neutral background for a medium close-up of your head and shoulders, since you're only going to have one shot for the whole video. Set up the web cam or video camera on the tripod and fix it in place for that shot. Check the lighting and sound levels according to the camera's instructions.

The Production

Now just do it. The great thing about digital video is that you can do it over and over again until you get it right—and it doesn't cost you any extra. And you can play it back instantly to see how you did. Make every run-through a dress rehearsal with the tape rolling. You'll be surprised at how few "takes" you need to get a finished product.

It's a good idea to ask a friend to help you by starting and stopping the recording, managing the "idiot cards," and giving you a human face to talk to. Some cameras come with remote controls, though, so you can go solo if you need to.

About the only "don't" to this technique is to not overreach your capabilities. Don't try to present the CBS Evening News with graphics, multiple camera angles, digital video effects, etc. Unless you have a multi-million-dollar production facility and staff at your disposal, you're not going to be able to approach that quality. All you want is a clean, glitch-free videotaped one-way conversation.

Just as an aside, you can increase the quality of your video if you want to invest a little more money in it. There are video production facilities complete with crews available for rent in most cities. Many quick print services have video conferencing facilities that can be used to make a video also. If you live in a small town with a local TV station, check with them, too. Your investment can start at a few hundred dollars and go up from there, though, so consider the option carefully. Remember, this show will be seen once by one viewer—it's not going to go into syndicated reruns and have a life in the international cable market.

Actually, that last sentence isn't exactly true. Your video presentation may have a surprising shelf life. One of the most incredible experiences with this technique I ever witnessed happened to another one of my clients.

This salesperson was trying to sell a sales promotion campaign to a very hard-to-reach prospect. This wasn't a typical Mr. Big, but was actually an elderly farmer who started a potato-chip business on the side. Like many such entrepreneurs he started small, producing a few bags for friends, then for local stores, slowly expanding his capacity and distribution as demand warranted. My client identified him as a good prospect for his sales promotion services and dreamed up a great campaign to sell him.

As you might have guessed, though, the farmer wouldn't see him. Wouldn't return his phone calls, respond to his letters—you know the routine. So the salesperson put his pitch on video and sent it to the farmer, expecting a quick response and already mentally spending his commission on the sale.

Except it didn't happen. Nothing. No response of any kind. He knew the video was delivered because he had the FedEx receipt. But the farmer didn't even acknowledge receiving it. And still wouldn't return phone calls. When the salesperson told me about it, we both just wrote it off to "win some, lose some."

A full year later we were proven wrong. That's when the salesperson received a phone call from a man who identified himself as the farmer's son. He said, "Dad retired last year and I took over the potato chip business. I found this video in his desk without any label on it and took it home to see what it was. The reason I'm calling is to see if we can still get in on that sales promotion you were trying to sell Dad?"

Whenever I advise a client to use the videotape technique, the negatives start rushing around in their brains. There's a simple positive answer to every one of them:

- "I don't have a camera." Buy one, rent one or borrow one.
- "I'm not a TV star." Don't try to be—just make your presentation as if the camera were Mr. Big.
- "I'll feel silly." If you're embarrassed about selling, get a new career.
- "It won't look professional." Don't try to film "Gone with the Wind," just sit comfortably in front of the camera and talk.
- "He may not have a VCR." If he's one of the less than 5 percent of Americans who don't, he'll find one.

After I saw the success of this tactic the first time, I started recommending it all over the country. One of my favorite success stories is when a rookie salesperson used the mystery video tactic to open the door to a chain of tire dealerships. The president of the chain wouldn't see her. He kept giving her the lame excuse that "those decisions are made by the managers' board" and refusing to admit her to a board meeting to make her pitch.

So this salesperson (being a rookie and not knowing any better) put her pitch on video and sent a copy of it to the president and to the manager of every store in the chain. She didn't know which ones were on the board, so she sent it to all of them. She made sure the DVDs arrived the day before the next scheduled board meeting. And the first words on her video were, "We know you have a lot of important matters to consider at your board meeting, but we hope you'll take 15 minutes to listen to this idea to increase your store sales."

She knew that the message got through because her phone rang the afternoon of the board meeting. It was the president asking her to meet with him to discuss a contract for her proposal. And that account turned out to be one of her company's largest within just a few months after the door got opened.

If you're going to be a creative seller, you've got to take a chance every once in a while. Work outside the box, as they say. Try something different, you might like it. Besides, what have you got to lose—he won't even see you, right?

Chapter 31
Presentations To Groups

You have the opportunity to use all of your persuasive skills and stagecraft to their fullest effect."

Selling is just like playing chess—the rules are the same every time but no two games are just exactly alike. And it's a good thing, too, since we'd all get bored pretty quickly if the games ever started repeating themselves. One of the variations many salespeople encounter is the need to make a presentation to a group rather than to a single prospect.

It may be Mr. Big and his assistant, a committee of decision-makers and decision-influencers, or even the board of directors. When you make a group presentation, you're generally working in a different physical setting that can range from chairs pulled around the prospect's desk to a conference room with a table the size of an aircraft carrier. You might even have to make your pitch in an auditorium complete with podium and sound system.

Regardless of the setting, the basic differences between a group presentation and a one-on-one call deal with the distribution and control of your written materials and handling the very different dynamics of large group meetings. It's important to remember, though, that all the other good sales techniques remain the same. Your goal is still to gather information about the prospect, for example, and you should still follow the five-page presentation format I introduced in *The Dynamic Manager's Guide To Sales Techniques*, including asking questions at the end of each page. Your stage presence and enthusiasm level are even more important when pitching a group, though, as is your ability to gain their attention and hold their interest.

Group Dynamics

The dynamics of group presentations can be interesting, to say the least. This is a sales presentation, not a floorshow, so you want to encourage questions and comments from the group. In fact, you should plan to ask some questions of your own just like you would if you were meeting with the prospect one-on-one.

Your questions can either be thrown out to the group as a whole or addressed to one person in particular, depending on which is more appropriate. You will find that agreement questions such as "Do you like this idea?" don't work very well in a group setting. There's too much danger of the group splitting into factions or a particularly out-spoken member shooting you down before you get into your presentation.

Information questions, though, such as "Who is your biggest competitor?" can work very well. Many times, they'll spark an intra-group discussion, which is a great time to listen closely and learn a lot. Watch the group dynamics to learn who the leaders really are. Obviously, you'll want to listen to what they say about their business, their market, and their competitors as well as what they say about your idea, your company, and your competitors.

You should welcome questions or comments that come from the group, even when they break up the flow of your presentation. If the question is one you don't want to answer yet, it's perfectly acceptable to say that you're going to cover that subject in a minute. Just make sure you do cover it before you end your presentation. If it's a question about your proposal that indicates the listener doesn't understand something, take the time right then to make it clear. If one person didn't get it, there are probably others who missed it, too.

Group Dangers

On very rare occasions a group presentation will turn ugly. No matter what happens, keep your cool. If you get a hostile question or comment, thank the person for sharing their thoughts with you, then deal with it just like you would handle an objection. If the whole room starts twitching in their seats, stop your pitch and ask them if you've said something wrong, then correct your misstatement.

The most common problem you'll face with groups, though, isn't hostility, it's keeping them on the track you want them to follow. It seems like every group has a leader or a loud-mouth (sometimes it's the same person) who wants to comment on every point you make, and everything everyone else says, too. Don't take it personally, though, because this person probably acts the same way every time this group gets together. In fact, you can usually identify this guy before he opens his mouth because the rest of the crowd will start rolling their eyes when they see his hand go up the first time.

I wish I had a magic incantation for you to use in this situation, but I don't. All you can do is stay pleasant and polite, not hesitating to change the subject back to your presentation before the loud-mouth can ask a follow-up question. Try to resist the temptation to put them in their place the way a stand-up comic deals with a heckler in a nightclub. Just grin and bear it and try not to lose your place in your pitch. Actually, the sympathy the rest of the group feels for you might well work in your favor

Another unpleasant situation is when the meeting degenerates into the dreaded "I Can Top That" routine. When the war stories start, everyone in the room seems to have a primal urge to contribute one. Each one has to be more horrible than the last one, of course, and the negative energy in the room just builds and builds. If it goes unchecked, you end up with an ugly mob on your hands.

Once again, the best tactic is to jump in before the momentum builds. The best rule of thumb is to interrupt after the second story is told. Don't let the third one even get started. Give them a polite "That's very interesting" and get back into your presentation. If you're really good, you'll be able to relate the benefits of your proposal to the problem that sparked the first story.

Handling Materials

Handling your written materials is actually easier in many ways when you are working with a group. The best tactic to control the pace of the presentation is to hand out one page of the presentation at a time. You never want to distribute the entire proposal at the beginning for the same reason you shouldn't just hand it to a single prospect: they'll turn immediately to the price and fixate on it. Instead, hand out each page in its turn. In a small room with a limited number of participants, you can handle this easily yourself—provided you can walk and talk at the same time. With a larger group you may need some assistance, which can be provided by the group members themselves. If you don't have a helper with you, just ask the people nearest to you to "take one and pass them on" to the people behind them. Your goal is to see that everyone in the group gets a copy—but that none have any page in their hand until you're ready to talk about it.

Larger group presentations often call for visual aids, which can both embellish and complicate your presentation. Whether you're using foam-board flip cards or a laptop with presentation software projected onto a big screen, be sure that you know how to use the presentation medium and have rehearsed with it.

Find out, if you can, just how large the room will be and how many participants you'll be facing. This will help you determine what kind of visual aids, if any, that you want to use. You may not want 24 X 30-inch flip cards for a group of four—unless they're going to be seated at the opposite end of a 20-ft. table.

Never count on the prospect to provide any equipment. There's nothing worse than arriving to connect your laptop to the prospect's projector only to discover that you need an adapter neither one of you has. Whether you're going high-tech or low-tech, bring every single item you could possibly need with you. This includes everything from extension cords and grounded-outlet adapters to monitors and projectors. If you need an easel for your flip cards, bring one yourself. I can almost guarantee that if you don't, the prospect's won't work or someone in another department will have borrowed it just before you arrived.

It's mandatory that you set up your visual aids before the group gathers in the room. I would rather skip the visual aids completely than stumble through a pitch while I'm fumbling with a "General Protection Page Fault" on my laptop. In fact, if it's not possible to get access to the meeting room and set up before the group gathers, play it safe and don't bother with the visual aids. It's better to make a neutral low-tech impression than a bad high-tech one.

If you're using a laptop, set up your software so that you don't have to click through several screens to get to your presentation. Create a shortcut to the presentation right on your opening screen. That way, all you have to do is click on it to start the show. Finally, check the view from the back of the room to be sure everyone can read your material.

No matter which format you use for your visual aids, design them as much like your written presentation as you can. Make each slide (or card) simple, clear, and to the point. Any bodies of text will need to be converted to bullet points, of course. This isn't the place to go into great detail on constructing slide presentations, but get yourself a good tutorial if you plan on preparing your own.

Group presentations are actually great fun to give. You get to practice your craft in a slightly different way from the normal routine. And you have the opportunity to use all of your persuasive skills and stagecraft to their fullest effect. Most group presentations involve prospects with large potential, so there's usually a lot riding on the effectiveness of your pitch. You'll make good use of your stage fright management skills.

Chapter 32
Team Presentations

"The choir always sounds better when they're all singing the same song."

The team call is when two or more people from your company gang up on a single prospect. It's not exactly the reverse of a group presentation, but it's close. Depending on whether your sales manager is involved or not, the purpose of the double team call can be two-fold: 1) to help you make the sale or 2) to improve your performance on subsequent calls. I'm going to deal with the first scenario. You have to cope with the second one (and your manager) on your own for now.

Team calls should make the prospect feel less like he's the target of a sales shark and more like he's the object of the company's affections. He'll get the strong message that the seller's company wants to work with him to solve his problems. He'll usually feel flattered that his business is so important that the selling company is devoting an entire team to getting and handling it.

The interpersonal dynamics of a team call are somewhat different from those of a group presentation because you need to manage your team members' behavior as well as the prospect's.

Team Members

Literally anyone in your company can be a part of the pitch team. Other salespeople, engineers, the chief executive officer, even a purchasing agent or shipping clerk can contribute productively to the sales presentation. Their involvement can make the sales call extremely effective. It can also raise some potential problems.

One of the most difficult dynamics to deal with occurs when your boss is the other half of your tag team. His or her presence raises all kinds of questions in your subconscious mind as well as the prospect's. What's the boss there for? Can you get any brownie points on the call? Among other things, the prospect may look to the boss for confirmation of every point you make. It's a tough situation.

The best strategy, though, is to try to concentrate exclusively on impressing your prospect rather than your boss. You'll have plenty of opportunities to kiss up to the boss but you may only have one chance to close this particular prospect. Hopefully, your boss will understand. And everyone on the team, including your boss, should be prepared to direct the prospect's attention back to you if necessary.

Team Call Preparation

Pre-call preparation for the team presentation is essential. You should each know what your respective roles are going to be on the call before you begin the presentation. Even if the presentation is one you've done together many times, rehearse it before you go into the meeting. This means everyone on the team, including your company's CEO. And the practice must be a full dress rehearsal complete with the actual props you're going to be using.

One of my most embarrassing moments occurred during a team presentation. It happened because we had not rehearsed with the actual materials we were going to use. There were four of us making a pitch that we had done many times together. Our presentations usually involved the top decision makers and were quite lengthy and detailed. We typically used a lot of boilerplate material, but the key points were always customized for the prospect we were pitching.

The climax of the pitch came when I would present our revenue projections for the prospect. I typically jumped into that page like a preacher at a revival, giving it everything I had. On this occasion, though, when I turned the page I saw the headings of the columns of figures carried not this prospect's name but the name of the company we had pitched the week before. The figures were correct, but they looked like they belonged to another company.

We all saw the simple little word processing mistake at the same time and everyone in the room was embarrassed, including the prospect. But the damage had been done. This little mistake completely undermined the "personal attention to each client" benefit that was our primary selling point. It cost us a $6 million client. The material had been proofread by three people, including me. But we hadn't used the actual materials in our rehearsal the night before. I'll always believe that we would have caught the mistake if we had followed that simple little rule.

In addition to the pitch itself, you should also rehearse the answers to particular questions and objections that you expect to crop up. It's important to know which person on the team is going to answer which question so that there's no fumbling when it arises. If the prospect asks you about delivery dates, for example, you don't want a long awkward pause followed by three people giving three different answers all at once. You also don't want your team leader to "hand off" a question to someone who's not expecting it.

You also need to organize your visual aids under the management of one member of the team. We've all seen blooper video where three outfielders collide under the same fly ball in short center field. You don't want that to happen to you in front of a room full of prospects, so make sure each piece of equipment and each piece of hand-out material is one person's responsibility. Your hand-outs, by the way, should be managed the same way they are in a group presentation—the one team member responsible for them passes them out with the order and flow you want.

Team Call Leadership

While we're on the subject of assigning responsibility, let's talk about leadership. Each team, even if it consists of only two members, should have a leader. That's usually the senior person on the team and will be the person the prospect will tend to address with questions. It doesn't have to be, but it usually happens that way. The leader will also generally be the one to open the presentation and ask the closing question. If there is any question about who's going to be the leader on your team, settle it before you go into the presentation.

But don't let the leader look like the Grand Poobah attended by his retinue. If the leader delegates all the menial tasks like handing out materials to the lowly lackeys on the team, the prospect is liable to sense a power display in progress, and react negatively. Eliminate this problem before it arises and make sure the leader is perceived as a member of the team, not its monarch.

On the other end of the scale, also make sure that every member of the team actively participates in the presentation. Each person should have a speaking role of some sort, preferably related to their role in the seller's plan to serve the prospect's needs. You don't want the prospect wondering why that guy in the corner isn't saying anything while you're trying to make the points in your presentation. The Metropolitan Opera may need spear-carriers, but your sales team doesn't.

In order to keep your team call focused on results, make sure everyone on the team understands these points about the upcoming call:

- What are we trying to do?
- If this call is successful, what will happen?
- Who are the key players?
- What happened on the last call?
- What are we going to ask them to do?
- Why should they do it?

The choir always sounds better when they're all singing the same song.

Immediately after the call, you should each separately jot down some notes on how it went, what you each learned about the prospect, what steps need to be taken to close the sale (if necessary), and how the presentation can be made better next time. Then compare notes. Only after this process is complete should any critique of individual performance be given.

Chapter 33
Negotiating Like A Pro

"You're negotiating to make the sale, not 'win' at the buyer's expense."

Do customers in your industry pay the asking price? Or do they routinely ask for a lower price, better terms, extra merchandise, rebates, slotting fees, or extended service? If you sell business-to-business, you've probably never had a customer agree to pay your asking price on the first pass. It's becoming more common in retail sales, too. What your customers are doing, of course, is practicing an art as old as commerce itself. They're negotiating.

Negotiation is that stage of the selling process that occurs after the commitment to buy is made but before the sale is actually closed. It's when the buyer and seller come to terms on the conditions under which the product or service is provided.

Sounds imposing, doesn't it? And it can be a complicated undertaking, which is why I suggest you approach negotiations as carefully as James Cameron approached the production of *Avatar*. You need to coordinate all the various components of the negotiation if you are going to produce a successfully orchestrated sale.

Negotiation is a matter of choices by both parties. One party chooses whether or not to offer something and the other one chooses whether or not to accept it. As you'll see, it's not always the seller who does the offering, nor is it always the buyer who does the accepting or rejecting. Nor is price the only item subject to negotiation.

When do you negotiate? If you're a creative seller, you only negotiate the terms of your proposal after the prospect has made the commitment to buy the idea you are selling. If the prospect doesn't like the idea, no amount of negotiation of the price or any of the other terms will make the sale happen. But once that commitment is made, you can assume that you will negotiate the sale in one way or another.

The price to value ratio is at the heart of every negotiation. Both the buyer and the seller negotiate both sides of that equation, giving gains on one side in return for gains on the other. When the needs of both the buyer and seller are met, the sale occurs.

Firm Prices

Some people are leery of negotiating a sale. They feel that the process is somehow dishonest or demeans them, their product, or even their prospect in some way. In fact, I often encounter sales managers who proudly point out that their prices are firm. They insist that every customer pays the same price and that's the one set by the sales manager. They would rather forego a sale than violate their holy pricing policies. These sales managers need a strong dose of reality—and they often get it in the form of declining market share.

There is nothing holy about a given price, nor is there any moral law that says that every customer is entitled to the same terms. In fact, certain religions make a pretty strong moral case for customizing prices and other terms according to each customer's individual needs. Don't get me wrong. There's nothing wrong with having a firm pricing policy. But let's not hide the reasons for it in some kind of moral cloud. Firm pricing is a matter of what management feels is best for the selling company. Ideally (from their standpoint), it controls demand to produce the maximum profit from the available supply. And having firm prices makes the administration of the revenue stream easier, which makes the sales manager's job easier. There's nothing wrong with that.

Free Markets

But there is nothing wrong with negotiating every sale, either. Humans have been doing it for thousands of years in one way or another. In fact, the most successful economic system yet invented, the free market economy, is predicated on the freedom of sellers to offer different value for various prices and for buyers to accept or reject them.

Isn't that what happens when your favorite department store puts an item on sale? Apparently, the store's customers made the choice to not buy that item at the previous price, and the store made the choice to offer it at a lower price as a result. Isn't that a form of negotiation?

Western retail negotiation just doesn't happen face-to-face (usually) like the haggling that occurs in a Middle Eastern souk. It's the same process, but the department store is haggling through the medium of its displays and signs rather than having hawkers standing in the aisles soliciting offers for the merchandise on the tables.

In business-to-business sales, nearly every sale is openly negotiated. There may be published price lists and standard terms, but very few buyers would keep their jobs if they didn't at least try to do better. And few sellers would keep the revenue flowing if they didn't make pricing adjustments to stay competitive.

Win/Lose Negotiation

So how do you negotiate honorably and successfully? By negotiating both value and price with the goal of striking the most favorable deal for both the buyer and the seller. If there is a morality problem with a negotiated sale, it's when one party's aim is to "win" the game at the expense of the other. If both the buyer and the seller can believe in and practice win/win negotiations, everybody's life is easier and they can sleep better at night.

Unfortunately, too many people engage in win/lose negotiation. They believe that the only way they can gain value is by taking it away from the other person. They view every transaction as a zero-sum game. This belief is anathema to the Creative Selling System. You can't build long term customer relationships based on taking advantage of the customer every time you sell them something. Sooner or later they'll figure it out.

When you engage in win/lose negotiation, you create an adversarial relationship with your prospect. That lifeblood of Creative Selling, information about the prospect's needs, is cut off at the source because the prospect soon realizes that you're using that information to gain the upper hand in the negotiations.

That's one of the main reasons, by the way, that the traditional consultive selling approach is so ineffective—many prospects fear that giving information to the consultive seller will just give him ammunition to use in future negotiations. So they clam up or even give misleading information to confuse the seller.

You can't create solutions to the prospect's needs unless you learn what those needs are. Without that information, your selling effort degenerates into a guessing game where you have to keep offering different proposals without having the feedback necessary to come up with good ones. And because your ideas don't very accurately meet the prospect's needs, fewer sales occur. The win/lose negotiation attitude may produce a larger single order today, but it reduces the probability of getting better orders tomorrow.

Win/Lose Disadvantages

Win/lose negotiation also produces conflict, which drastically reduces the efficiency of the buying/selling process. Both parties waste valuable time plotting negotiation strategies, floating trial offers, and delaying commitment until they are reasonably sure that the other side has given up as much ground as they are going to give up. "Never leave money on the table" becomes the goal of the seller rather than "Create a satisfied customer." That's no way to make someone a customer for life.

Win/lose negotiation focuses almost exclusively on price, with a resulting denigration of value. The buyer may get "more for their money" but that's a misperception they have just because the seller lowered their price. In the world of win/lose negotiation the buyer is only deluding himself if he thinks the seller hadn't jacked up the asking price in the first place.

In absolute terms, they may get less value than if they paid a slightly higher price. That's because sellers who are caught in win/lose negotiation retaliate, either intentionally or not, by lowering the value delivered. Production and shipping priorities tend to favor the customer who pays a higher price. After-sale service does the same. Special offers aren't offered to the win/lose buyer because the seller knows they'll try to knock the price down even further. Consequently, that buyer may miss some real values at bargain prices.

And buyers who lose in win/lose negotiation retaliate, too. If they feel they've been pressured into a corner on the price, they'll remember that and get even next time. They'll actively look for another supplier. They'll pay the invoice at the last possible moment. They'll not think twice about canceling an order at the last moment if they can.

Squeezing the last nickel from a deal may feed the ego of the squeezer, but it doesn't endear him to the squeezee.

The only time you should engage in win/lose negotiation is when you aren't concerned about repeat business. That's why some negotiated transactions have such a reputation for being no-holds-barred affairs. Real estate, business ownership sales, and other such one-time transactions are often conducted on a win/lose basis because the two parties will not generally have any economic connection or even contact after the sale closes. But if you want to do business with the other side later, a win/lose attitude isn't wise.

Negotiation And Stress

Negotiating has earned its reputation as an unpleasant process in large part because it is inherently stressful. Stress is produced when something or someone blocks a person from obtaining a desired goal, which just about defines the process of negotiation. Each party is blocking the other one in some way. "I won't buy unless you give me this" is just another way of saying, "You can't obtain your goal (to get the order) because my demand (to get the concession) is blocking your way."

Two other stressful things happen in negotiation. The blocks generally get bigger and bigger as the easy concessions are made early and the tough ones—the big price cut or the large volume order—are left to the end. And, the closer you get to the end, the closer each person feels to achieving his or her goal. The carrot is dangled closer and closer to the donkey's nose.

Stress, stress, stress. That's the real reason many people feel uncomfortable when put into a negotiating role. The uncertainty of the outcome is stressful. The pressure to make multiple decisions is stressful. The fear of feeling outfoxed is very stressful. It's certainly a lot less stressful to say, "Sorry, our prices are firm. Take it or leave it." You get the pain over with.

Win/Win Negotiation

Negotiation doesn't have to be that way. I'm not saying that you'll eliminate the uncertainty, the decision-making, or the possibility of leaving some money on the table, but you can make the process less stressful if you have the right attitude.

The better way, of course, is win/win negotiation, where both parties recognize that the value side of the equation is not finite. If you can focus on building the value of the deal, both the buyer and the seller generally win. Win/win negotiation is at the heart of the Creative Selling System because it focuses on need satisfaction.

It's an attitude thing. Win/win negotiators may start from positions far apart, but they know that they're going to work with each other to come together somewhere in the middle, not drag each other from one side to the other.

This type of mutual conflict resolution builds trust, which opens the doors to better communication of needs. That's why creative sellers have to practice win/win negotiations; to get the information they must have to meet the prospect's needs.

The lack of conflict builds efficiency into the buying/selling process. I remember once trying to negotiate a television advertising schedule with an advertising agency that practiced win/lose negotiation. If they would have approached the situation from a win/win frame of reference, we could have struck a deal within minutes. But, because they were intent on squeezing the dollar until Washington screamed, the negotiations went on for two weeks. They still didn't get a better deal, but they wasted a huge amount of their time (and mine).

Value Not Price

The focus of win/win negotiations is generally on value, not price. The seller will have a tendency to add more value to the package rather than cut the price and the buyer will have a similar tendency to ask for more value rather than to demand a lower price. And both parties are more likely to meet in the middle because they're not "giving up" money, which is a difficult, unpleasant action.

The final solution better meets the needs of both parties. The seller gets a larger sale in terms of dollars and the buyer gets a better solution to their need in terms of value. Most importantly, a foundation is laid for a constructive future relationship.

"Only in the land of milk and honey," say the skeptics among you. "It's a tough old world out there. Dog eat dog. Every man for himself and the devil take the hindmost."

You skeptics are right about some things, of course. It is a tough old world. But I've found that the people in that tough old world are pretty nice—if you're nice to them first.

Somebody has to make the first move. The next time someone asks you for a lower price, try offering more value instead, then wait to see how they react. If they're intent on pounding down your price, you'll find out soon enough. But you'll be surprised at how often people will respond positively, opening the door to a trusting relationship.

Information Is Power

In all types of negotiation, information is power. Win/win negotiation is no exception. In fact, the more information both parties have, the smoother and more productive the negotiation can be. The things you want to know are much the same as those you want to know about your prospect when you develop your proposed idea for them.

Remember that they will want to know the same kinds of things about you and your position, so be prepared to offer some of that information under the right circumstances. Conventional wisdom says that you should play your cards close to the vest but conventional wisdom is often wrong. Sometimes the exchange of information can be a transaction within a transaction that takes the edge off the larger negotiation.

Here's a partial list of common types of information you should have before you enter your negotiations:

- What are the prospect's apparent needs?
- Do any underlying needs exist?
- What are the alternatives to your proposal?
- What are the advantages/disadvantages of the alternatives?
- How do your competitors fit into the alternatives?
- What is the prospect's financial position?
- How big a factor is the price?
- How strongly are they committed to the proposed idea?
- Are there other decision-influencers?
- What deadlines are they facing?
- Are they negotiating to win/win or win/lose?

You have many sources of information at your disposal. The prospect himself is the best one, of course, and if you've been listening to him as well as talking to him, you'll have picked up the answers to many of these questions already. Don't overlook your company's files, either. A given prospect may be new to you but not to your company, since the salesperson who preceded you in the territory may well have had some contact with the prospect.

I've also always found it useful to get to know as many of my customers' employees as I could. You certainly want to know Mr. Big's secretary or assistant as well as the receptionist and telephone operator (if there is one). But don't overlook his salespeople, clerks, shipping manager, buyers, purchasing manager, bookkeeper, etc. You never know when they're going to reveal an interesting tidbit of information that you'll find useful during negotiation.

Mr. Big's competitors and other vendors are also important sources of information. A caution in this area, though: Always consider the source when judging the truthfulness of any bit of information. A little knowledge can be a dangerous thing, especially when it's exaggerated by a partially-informed employee or a competitor with their own agenda. Just as information can be helpful in negotiation, disinformation can be disastrous. Anyone who has tried to make money in the stock market by trading based on "tips" can attest to that danger. Another word of caution: You don't want to become known as a carrier of tales or rumors. Such a reputation can have very unpleasant far-reaching consequences. Your strict policy should be to have open ears and a closed mouth at all times.

Honesty in negotiation is important in another sense. Be honest with yourself about your own position. You tend to underestimate your own strengths and weaknesses because you are more aware of them than you are of the buyer's. Remember, the buyer probably doesn't know that you're just one sale away from winning that trip to the Bahamas. If you reveal that little fact, you'll probably pay for it by suffering through a more demanding negotiation.

Everybody has their favorite "rules" for negotiating. But rules can be dangerous if you don't temper them with some simple common sense. I've learned the hard way that you can out-smart yourself if you try to get too fancy in your negotiating maneuvers. Let's look at some of the common tactics to consider and examine them closely for pitfalls.

Time Pressure

One of the factors never to be overlooked in any negotiation is time. Time pressure works for and against both parties, often in interesting ways. Anyone who has been involved in union negotiations, for example, knows that the largest concessions always come just before the strike deadline. In fact, sometimes that's the first time any concessions occur! Knowledge of the deadlines faced by the other party can be a powerful tool.

The pressure to come to an agreement is generally greatest on the party with the nearest deadline. Magazines are much more inclined to negotiate liberal terms for ad space the day before the issue closes than they are the week before. The prospect whose insurance policy is about to lapse is more eager to renew the policy than one with a 90 day grace period remaining. Know your prospect and know their deadlines.

One way to use time to your advantage is by making small concessions one at a time, drawing out the negotiating process if that is to your advantage. On the other hand, you may need to bring the deal to a close, in which case you may want to make a BFO, or best and final offer.

As a seller, though, don't be surprised if the buyer calls your bluff. They have nothing to lose and plenty to gain by telling you your BFO isn't good enough. If you back down and make a further concession, all you've done is prove to the buyer that you're a bluffer—and that your word isn't any good.

The time to make a BFO is when you discover you're negotiating with yourself. You can tell that's the situation because the other party isn't offering any concessions—you're the only one making any movement. It's one of the most frustrating situations you can face. You make all the moves, getting nothing more than a "that's not good enough" response from the prospect. The time to take a chance and make your BFO is when you have nothing to lose.

Starting High

I used to be a strong advocate of aiming high—making an outrageous offer so that I'd have plenty of room to come down when the buyer made a counter offer. Besides, I believed, low offers signal weakness.

I eventually learned that if the first offer was too high—outside the realm of what's reasonable to the buyer—then the buyer just might not make any counter offer at all. Then where was I? If I lowered my offer to try to re-start the negotiation, I was really signaling my desperation and letting the buyer know that concessions could be won.

The first step in the Creative Selling System is gathering information about your prospect. And one of the key pieces of information is an estimate of the prospect's spending potential. This not only gives you a goal to shoot for and an idea of how to structure your proposal, it gives you a good guideline for where to start your negotiations. As long as you begin with a proposal in the ballpark your prospect is used to playing in, you're not likely to scare them off.

Take the time to do your homework and use one or more of the estimating methods I covered in *The Dynamic Manager's Guide To Sales Techniques*. Even if you didn't use those figures to structure your proposal in the first place, they will give you a sense of what's possible for your negotiation.

Judge the reasonableness of your opening offer carefully. My rule now is that my opening offer is one at the high end of what the prospect could accept with no further changes if they were so inclined—and one I could defend without stretching my credibility.

Lowest Acceptable Alternative

It's also good to practice a little mental discipline. Right at the beginning of the negotiation, establish in your own mind the lowest acceptable offer you'll take. That way, you have a sense of how far you can go before you start cutting into profit margins, production capacity or whatever benchmark your company uses. As the negotiations proceed, you know where you are at all times. That sense of security gives you greater confidence during the process.

Establishing the lowest acceptable alternative in advance does something else. It keeps you in a win/win frame of mind because you don't have to worry about losing! As long as you know the point at which you will walk away (and stick to it) you can't lose anything.

As you may have noticed, we've now set an upper and a lower limit to pricing. This range makes it much easier to build a few small concessions into your proposal, or plan some value items you can add as the negotiations proceed. This helps you avoid making that big concession all at once, leaving you with no place to go if the buyer rejects it.

Never Give Without Getting

One rule I've found very helpful is to never give a concession without getting something in return—or at least asking for something back. If you don't do that, if you simply give concession after concession, pretty soon you'll find yourself in an ugly position similar to negotiating with yourself. Only in this situation, the buyer keeps the process going by making more and more demands. You can control this to a large extent by asking for something in return.

If the customer asks for something like free delivery, for example, you can respond with, "If I can waive the delivery charge, will you invest in an extended warranty?" It's a not-so-subtle reminder that negotiation is a two-way street. It's also a graceful way to avoid saying "no."

Speaking of "no," this is a word that should almost never be used in negotiations of any kind. It's so final, so definite, so negative that it should really come into play only when you've been pushed to the edge of the cliff and the buyer demands that you jump off. To avoid being pushed that far, try saying "maybe."

The Power Of Maybe

If you are negotiating in a win/win mode, "maybe" keeps the door open to add value items until the entire deal is clearly structured. When two people sit down at the negotiating table, they usually each have a list of items they must have, ones they'd like to have, and ones that they'll take if offered. One form the negotiation can take is for both parties to exchange lists, then discuss each item.

For this format to work properly, of course, there must be total honesty and complete trust on the part of both parties because you have to be sure there are no items held back to use at the end. Because of this requirement, this type of negotiation seldom occurs in its purest form. The temptation to have a few cards up the sleeve is too great.

A common negotiating strategy for buyers is to refuse to give you any information about what they're willing to do other than what you need to know to give them a proposal. When you're faced with that situation, saying "maybe" is the only way to get more information. If you say "yes" or "no" to each item as it comes up, you're handing complete control of the negotiation over to the buyer.

Since you can seldom be entirely sure you're not going to be faced with a demand for a sweetener at the end, you don't say "yes" or "no" to any single item until all items are on the table. You just say "maybe" to each one until you are pretty sure you have seen all the items the other person wants. Then you give a conditional "yes" to a package of values that you are comfortable giving. The condition of the offer is, "If you buy this exactly as offered, I'll give it to you at the agreed price." If the prospect agrees to this deal and then tries to get more in the package, you're able to say with a straight face that you have to revise the price.

Structuring Your Proposal

The seller's want list is usually contained in the proposal as offered. As I mentioned before, it's usually a good idea to build some possible concessions into your proposals in anticipation of the negotiations. The number and type you use will, of course, be determined at least in part by whether this is a new prospect or a repeat customer, since you won't know the negotiating habits of the new one but you will probably have some knowledge of how the current customer behaves.

You may also want to hold back some value items you could add later in the negotiation as a sweetener. These can be optional features that you can throw in at little or no cost such as extended payment terms or any number of items from your value list that you use to close the deal.

There are a couple of cautions to this practice, though. For one thing, if you consistently hold back and then give the same item to a customer, they (and you) will consider that item a standard part of future deals and it will lose its value as a sweetener. You also have to be sure that your sweetener isn't offered until the end of the negotiation. If you even hint at its existence earlier, you will lose its impact in your closing.

What are some of the value items you can offer? They certainly vary depending on the product or service you sell. Keep in mind, though, that "value" doesn't have to mean "free stuff." Value comes in many forms—always in the perception of the receiver. Consider some of these items of value that can be offered in one form or another by the seller to the buyer or vice versa:

Terms of the Sale

- Payment due dates
- Size of credit lines
- Carrying charges
- Discounts for prompt payment
- Length of grace periods

Product/Service Features

- Delivery dates
- Production line priority
- Special packaging
- Service guarantees
- Warranty extensions

Related Items

- Product exclusivity
- Advertising support
- Trade promotion

Future Sales

- Price guarantees
- Contract extensions
- Cancellation privileges
- Volume rebates

Miscellaneous

- Quick decisions
- Referrals
- Contract length

- Volume of order
- Share of business

Some of these items are price-related but most are not. All, however, represent a form of value to either or both parties in the negotiation. This is certainly not an exhaustive list—I'm sure you can develop a list of your own that relates specifically to the product or service you sell. Even two or three items that carry little cost to the provider and high value to the receiver can be good negotiating tools.

When you're faced with negotiations to close a sale, look on them not as a hassle to be endured, but rather as an opportunity to close. When you negotiate this way, trading value given for value received, you are perfectly positioned to use the negotiated close.

Always keep the ultimate goal in mind: you're negotiating to make the sale, not "win" at the buyer's expense.

Chapter 34

Case Study: Should Retail Art Galleries Negotiate?

"If a customer asks for a lower price, remember that it's just a business transaction, not a judgmental comment."

"Is this your best price?"

Few customer questions cause more consternation than this one—and few receive such diametrically opposed answers from gallery owners. There are no shades of gray when it comes to negotiating with retail customers; you either do it or you don't.

"You have to give and take," says Ana Leyland, owner of A Mano Gallery in New Hope, PA.

"We don't do it," flatly replies Diane Magnarelli, co-owner and sales manager of The Capitol Craftsman in Concord, NH.

Many factors enter in to a gallery's decision to negotiate prices, some practical, some philosophical. Magnarelli, who oversees both the craft gallery founded in 1979 and a jewelry store next door, sticks by her principles. "How can I wait on one customer today and charge them one price, then charge another customer a different price tomorrow?" she asks. "We don't pick and choose who gets the best deal. That means we go home and sleep well."

Leyland, who has operated A Mano Gallery for 25 years and opened a second store in nearby Lambertville, NJ, 12 years ago, takes a more pragmatic approach. "We're here to transfer ownership, not have a store full of merchandise," she says. Leyland has a down-to-earth attitude toward customers who ask for a lower price. "Everyone has a different personality," she says. "Don't get upset about an offer. You can always say 'no.' It's just the nature of people; they always want to get a better deal."

Like most gallery owners who don't shy away from negotiating with customers, Leyland considers numerous factors when deciding how to answer the request for a better price. One is the store's previous relationship with the customer. "We have customers who have been coming to us for 25 years. How can you not give them a discount?" she says. Another is how and when the customer raises the issue. If a customer loudly demands a better price in front of a store full of other customers, Leyland automatically turns them down. "It just puts everyone in a difficult situation," she explains. "If the customer comes up to me quietly and asks to deal with me, it's different."

That's her defense against the slippery slope many gallery owners consider the gravest danger of negotiated retail prices. "If you give Sally a deal, she tells five of her friends, and suddenly it snowballs and you're doing it for everybody," explains John LeBrun, who generally avoids the practice in his shop, the Barclay Gallery and Garden Café in Milwaukee. For particularly good customers, LeBrun takes a more oblique approach: "If they ask for a deal and they're spending a couple of thousand dollars, I'll offer them a gift card worth 10% off that they can use at a future time. In essence, I'm getting them back and halving my out-of-pocket cost."

LeBrun, like many gallery owners, bases his decision in part on how much the customer is spending. "I've had people come in and offer $40 for a $50 cat clock," he says. "I tell them, if it's not worth $50 to you, just don't buy it."

Sherry Armstead opened Art on Symmes in Fairfield, OH, four years ago after a long and successful career in real estate, which made her very comfortable negotiating with her customers. She estimates 20% of them ask for a better price, then adds, "It seems like I've seen more people ask in the last year and a half. It's a trend that's gaining momentum." As a result, Armstead freely admits, "I'm starting to build negotiation room into my initial prices."

This practice is growing as more galleries (and other high-ticket retailers) negotiate with more customers. LeBrun says that's one reason he doesn't generally work that way. "If I did, I'd be playing games with how I price things in the beginning in order to discount, and I don't think that's fair," he says.

Armstead doesn't hesitate to take the whole process a step further, sometimes initiating negotiations in an aggressive approach to close the sale with a customer who wavers in their buying decision. "I might say, 'What would it take for you to take this home today.' That works about 70% of the time," she observes.

She almost never takes more than ten percent off the price, however, a figure that seems to be pretty standard among the gallery owners we talked to who are willing to negotiate in some way with their customers. "You have to know what you paid the artist, how much was the shipping, how long has the piece been here," Leyland says. "You also need to know how the customer is going to pay for it. Will it be cash or am I going to have to pay the 3% to American Express? All these things play a role in what you can do."

You also need to read the individual customer's psyche. LeBrun says, as a customer, "You always feel like you're getting a bad deal" if you've just negotiated a price. You might feel a moment of triumph at the time, but then you wonder if another customer did even better.

Armstead, though, points out the other side of the coin: "I've had people I wouldn't negotiate with walk out."

Here are a few helpful negotiation tactics for retail salespeople:

- Stay cool. If a customer asks for a lower price, remember that it's just a business transaction, not a judgmental comment on your artwork, your gallery, or you.
- Know your limits, but don't go there right away. If the customer can talk you into two small concessions rather than one big one, they're more likely to be satisfied with the deal.
- Ask for something in return. A customer may be willing to use cash rather than a credit card, put their name on your mailing list, or give you something else of value in return for a lower price.
- Use negotiation to close the sale. "If I give you this price, will you buy it now?" is a great way to separate buyers from lookers.

In today's economy, you can expect more and more retail customers to test the firmness of your prices. If you keep your wits about you and exclude emotions from the process, though, you can use that trend to build your sales.

Chapter 35
Retail Up-Selling

"When you take the sales initiative, opportunity knocks a lot louder."

Back in the good old days, when retail stores had living, breathing employees who helped customers choose their merchandise, it was standard procedure for the salesperson to try to increase the size of each individual sale. They did this very effectively in several ways that can be adopted by today's retail shop owners who are interested in increasing the top line on their income statements.

One of the first is simple up-selling, where you guide the customer to a selection with a higher price point than the one they came in to buy. In an extreme example, let's say that the customer came to your hardware store to buy a wrench. An up-seller would make at least an attempt to sell him or her a complete set of wrenches instead. Outlandish? Maybe, but you never know until you try. And, as long as the suggestion is done quickly and without pressure, the customer won't mind.

A good way to manage this kind of interchange with the customer is to ask them what problems they're having while you're getting the item they came in for. That's also the time to get some basic information like what kind of project they're working on so you can give them accurate advice. Then, even if they say "no thanks" to the suggestion, you can reply with "Let me at least give you a price so you can think about it." There's no pressure on the customer in up-selling this way.

Add-ons

Another sales-building strategy is to suggest add-ons to the original purchase. Back when men wore coats and ties to the office (is anybody besides me old enough to remember that?), you couldn't buy a jacket in a men's store without the salesperson offering you a shirt, a couple of ties, and a pocket handkerchief (now I'm really dating myself). The modern shop owner can and should do the same thing. At a garden center, for example, once you've sold the customer a rose bush you should suggest new pruning shears and maybe some long gloves.

Add-ons should be, but don't necessarily have to be, related in some way to the customer's original purchase. It's also helpful if they have a lower price point. They are truly impulse purchases for the customer, although the impulse originates with the shop salesperson.

There is no reason these same tactics can't work for service revenues, too. The garage customer that buys a set of adjustable shocks, for example, might also be interested in a chassis tune. One incentive for the customer to make the additional purchase might be that you can save him or her some money by doing both jobs at the same time. It can also save the customer something else that's valuable—time.

Up-sell Bargain Hunters, Too

There are some situations where you might think that up-sells and add-ons aren't possible, like when a bargain-hunting customer comes into the shop and says, "I'm looking for such-and-such, and I only want to spend X dollars." There are several ways to deal with that kind of lowballer. The first is to call their bluff and see how serious they are about their budget by telling them you don't have anything in that price range and offering to show them secondhand merchandise or a cheaper job. Note that you're not refusing to meet their needs, just their price. You're also sending them a not-so-subtle message that their expectations may be too high without telling them flat out that they're an idiot.

Another way is to just ignore what they say about their budget and start at the high end of the market and work your way down. One advantage of this approach is that it gives the customer a chance to see options they might not even know exist. What's more, after they've seen that royal banana split, it makes their plain vanilla cone look a whole lot less appealing.

Yet a third approach is to give them alternatives and let them choose. Even if Product A and Product B are both priced higher than they say they are willing to pay, it's always very possible that their budget will change if you do a good job of selling the higher-priced options. This is also a good way to find out what's really important to them, both in terms of what they are looking for and how much they are really willing to pay.

Sell The Right Thing

A similar customer with pricing on the mind may insist they can get by with a cheaper product even when you know they are ultimately going to be dissatisfied with it. It's important to sell this customer the right product the first time if at all possible, because they will probably blame you for their dissatisfaction later—even if you sold the cheap product to them under protest. Even worse, they may spread the bad word to their friends. Selective memory is a powerful force for evil.

One way to up-sell them is to play up the differences between the cheaper and the better products while you stress the very small differential in their prices by breaking it down into smaller amounts. Over the life span of two brands of high performance tires, for example, how many pennies per mile does the twenty-dollar price difference amount to?

Good salespeople always have their eyes and ears open looking for opportunities to up-sell their current customers. Here are some good ways to find more of them:

- Be alert to changes. Has the customer bought a new car? Of course, that's an obvious opportunity to start selling. But how about if they've moved to a new house with a bigger garage? Can't you envision that rack full of tools they have room for now?
- Disappointment breeds more sales. Let's be frank: if your customers won every race they entered, they wouldn't need you, would they? So when you hear one grousing about coming in second all the time, make a few well-chosen suggestions about how they can move up a notch while you're empathizing with them.
- What's new? New products are coming into the vibrant performance market every day and you owe it to your customers to tell them about them! An email newsletter can do the trick—and so can a simple telephone call.

When you take the sales initiative, opportunity knocks a lot louder.

Seller Reluctance

You and your other salespeople may be reluctant to use these tactics because of expected customer resistance or even resentment. But as long as you watch how they are reacting, listen to what they're saying to you, and don't try to cram something down their throat, that problem won't be nearly as bad as you think. Remember, you're dealing with somebody who has already decided to spend some money with you, so they must be pretty comfortable with the way you do business.

The biggest obstacle to increasing your sales this way, however, is simple laziness. It's a lot easier to just give the customer what they ask for, take their money, and say goodbye. When you do that, though, you're actually doing the customer a disservice because you can't be sure that what you sold them will really meet their needs. How much do they know about what they are buying? Do they really understand what alternatives they have or what the differences are between various products? Up-selling is a good way to get to know what they truly need, which puts you—the professional—in a position to make sure they buy the right thing.

When you understand it that way, you realize that you are creating value for the customer while you are bringing more dollars into your store. That's about the best formula for business success I've heard since someone advised me to buy low and sell high.

Chapter 36
Creating An Effective Retail Sales Environment

"Every interaction with a customer is a transaction whether they buy something or not."

Many factors determine success in retailing. You have to have the right inventory and offer it at the right price. You need a shopping environment that's clean, well-lit, and inviting. More than anything, though, you need a staff that's both capable of helping the customer and eager to do it. While the time and effort you put into creating an effective retail space is important, it will go to waste if somebody doesn't treat the customer properly once they're in it. To make sure your staff maximizes each customer interaction, train them to do three things for every shop visitor: greet them, help them, and thank them.

Greet and Acknowledge

People like to be treated right, and that starts with a greeting when they come through the door. You don't need to throw your arms around them and kiss them on the cheek, but a simple "Hi! Can I help you?" lets them know that the staff is eager to help. Even customers who don't want assistance right away generally appreciate some acknowledgement of their presence. This should be done, by the way, even if your harried sales person is helping another customer in another part of the store. All they have to do is say, "Make yourself at home, I'll be with you in a moment."

What about the person who says they're "just looking"? Should you ignore them until they summon you? Yes and no. First, keep in mind that you want them comfortable in the store—the more time they spend in your aisles, the likelier they are to buy something, so don't be afraid to encourage them. In fact, a good response is something like, "Great! Glad you came in today." But you also don't have to go away and just hope they find something to buy. Follow up your greeting with a non-threatening question like, "Have you shopped with us before?" If the answer is no, give them a quick description of who you are and what you sell. If it's yes, let them know about any sale or promotional items you might be offering today. Then repeat your offer to help. You might be surprised at how many times a standoffish customer loosens up after a little conversation.

Listen and Help

We sometimes fool ourselves into thinking that people are so used to shopping unaided in the aisles of mass-market retailers that they don't want to be bothered by pesky sales people, but nothing could be further from the truth. What customers don't like is a clerk hanging around putting silent pressure on them to make a decision. While there may be a few independent souls who want to browse unaided through a plan-o-gram full of merchandise, most people appreciate the expert advice and guidance of a knowledgeable retail sales person, especially when they're shopping for something more complicated than a bottle of shampoo.

A good retail salesperson does their best work when they help a customer figure out what they need in order to accomplish their goal or fix their problem. Which means, of course, that your staff has to know what they're talking about. They need to know the lines you carry and what the products do—and don't do. They need to be able to answer the prospect's questions and even to suggest questions that the prospect should be asking.

If they don't know the answers, they should know where and how to get them—and make it clear to the customer that they're willing to do the extra work cheerfully.

Helpful service like this means the sales person needs another set of tools, too: good communication skills. Sometimes, it's not enough to just ask the customer what he wants. The sales person may need to do a little probing about the customer's needs or desires before he or she can suggest a good solution. They need to know what kinds of questions to ask and—even more importantly—they need to listen to the answers. Some customers will be able to tell you exactly what they're looking for, what size they want, and even where it's located in your inventory. A far greater majority of them, though, are like patients in the doctor's office; they need somebody to listen to their symptoms, to tell them why it hurts, and to prescribe something they can do about it.

Having shelves full of merchandise is fine, but it's almost impossible to up-sell a customer if you just rely on the quantity of SKUs you offer. Even worse, impulse purchases might seem to be more likely, but they are just about non-existent in a cluttered, claustrophobic environment. The most successful retail operations have showrooms that make both of these profitable events happen more often. Here are some tips for making the most of your selling space:

- Your front window is the first impression many customers get, so make sure it's an appealing one. It should be clean (including the glass), well-lit, and arranged in an uncluttered, entertaining way. Choose the merchandise you're displaying carefully and remember that it will fade in the sun. Most pros suggest cleaning the space and re-doing the arrangement about once every six weeks.
- Keep the entrance area free of clutter. Customers—especially new ones—generally stop when they come through the door to look

around and get their bearings, so give them a little room—and the sight lines—to do that. Avoid big displays just inside the door that might block their view of whatever it is they're really shopping for.

- Keep your space brightly lit, not just because it makes the merchandise look more appealing, but because it gives a sense of energy and motion to the shopping experience.
- Silence is deadly, so crank up your CD player or radio. Almost any kind of music is good, just as long as it's not so loud that the customers and your sales staff can't hear each other.
- Take a tip from the supermarket industry and arrange your merchandise on shelves or racks in ways that encourage impulse buying. Put related items like winter hats and gloves near each other and remember that the items that sell the best tend to be displayed just below eye-level. Generally, goods located above the customer's head might as well be hidden in the back room for all the attention they're going to get.

Finally, keep in mind that every interaction with a customer is a transaction whether they buy something or not. Both you and the customer get something from every conversation; you get a chance to qualify them for future business by finding out what kind of lifestyle they have, the size of their family, and other important details that affect their purchasing intentions. They learn (hopefully) that your staff is knowledgeable and eager to assist and that you carry the kind of products that can help them achieve their goals—information that will bring them back again. So, even if they don't make a purchase, be sure to thank them for coming in and invite them to come back soon.

Chapter 37
Case Study: Intangibles In The Auto Aftermarket

"Selling services requires strong communication between you and the customer."

According to most automotive shop owners, online discount parts retailers are the biggest single threat they face. But the local car restyler usually provides something the online retailer can't: hands-on service for the customer's car or truck. Shop services like installing wings, applying spray-on bed liners, and tweaking custom lighting systems are both profitable and highly marketable, and they can't be delivered at cut rates over the Internet!

But selling services to a customer is different from selling them a product. It requires a much higher degree of trust, an emphasis on your shop's performance record, and, above all, stronger communication skills—both on the talking and on the listening side. When you're selling parts, you can pretty much put the merchandise on the counter, let the customer look at it, and wait for them to say yes or no. When you're selling services, it's not that simple.

The first problem, of course, is that most shop services aren't tangible. The customer can't hold them, inspect them, or take them out on trial before they hand over the cash. That makes it tough for the customer to visualize what he is getting for his money and increases buying resistance accordingly. It also makes it very difficult for the customer to compare alternatives. If they're thinking about buying grill guards, they can hold their possible choices in their hands and compare them. If they're considering a wild flame paint job, they won't know if it's right for them until after the work is done. They're buying on faith.

That's why everything you can do to make your services as tangible as possible helps move the customer along the path to saying yes. How do you make a service tangible? Show it being done, for one thing. Take the customer into the shop and demonstrate the work in progress on someone else's car if you can. If that's not possible, keep some pictures on hand. Photos of someone else's upholstery being installed will help them more readily imagine what's going to happen to theirs. Another technique is to hand the customer a lengthy printed list of all the steps you take for a given job. A forty-seven-point checklist for a sunroof installation inspires a lot more confidence than a job description that reads "parts and labor."

Build Trust

Ultimately, the customer has to agree to the job based on their trust in you and your staff. They have to believe that the job will deliver the benefits you promise, that you know how to do it right so you won't cause any damage, and that your price is fair. That's a lot to take on faith.

There are several things you can do to build customer trust besides greeting them with a winning smile. One is to prominently display all those certificates you and your staff got for every class or training program you ever completed. Put them on the wall along with your show awards, customer testimonials, and manufacturer certifications. They'll look great next to the pictures of your own show cars and the ones of your customers holding up all their trophies. When you run out of wall space, put a scrapbook full of them on the counter for your customers to thumb through while they're thinking about that window film installation you're trying to sell them.

You can also offer the names and telephone numbers of satisfied customers—before your prospect asks for them. Don't be shy about telling the customer how many jobs just like his your shop has completed successfully over the years, either. Your goal isn't to boast about your shop, it's to help the customer feel more secure in making a decision. The more reasons you can give him to trust you, the more likely he is to say yes and the fewer problems you'll have later as the job unfolds.

Talk and Listen

Above all, selling services requires strong communication between you and the customer. It's essential that you explain exactly what you're going to do, why it needs to be done, and how much it's going to cost. It's even more important that you listen carefully to the customer to make sure that you're both on the same page. Does he understand what you're proposing? Is it what he wants? Does he have any unasked questions?

Establishing and maintaining open communication is especially important for a service job because you often encounter unexpected problems as the work proceeds, which can undermine the trust you've built up with the customer unless the news is delivered properly. No one wants to leave their car in your shop for a dash panel upgrade only to come back and learn that a major instrumentation repair has been added to their bill as well. The time to talk to the customer about unanticipated repairs is before they're done, not afterwards.

Another source of customer dissatisfaction that can be eliminated with better communication is pricing. Some routine, straightforward jobs can be sold at a published flat price. Most of the work you do is probably not simple and routine, however, and you don't really know how much time it's going to take until you do it. Flat rate manuals can help, but they're far from the total solution, especially for complicated work that comes with high expectations. Again, the solution is openly communicating with the customer at the beginning of the transaction.

Emphasize that the amount of labor, parts, and material required for the job is an estimate. It's based on your experience with similar jobs so it should be pretty accurate, but it's still just an estimate, not a guarantee. Explain that you'll do everything you can to keep the amount of hours under the estimate and assure them that you'll let them know as soon as possible if it looks like there's going to be an overrun or if there are additional parts required due to an unforeseen complication.

Then do it! Make sure you have telephone numbers where the customer can be reached during the day while the work is being done and call whenever there's the least question about any item beyond the estimate. It's a great temptation to skip the call in the interest of time, but it's a false economy if the customer blows up when he finds out about the work later. Even if the work is absolutely necessary, it's going to leave a bad taste in the customer's mouth and make them hesitant about trusting you in the future. And those kinds of grudges not only last a long time in the customer's mind, they linger on the word-of-mouth grapevine forever.

Service is the heart of the restyling business. With the growth of online retailers who can sell parts below the brick and mortar shop's costs, selling those services is more important than ever. Following these simple guidelines can make the experience less painful for the customer and more profitable for the shop owner.

Chapter 38
Sales Promotions With Consequences

"The customer who responds to the sales promotion has little or no loyalty to the product behind it."

Many companies turn to sales promotions of one sort or another to build both short term sales and long term market share. While a strong case can be made that promotions—especially those that are heavily price-oriented—induce people to buy more product, they aren't necessarily contributing to the health of the business.

The dangers of sales promotions are illustrated well by one of the persistent bad practices that swept through the media sales business from time to time. It's "incentive travel" offered to accounts who are either new advertisers spending a minimum amount or current advertisers who increase their spending with the sponsoring medium by a similar amount over a given period.

Those who qualify this way typically get a free trip for two to some nice vacation spot where they'll be traveling with the TV or radio station management and the other advertisers who qualified. Many other businesses will offer similar sales incentive promotions like this to quickly generate revenue growth.

This type of sales promotion always seems to generate loads of "new revenue" the first year it's run. Of course, there's no way of knowing whether the customers would have spent that money anyway or whether the same amount of sales effort put into sound sales practices would have produced the same results. All the station knows is that the travel promotion "generated new revenue."

Since it worked the first time, you do it again, right? The second year, though, you're faced with a dilemma. What's the threshold for qualifying for a trip? Those "new accounts" who signed on last year now have to increase their spending significantly to qualify because these trips aren't cheap. And the long-term customers have to do the same. The third year the problem gets worse.

It doesn't take the advertisers long to figure out, though, that they can insure getting a trip every other year if they cut their spending during alternate years because the spending minimums are always based on a previous period's spending! So the broadcaster enjoys a real roller-coaster ride as their long-term customers take advantage of their "new business" promotion.

So should the broadcaster avoid that problem by offering the trip only to absolutely new customers? They can, but what kind of message does that send to the long-term advertiser about how much the station values their business? Not a positive one. If you're going to reward a customer for doing business with you, shouldn't you reward the most profitable customer first? And there is no way that a new account is dollar-for-dollar as profitable as an existing one.

Sales promotions of this type are losing favor in many fields. There's been a decided swing away from sales promotion spending that generates only short-term sales and toward marketing spending that establishes loyalty and repeat sales as well as immediate sales.

Price Promotion And Market Share

The most popular type of sales promotion is the price promotion. Like the rationalization for nearly every sales promotion, price promotion is justified on the grounds that the company is building market share by doing it. That's true only in the most superficial sense.

The purpose behind building market share is to increase the base of brand-loyal customers who will make future purchases—without incurring further sales promotion expense. In other words, today's market share has no value if it is not an indicator of tomorrow's. If the share comes—and goes—when the price changes, it's not a true indicator of the company's future prospects.

Let's do a little math to illustrate the point. Here's the situation: Your product costs $10 to make and you normally sell it for $15, making a $5 profit. I'm going to keep it simple by assuming that you have one customer who buys it once per quarter (four times per year), so your gross profit is $20 per year. Now let's do some sales promotion to increase your market share.

"Attention Shoppers! For a limited time only, you can buy our product for just $12—you save 20 percent!"

The discount is $3 and let's say that the promotional advertising cost is $2, so you're selling your product at cost to build share.

The response is great. You get another customer right away (doubling your market share!). Of course your existing customer also pays the lower price, so you've effectively doubled your sales and wiped out your profit for that quarter. It looks like this:

Gross Sales with no promotion equal $15, less cost of goods sold ($10) and promotion expense ($0), leaving a gross profit of $5.

Gross Sales with the promotion equal $24, less cost of goods sold ($20) and promotion expense of $4, leaving a gross profit of zero.

But zero profit today is okay, because you're building market share for future purchases, right? And those future purchases are supposed to be profitable, am I correct? Which means that both customers will have to pay full price and there will be no promotional spending in subsequent quarters.

Good theory, bad practice. Since the new customer is price sensitive (or he would have bought the product without the price cut in the first place), how likely is he to make a subsequent purchase at a higher price? Not very.

What's more, what's going on in your current customer's head? His next purchase after the promotion will have to be at the original higher price—which represents a 25 percent increase over the most recent price he paid (the $12 promotional price plus a $3 increase to the $15 original price equals a 25 percent increase). He'd have to be pretty darn loyal to your brand to put up with that.

So the result of this sales promotion is a temporary increase in market share, elimination of profit, and endangering the current customer relationship.

The better way is to build market share by promoting the value of your product, which reinforces the brand loyalty of the current customers and attracts new ones (who are not necessarily price sensitive) at the same time. You still incur the promotional expense, but you build profitability anyway by increasing higher margin sales.

What most companies have found is that the customer who responds to the sales promotion has little or no loyalty to the product behind it. When a competitor offers a promotional incentive, they switch without thinking about it. And the sponsor of the original promotion loses his investment in that customer.

You should adopt a similar strategy for growing your business. It's fine to offer periodic sales promotions to generate new business, but you should devote just as much time and effort into "advertising" to keep your current customers. The "advertising" you do is in the form of servicing your current accounts, treating them like the valued customers they are. The message you should send is that you'll never take their business for granted.

Chapter 39
Creating Repeat Sales

"Idea power works on renewals the same way it works on new prospects."

Your current customers are your best single source of new business. They know you, they know your product, they have demonstrated their willingness to purchase. What's more, you know them, you've learned about their needs, and you've invested a significant amount of your time in the success of their business. You should work to protect that investment and encourage it to grow the same way you manage your investment portfolio, making adjustments periodically to maximize the return on your investment.

Your current customers are also your company's most profitable customers. The heavy start-up costs have been absorbed and written off already. The current customers have passed the credit checks, had their account data fed into your computer, been educated about your billing practices, learned how to use your customer support and service staffs, and otherwise incurred the typical back-office expense necessary to start doing business with a new account.

They've probably also passed the most expensive stage of incurring initial selling costs. You've used the get-acquainted offer, the short-term trial contract, and the sales promotion expense to bring them into the company. You've done your basic research, invested your time in preparing the initial proposals, tracked down the decision-makers, and made all the follow-up presentations to make the first sale. Once you've done these things, you generally don't have to do them again. You can skip or abbreviate at least some of these time-expensive tasks.

You can concentrate on keeping the current customer happy and increase your business with them while you go about developing other new accounts. As you've probably guessed by now, you have to do both tasks to build a successful account list or territory. There is no rest in sales unless you decide you're not going to grow your business both ways. And if that's your decision, you'll have plenty of time to rest—in the line at the unemployment office.

Customers For Life

Your goal for every customer should be to turn them into a customer for life, a popular concept that's made the rounds in the last few years. Bowl them over with your service. Become such an integral part of their company that you have your own desk in their office. Know their needs so intimately that you develop solutions before the customers even discover the needs themselves.

Out of all your customers, you won't have very many with that kind of relationship, but when you do, you'll profit from it. I've been fortunate enough to have a handful of such customers with whom I've done business both when I worked for other companies and after I started my own. A few of them have represented millions of dollars in income over the years. You can enjoy the same kind of long-term relationship with your best customers if you practice just one thing: never stop selling them.

They may become your friends; in fact, I hope they do. They may come to rely on your service or products to the exclusion of all others. They may tell you that they'll always be your customers and sign long-term contracts to prove it. But if you take them and their business for granted, you'll regret it someday.

You'll also be sorry if you rely on them as your sole or main source of income. Having one dominant customer is a dangerous situation because there are too many variables outside your control—and theirs. "For life" is a long, long, time.

Situations and people change. What was the foundation for a wonderful relationship two years ago may not mean anything today. Your relationship with your customer for life has to develop and change the same way your relationship with your spouse or significant other evolves over time. That's the only way the relationship will stay vibrant, alive, and satisfying to both of you.

So never stop selling them. Every time your company comes out with a new product or service, pitch it to your current customers first. If it's really a "new and improved" model, don't you owe it to them? If there's a limited supply, shouldn't your best customers get first shot at it? That should be one of their rewards for being a loyal customer.

And always look for ways to add value to their current purchases from you. If your company sees fit to offer an inducement to new customers, shouldn't your best current customers get the same deal? It's a real slap in the face if they don't. And if the new business incentive is a small price to pay for a new account, it's an even smaller price to pay to keep a current one. That's one of the management dilemmas behind sales promotions.

Continual Selling

The best way to make sure the long term customer knows you're not taking them for granted is to make it a practice to continually sell them. Advertising works best when it's presented constantly over time. The message and the medium are important, but the repetition of the message—the frequency with which a customer sees the ad—is paramount. Good customer relations are built the same way: continual selling.

As you practice continual selling, watch out for a few pitfalls. In most businesses, long-term orders are encouraged. A contract to deliver the product or service in increments over a period of several months is generally considered more valuable than a series of contracts to deliver the same volume written one month at a time. The security of the long-term contract is often so important that the vendor will grant a discount or other special terms to the customer who signs one. Salespeople recognize the value, too, because they know that it's much more efficient to sell one contract than twelve.

But there's a downside risk in long-term contracts, too. The salesperson often believes, either consciously or subconsciously, that they've secured all the business they're going to get from that customer, so they stop selling them until contract renewal time comes around. In some cases (which are all too frequent), the customer won't even hear from the salesperson again until it's time to renew. This attitude not only impairs the relationship with that customer, but it blinds the salesperson to many good opportunities in the interim.

I'm sure that your company has a continuous stream of new products, repackaged lines, sales promotions, and maybe even a price change or two. The first place you should prospect to sell these is among your current customers. They've already shown their willingness to buy from you, so keep the boiler stoked by continually feeding it new fuel.

Your customer's needs may have changed or new ones arisen since they signed that long- term contract. The contract itself may have left some money on the table or there may well be a "contingency fund" in the customer's budget held back just for last-minute opportunities. You'll never know unless you constantly offer them additions to their contract.

Another advantage of continual selling is that you are trying out new ideas on the customer all the time. That gives you frequent feedback on what the customer likes and doesn't like, needs and doesn't need. Whether you sell any add-ons or not, this is very useful information when it comes to renewal time.

Long Term Contract Renewals

If you've been selling for any period of time, you've learned that contract renewals, even with your very best customers, are far from automatic. That's why you should develop a renewal strategy that's as complete as your plan for selling a new major account.

First, when you start working on that renewal, try to move the decision date earlier every time. There's a real pragmatic defensive reason for this. Just as you monitor your competition, they're constantly monitoring your accounts, too. And they're probably just waiting for the opportunity to get in there with your biggest account at renewal time. Can't you just see them lurking in the shadows?

The best way to foil their attack is to preclude it by locking up the renewal early. If you wait for the prospect to tell you it's time for renewal, it's too late. You should be the proactive party in the transaction.

Do your estimate (or re-estimate) of their spending potential, study their needs as you now know them, and put that proposal for the renewal on the table as early as you can. You'll stand a good chance of getting an early renewal at the best and will have set the standards for the competition at the worst. It's generally better to be defending your position than assaulting someone else's.

And when renewal time rolls around, make sure you set your sights high enough. Don't let your expectations be limited by the size of the last contract.

Human beings have a bad tendency to categorize each other. In sales, you tend to sort your current customers into boxes—and the size of the box is not based on their total potential as a revenue source but on what they spent with you the first time you sold them.

This system of classification is even worse when you take over an account that had been handled by someone else, like your predecessor in the territory. There's a particular danger of improper classification, by the way, with some computerized sales automation systems since they can't take into account what should be, only what has been. And many time management systems encourage you to rank your prospects by dollar volume and allocate your time accordingly, so the error can be compounded.

If you sort your customers into boxes based on their previous spending with your company, you're putting yourself into a box, too. And that box limits the potential for growth in your commission check. You should have no more pre-conceived ideas about your current customers than you do about new prospects. You must not let past spending be the sole determinant of the size of future proposals.

Remember, too, that the stereotyping process works both ways. Just as you've classified the account based on its past spending, the buyer has probably classified you based on the size of the proposals you have offered. If you've been selling them small deals, you're grouped (mentally at least) as an unimportant vendor. If the amount they spend with you "moves the needle" on their income statement, you'll be in a much larger box.

I recommend periodic reviews of current account potential along the lines of the initial research on prospective new accounts described in *The Dynamic Manager's Guide To Sales Techniques*. There's no law that says you can't do that same kind of research into your current accounts. In fact, you would be doing the customer a real service if you took the time to analyze them that way.

Start with a fresh needs analysis as if you were getting ready to pitch a new account—then add the knowledge you've gained during the term of the current contract. Has the competitive scene changed? Has the customer made any changes in their business? The list of questions is endless but they should all give you a clearer map of the route to a sizable renewal.

Then look outside the box and estimate their revenue potential. If there's a discrepancy between the estimate and their actual spending, you may have identified an opportunity.

Renew With Ideas

But above all, don't forget the actionable need-satisfying idea! A good creative seller will base the renewal proposal on a fresh idea for the customer. Since you know their business intimately now, your ideas for them should be real barn-burners.

Idea power works on renewals the same way it works on new prospects. It more firmly establishes you as a resourceful ally of the customer. It separates you from the competition. It moves you and your proposal farther up the decision-making chain. And there's that key advantage of idea selling, which is its focus on value rather than price.

A typical contract renewal usually starts with you and/or your sales manager deciding how much more to ask the account to spend. That amount generally is determined by the budgeted revenue increase your company has imposed on your sales manager and has nothing to do with the customers or their needs.

So the two of you look at what the customer spent last year, what prices they paid for what inventory or services, and you put together a proposal for the same thing with an additional item or two plus some unit price increases. Sound familiar?

When you pitch this insightful piece of work to the customer, Mr. Big's going to consider it with two things in mind:

1. "Since this is the same thing I bought last year, am I satisfied enough with it to buy it again?

2. And if I buy it again, can I get a lower price?"

Then he'll pull out the proposal which your competition has given him and compare the prices. Since they've had a year to study what Mr. Big bought from you, they've undoubtedly offered their version of it at a lower price. Even if they haven't, Mr. Big is going to tell you that they have.

Being the saint that he is, Mr. Big will also inform you that he wasn't entirely happy with what you sold him last year and has to have a better price this year to justify buying the same thing again. And since you can't prove either point otherwise, you have to negotiate the renewal on price.

But what if you had followed the Creative Selling System to set up your renewal pitch? You'd be presenting a new idea to Mr. Big rather than the same old thing. And since your idea is based on the intimate understanding of his needs you have gathered during the last year of servicing the account, it should be right on Mr. Big's target. Can he compare your new proposal with the competition's? They've come in with last year's model while you've presented a completely redesigned, up-to-date, forward-looking alternative. Which looks better?

How about comparing the new proposal with the old contract? If he says he wasn't satisfied with the old deal, he's playing right into your hands. Once again, what you are offering isn't the old deal—it's something new. He can't compare prices—it's apples to kumquats.

Idea power is awesome.

Unhappy Customers

There's another reason to continually sell a current customer. If you don't, you may not know that they're unhappy until it's too late.

I always shudder when I hear a salesperson say that their job is to get the order and it's another department's job to service the accounts they bring in. That tells me right away that their company experiences a huge amount of account turnover. As you probably know, most unhappy customers don't complain on their own initiative—they just go elsewhere. If the only time you see the customer is when it's time to renew the contract, you may not have been around enough to hear the complaints.

If you rely on the service department to tell you when a customer's unhappy, you're living in a dream world. They haven't got time for that—there are customers to be serviced! Nor do they get paid the big bucks like you salespeople do. What do they care if the customer's not happy? From their income standpoint, they get paid the same whether there's one customer or 20 to take care of. Short sighted? Maybe. But true just the same.

But if you are on the customer's doorstep every week or so trying to sell them an addition to their current contract or order, you'll hear about it if they're unhappy. And wouldn't you rather know now while you can do something about it, instead of at renewal time after they've been stewing about the problem for months? Which way gives you the clearer path to renewal?

Chapter 40

Case Study: Chacon Autos Steers Through A Downturn

"How a company that sells primarily to customers with damaged credit exceeded sales expectations while most of the auto industry struggled."

Few sectors of the economy took a worse beating during the 2007-09 recession than the automobile business. Yet Dallas-based Chacon Autos didn't merely manage to survive, it thrived. The family-owned and -operated company actually generated year-over-year profit growth during an economic downturn that drove two of America's big three automakers into bankruptcy and shuttered nearly 2,500 of the nation's new auto dealerships. The 52-year-old firm relied on a disciplined marketing approach, some prudent cost controls and the flexibility of family management to beat the odds.

"Knowing each other's strengths and weaknesses probably helped us through the downturn," adds Darrell Chaney, 52, the younger of two second-generation brothers who operate the business along with a healthy contingent of third-generation family members. None of the family employees carries an official title, but 55-year-old Gary, Darrell's brother, is the chief executive.

Chacon operates two Suzuki dealerships and six used-car stores in Dallas-Fort Worth and San Antonio. Used cars represent 90% of sales, which total about $80 million annually. The Dallas Business Journal ranked the company the 89th largest privately held concern in the market in 2009. Chacon has about 160 employees.

The company primarily markets low-mileage used cars to customers with damaged credit. It also finances nearly all of them itself, a risky but highly profitable service that contributed to its performance during the downturn. "In a way, we have two separate businesses, a car sales business and a finance company," explains Gary Chaney. "To some degree, we have a built-in buffer."

The "buy-here-pay-here" approach was key to the company's success when William Chaney and two partners (one of whom was a cousin) turned a gas station into a car lot in 1958. The company name came from combining two of their names, Chaney and Conway. According to Gary, his father saw a niche in the market full of customers who needed a car but also needed credit to buy one. There were plenty of new and used car dealers, but not very many places where customers with less-than-stellar incomes could get a car loan.

Over time, the three men acquired two other lots, then split amicably in 1986 so they could more easily pass the businesses on to their respective offspring. Today, the other two companies, Public Auto Sales and Auto USA, are friendly competitors, although Chacon is by far the largest. William transferred control to his two sons, Gary and Darrell, in 1992 and passed away in 2009. The two sons steadily added used car locations in the Dallas-Fort Worth market as opportunities arose, then opened in San Antonio in 2003.

Today, Gary handles accounting and the back office, while Darrell oversees customer finance. "We kind of divide up sales," says Gary. "Since our kids started working here, we turned some of it over to them, too." Their 83-year-old mother, Christine, not only is the ex-officio chairwoman of the board but also sells cars and processes loan applications six days a week, just as she has since the firm was founded. All told, seven family members work full-time in the company and two more plan to join soon.

Focus on Customers

Most Chacon customers have a job but might have a poor credit score that precludes them from getting a car loan from a bank.

Their biggest need, according to Darrell, is for dependable transportation. Consequently, the company stocks primarily one- or two-year-old used cars with less than 40,000 miles on the odometer. The cars are bought at auction and normally sell for about $15,000 with a 20% gross margin. Gary says Chacon doesn't sell "beaters," high-mileage used cars that can be bought for a song, marked up 400% and sold to desperate buyers.

The company's standard formula calls for a 15% down payment with the balance carried over three years at 18% APR, giving most customers a monthly payment around $450. At press time, banks in the Dallas-Fort Worth market were charging as much as 11% for similar loans to creditworthy customers.

Chacon processes its own loan applications and funds its financing with lines of bank credit. The company has had a 23-year relationship with one local bank but uses others as well, Gary says, mainly because the business has grown so large that it's both prudent and necessary to have multiple credit lines. "It's been a little tough," Gary acknowledges. "Because of all the challenged credit with homeowners, we've had a little bit of resistance from the banks." On the other hand, he points out, "Low interest rates help our spread somewhat, but they also increase our competition."

The economy stressed some customers, of course, driving repossession rates toward the high side of the normal 25% to 35% range. Financial woes also lowered the frequency of trade-ins by customers who typically had bought a new used car during the third year of their loan. Again, though, there was some silver in the economic cloudbank, since people who might have been new-car buyers in the past chose late-model used cars instead.

Chacon got into the new-car business with a Suzuki franchise in New Braunfels (near San Antonio) in 2004 and added another location in Dallas in 2006. This enabled the company to serve both ends of the market. Gary's son Greg Chaney, who runs both the new- and used-car stores in San Antonio, says, "New cars tend to attract a different customer. Plus, in new cars, we have third-party financing available." The new-car stores are a source of used-car inventory for all the locations and have used-car sales lots, too. Greg serves as chairman of the national Suzuki dealers' advisory board.

Retired public school principal Dretha Burris bought a year-old Suzuki from Chacon in 2007. "I believed that their prices were reasonable," Burris says. "They were honest with me about the value of my trade-in. Their customer service and follow-up were excellent." Burris says she intends to buy her next car from Chacon as well. "In the Dallas area, their reputation is that they work with people other folks won't. They're known as an honest, dependable dealership." While she financed her purchase through the teachers' credit union, she says she wouldn't hesitate to get a loan from Chacon if she needed it.

Close customer relationships are essential to Chacon's success, family members say. "When you're family-owned, it means a lot to the customers," says Christine. "We've been in business so long, they tell their friends about us." She says many customers have bought three, four, or even five cars from Chacon over the years and it's not unusual for third-generation customers to do business with the dealership. "When Gary and Darrell were first starting out, I told them to always be patient with the customers," she adds. "You have to have a listening ear because each customer has different problems and different situations."

Chacon systematically nurtures those close customer relationships. Joey Chaney, Darrell's youngest son, explains that many customers make payments in person, a practice the company encourages. "When they come in to make their payment," he says, "we can see what kind of shape their car is in. We can also check their balance and, if it's low enough, we encourage them to trade in on another car. That's something I learned from my grandma." Running a credit operation facilitates the system. "We try to structure deals so [customers] can trade in without having any cash for a down payment and they'll still have some equity and their payments will stay about the same. That way they get an upgrade." Gary estimates that repeat business amounts to about 30% of total sales.

Long-term Perspective

Joey, 22, has been working at the Grand Prairie location as assistant office manager since 2009. His brother Josh, 29, approves car sales and loans, handles account collections, repossessions, and bankruptcies at another of the Dallas locations. Their middle brother, Jacob, 27, is joining the company this year. Joey tried college for a year, then worked for a courier service. Like his dad, his uncle and most of the third generation, he grew up in and around the stores. "My first job was at the Haltom City store when I was 16. I painted a fence," he says. "I gradually worked my way up. There aren't any gimmees for anybody at Chacon. You work your hardest and do the best you can. Family members also earn the same as everybody else."

Victor Junco is a non-family member of the management team who has worked for the Chaneys for seven years, most recently in the San Antonio store. "Gary and Darrell are very adamant about making sure every family member earns their wings," he says. "They have several non-family members in important positions, too."

The company has a firm rule that family members must work somewhere else for at least two years before joining the family firm. Joey's father, Darrell, spent some time working in a grocery store. "Dad told me I needed to find a job when I was 16," he explains. Later he worked in the collections department of a credit union for four years. Gary was in management for several years at a local retailer. He came to work for Chacon in 1987, when he was 32. His daughter Stefani Musick, 31, worked as a finance officer with the CIA in Langley, Va. She has her CPA and oversees all accounting for the company. She met her husband, Rock (yes, Rock Musick), at the CIA.

Stefani believes family ownership has contributed heavily to the company's ability to weather the downturn: "One thing that helped us is that everybody kind of grew up in the business. We've seen good times and bad, especially my dad and uncle. They really have 50 years of experience to draw on." She adds, "We have a good business model, but we can tweak it if we need to. I don't know if we could be that flexible if we weren't a family business."

Unit sales, which normally run around 4,500 cars per year, were off about 20% last year, but profits were up, according to Gary. He explains that the company tweaked operations as the downturn deepened. "Some of it was a refocus on certain types of cars that had higher gross margins. That helped our turnover and we were able to reduce some of our debt," he says. "We didn't lay anybody off, but we let a few positions remain unfilled for a while."

Stefani says such decisions aren't reached through a formal process. The board of directors consists entirely of family members: Gary, Darrell, Greg, Stephanie, Josh and Christine. "If it happens that we're all in town at the same time, we may sit down as a group and talk about direction and things like that, but more of that type of communication takes place informally," Stefani explains.

As essential as it is to the company's success, the credit approval process is rigorous but informal, too, a philosophy that probably wouldn't be viable under non-family corporate ownership. "We understand our customers' problems," Gary says. "If they lose their job or just have trouble making their payments, we try to work with them."

Credit approvals are made at each location, not through a central credit office. "With these kinds of customers, you can't just plug some numbers into a computer," Junco says. "You have to know the local economy and the people." There are company guidelines to be followed, but decisions are made on the spot.

Above all, says Darrell, the company must stand behind its people. "Mom and Dad taught us the importance of integrity—although keeping your word and maintaining your integrity in the automobile business is very tough," he says.

The family is confident the company's future is bright. As Stefani says, "There will always be people with damaged credit, and they will always need cars to get to work."

Continued family ownership and management are apparently assured, too. According to Stefani, the company is actually owned by a generation-skipping trust established by her grandfather, so the third generation has a vested interest in its success today. Management-wise, she says there is no hurry to choose a leader from among her siblings and cousins. "We've had a lot of success bringing the third generation into the business. We're really fortunate that we all get along."

The transition won't occur in the immediate future, although it's not going to be delayed interminably, according to Gary. "Dad relished the idea of turning the business over to us," he says. "He was in his late sixties and he hung around for about ten years afterward, but he was happy to turn it over. I'll be happy to do it when it's my time, too."

Originally published in Family Business, www.familybusinessmagazine.com.

Chapter 41

Keeping Your Business Customer-Friendly

"Customer relationships can't be taken for granted because even the smallest molehill can turn into a mountain."

Most small business owners would quickly agree that it's easier to lose a customer than to get a new one. It's a lot more expensive, too, if you count not only the cost of replacing that old customer but the business you've lost until you do. Unfortunately, there's also a third cost that's impossible to quantify but may be the most expensive of all—the damage the bad word of mouth can do to your future business from other potential customers. In other words, keeping the customers you have may be the best way to run a profitable business.

We like to think that things like the quality of our company's products or service and the fairness of our pricing are the most important factors when it comes to building customer loyalty. To a certain extent, that's certainly true. But there are several other things we do (or don't do) in our operations that can sour the customer's feelings toward us and, all too often, drive them into the welcoming arms of our competitors. Most of those things seem like such small items that we can't imagine losing a customer over them. But customer relationships can't be taken for granted because even the smallest molehill can turn into a mountain if we're not careful.

There are several areas of business operations where mountains are likely to grow. One of the first places to look is your telephone, often one of the first points of entry to your business for your customers. When the customer calls, does it sound like you're glad they did? Or does the way you answer the phone send the message that their call is an intrusion? If you answer the phone with a supposedly neutral statement like, "Dave's Guitar Shop," you're making the customer work to justify their call to you. If you just add something a little friendlier such as, "Can I help you?" it makes the customer feel wanted. This applies when a real live human answers the phone, of course.

Telephone Mechanics

If your customer's first telephone interaction with your shop is with an automated attendant, some different rules apply. Since most people detest dealing with machines, it's essential that you make their experience as painless as possible. Here are some guidelines for setting up your automated telephone answering system:

- Make the welcoming message cheerful and short.
- Offer an immediate option—like "press zero"—to speak to a real person, then repeat it after the other options.
- Keep the number of choices to a minimum. If your customer has to wait to hear, "Press twelve for the parts department," you've lost them.
- Label your choices by functions the unfamiliar new customer will recognize, like "parts," "machine shop," and "estimates," instead of "Charlie," or "Susie."
- Don't make them press more than one number before they're connected to a human.
- If you absolutely must use a voice mail system, make sure it's customer friendly, too. Everyone's greeting should be pleasant and promise a return call as soon as possible. At the end of each mes-

sage, repeat the option to "press zero" for an operator.

Whether you use a voice mail system or have someone who takes messages, make it an absolute rule that every customer message gets returned that same day—although within an hour is even better. Even if you have to call back to say you can't talk to them now, make an effort to acknowledge the call.

The degree of customer-friendliness of your telephone system is easy to test. Just take a page from the manual of the retailers who employee "secret shoppers" and call your shop from outside to see what it sounds like. Put yourself in the customer's shoes and ask yourself if the person that greets you—recorded or live—sounds like he or she is smiling. Listen to the entire greeting and ask yourself if you feel welcome. If you have an automated attendant, press every option at least once to see what happens. If you end up in voice mail purgatory—where you don't know if the message you're leaving is for the right person—you know you've got a potential problem.

Signs of Aggravation

Now look around the shop and see if there are any other customer-aggravating items. How about signs that explain your policies to customers? Do they read like they were written by Joseph Stalin? It's really not necessary to scold your customers when you tell them where to park, make them stay out of the service area, or keep their hands off your tools, although it may seem like you have to sometimes. "No Customers Allowed" sounds pretty nasty, especially compared to a sign that gets across the same message by reading, "Employees Only, Please."

You sound a lot more customer friendly (and professional), too, when you explain why you have the rules you have. Add "Insurance Rules" or

"OSHA Regulations" to the "Employees Only, Please" sign and you've made your policies sound a lot less arbitrary.

When it comes to rules, it's not a bad idea to review yours every once in a while. Look at things like your hours of operation, availability of merchandise, deposits, and return policies to see if they serve a real purpose beyond irritating your customers. Do you close so early in the day that customers don't have a chance to pick up something they need after they leave work? If a customer has to take off work, it's an additional cost to them of doing business with you. The same holds true for when you open—can they drop off an item for repair and still have time to get to their job? Saturday and Sunday hours are customer-friendly, too. And if you want to really do it right, offer to accommodate customers by appointment at other hours when you're not normally open.

Most customer relationships are built on good communications, of course, which raises a couple of other questions: Do you call the customer when their job is ready or make them call you to find out if it's finished? If the work's not going to be done when you promised, do you call to warn them? It takes a little time and effort on your part, but the customer who gets such a call generally recognizes the thoughtfulness. Besides, it demonstrates that you respect the value of their time and, by proxy, appreciate their business.

While I'm ranting, whatever happened to saying "thank you" to customers? From the almost total absence of that phrase in most businesses these days, you might think it had been put on something like the FCC's list of forbidden words. Another phrase seems to have replaced it, the one you hear when the cashier at the grocery store hands you your change and receipt and says, "here you go." What the heck is that supposed to mean? Even worse, when the customer takes the change, their inclination is to say "thanks," which sounds as if they are expressing their gratitude to the store! What's wrong with this picture?

If you want to make your shop truly customer friendly, make it a practice to thank the customer every chance you get. "Thanks for calling," "thanks for letting us work on your car," even "thanks for coming in" are the right words to use when dealing with the person who keeps you in business.

These may seem like little, picayunish details when compared to major factors like how well the product works after the customer gets it home, and they are—individually. But when you add them up, which is what happens when the customer comes into your shop time after time, they grow. Add enough aggravations, and the next thing you know, you've built that proverbial mountain out of a molehill.

Chapter 42
Three Sure Ways To Drive Away Customers

"Is the customer always right? No, but they should never be told flat out that they're wrong, either."

One of the easiest things to accomplish in any business is to lose a customer. Good ones are hard to find, but they're easy to lose. A certain amount of customer turnover is to be expected; people move out of town, suffer pocketbook problems, even experience lifestyle-altering events like getting married and having kids that change their buying habits. On top of that natural attrition, though, is the kind we create ourselves. It's the result of the things we say, do, think, and ignore that drive our customers away.

Losing customers is never intentional, but you wouldn't know that from the way some business owners and their employees treat the people who pay the bills. They inadvertently insult them, frustrate them, embarrass them, and confuse them in numerous ways that make the customer hesitate before coming back to the shop for more. Some of the problems come from poor attitudes, others from simple misguidance. Often, we think we're doing the right thing when it's actually the worst possible thing we can do from a customer relations standpoint.

Here are three common ways we treat our customers that are almost guaranteed to drive them away.

Be A Know It All

You're the expert. Let's say you are in the automotive restyling business. You've spent years learning the tricks of your trade, the special skills that let you tweak a convertible top until it's watertight or lay down a pinstripe with the precision of a NASA engineering draftsman. That's probably why your customer brought his ride to you in the first place; if he could do it himself, he wouldn't need you. But that doesn't mean you have to rub his face in it.

Let's face it, tricked-out wheels are all about ego. My car is cool and it makes me cool. It's a reflection of my self-image, my style, my place in the world. If I ask a question, please don't make me feel stupid when you answer it. You may be able to prove you're smarter than me, but it won't improve our relationship. If I have an idea or suggestion on what I want done to my car, please don't ridicule it. Even if what I want you to do violates all the laws of physics, you don't need to belittle me when you tell me it can't be done.

It's all about respect for the customer, an attitude that's reflected in the words you choose and even the body language you use when dealing with them. Here are some phrases that you might use to raise the customer's self-esteem:

- "I can see how you might think that…"
- "Good question!"
- "That's an interesting idea, but…"

Above all, no matter how hard it is, resist laughing, snorting, or shaking your head in disbelief when the customer asks a question or makes a suggestion.

Give Them Unpleasant Surprises

When you are in a service business, not every job goes as planned. That's why, depending on the kind of work you do, you give your customers an "estimate" instead of a firm price before you begin. If you're smart, that estimate is in writing, and if you're even smarter, you ask the customer to sign it before you touch their job. Even then, though, misunderstandings occur and customer relationships can become strained. No one likes to get a bill for more than he expected.

It happens all the time: a manufacturer raises the price of a key component after you've figured the old price into the job; you remove a panel only to discover a crack in the supports underneath, one thing leads to another and before the job is done the man-hours you originally estimated turn into man-years. You can't just absorb these unexpected costs, nor should you. But you can't just pass them on to the customer either, at least not without his prior approval.

Your future relationship with your customer depends in part on the way you tell him his bill is going to be higher than he thought. Your goal should be to convince the customer that you're not trying to pull a fast one. Express regret that you have to deliver some bad news, then give them the details—and the more details you include in your explanation, the higher your credibility will be. You don't have to be defensive or apologetic, but let him know you share his pain. If you're open, honest, and above all timely, you'll keep that customer.

Fight Their Complaints

You can't please everybody. Some days, in fact, it seems like you can't please anybody. The paint color is a shade lighter than the customer thought it was going to be. There is a squiggle in the upholstery seam that only the customer can feel. The shelf is higher on one side than it is on the other—you can't see it, but the customer can. How do you handle impossible, irrational complaints? (No, a slap upside the head is not a viable solution.)

The first step in handling a complaint—rational or otherwise—is to hear the customer out. Listening is the most important skill in customer relations, so remember the first rule: you can't listen if you are talking! Let the customer talk first. Don't pounce on what they say by trying to give them an answer before they're finished. A remarkable number of complaining customers just want someone to listen to their problems, so learn to offer that particular small service automatically.

Is the customer always right? No, but they should never be told flat out that they're wrong, either. Soften it a little by using phrases like

- "I can see why you feel that way…"
- "Let me look at that again…"
- "I understand what you're saying…"

Then make an adjustment if you can, or explain—politely and respectfully—why you can't. It's tough to generalize because complaints can vary from the frivolous to the catastrophic, but the key factor in the customer relationship is the way you communicate with them about it.

You may have to shave your profit on a job to make the customer happy, but it doesn't really happen all that often. There are people who try to get something for nothing, but if we start by assuming that the customer is trying to take advantage of us, we're never going to resolve the problem to either their satisfaction or ours. In fact, the damage to our relationships with good customers far exceeds any loss we'll experience by giving in to the unfair demands of the single crooked complainer.

Chapter 43
Dealing With Difficult Customers

"Separate the person from the problem and focus on their interests and goals, not on the problem."

We've all had them: the customer who refuses to be satisfied. Sometimes they whine like nine-year-olds; other times they rant and rave about our merchandise, our service, or even our parentage. One way to deal with them involves a baseball bat but, attractive as that solution may be, it's not really viable. Your goal when dealing with a difficult customer is to solve today's problem in a way that lays the ground work for tomorrow's order. Smacking them in the head interferes with that process. The better way is to apply some of the simpler principles of sales psychology and see if you can't turn that steaming monster into a happy, satisfied repeat customer.

The root of most customer problems is stress, usually stemming from what they perceive as an obstacle you've placed in their way. They may feel you're not giving them what they thought they were supposed to get from you, or that what you are providing doesn't satisfy their needs. Regardless, the first step in reducing the stress level is to find out what's really bothering them.

Defense Is Offensive

That's much easier said than done. All too often, our first reaction to a complaint is to get defensive. The customer makes a less-than-pleasant comment about the design of a product we've slaved over for hours and it's like somebody peeked into the bassinet and told us our first child was an ugly baby. How dare they!? We have to keep our primary goal in mind: to make more sales. It's very satisfying to create beautiful designs, but the only award that counts is the one that ends up in your bank account and that prize comes from a very opinionated judge, your customer. So, if the customer likes it, it's good. If they don't, change it! And do it cheerfully, because if you're snarling under your breath, you're telling that customer that you think they're wrong. No one likes to be treated with condescension.

Sometimes, we immediately jump to the conclusion that they're trying to get something for nothing or to bad-mouth us into cutting our price. There are people like that out there, but there are a lot fewer of them than we think. If we start from a defensive posture, we're bound to make the problem worse instead of better. Orlando-based organizational management consultant Dr. Arnie Witchel advocates what he calls "negotiation jujitsu" when faced with a difficult customer. "In jujitsu," he says, "you go with the force to disarm your opponent, not against it. If a difficult customer is pushing hard on you, do not push back! Reframe any attacks on you or your company with questions that seek to clarify the situation and concerns. Don't resort to hostility!" He points out that you have to separate the person from the problem and focus on their interests and goals, not on the problem itself. If you do that, if you approach the situation with an eye on removing obstacles that block what the customer wants to achieve, you're more likely to arrive at a collaborative, mutually-satisfactory conclusion.

Practical Suggestions

Here are some ways to improve communication with difficult customers:

- Be receptive. Tell the customer you want to hear what they have to say, then give them a chance to say it.

- Put on their shoes and walk around in them for awhile. If you were faced with their frustration, how would you feel? And, just as importantly, what would you expect to be done to correct it?
- Use descriptive, non-judgmental words. Instead of saying "that's wrong" try "that's one way to look at it."
- Set limits on the problem by excluding things that happened in the past or aren't relevant to the current situation.
- Break the problem up into smaller pieces and try to reach an agreement on each one.
- Emphasize the things you have in common. "We both want the recipient of your gift to be happy," for example.

Listening is the most important skill a sales person can possess in every situation, from trying to get an appointment with a new prospect to making a presentation to your biggest client. It's essential when dealing with a difficult customer, so remember the first rule of listening: you can't listen if you're talking! Let the customer talk. Don't pounce on the things they are saying by trying to give them an answer before they're finished saying them. In fact, watch out that you don't just pretend to listen when you're actually phrasing your answer while they're talking. A remarkable number of difficult customers just want someone to listen to their problems, so learn to offer that small service automatically.

Something else to keep in mind is that "I'm sorry" may be the two most powerful words in customer relations. They're certainly applicable if you or your company messed up an order or have something else for which to apologize, but they also show empathy for the customer's feelings regardless of who is to blame. Those two simple words go a long way toward removing the "me against you" attitude that pours gasoline on a smoldering customer's fire.

If you really want to "wow" the customer, accept responsibility for the solution, even if you don't deserve it for the problem. Fear that their problem is going to get short-shrift causes more customer stress than any other single factor. It's no wonder, when we live in a society where way too many "customer hotlines" are answered by call-center operators on the other side of the world whose standard answer to a complaint is to file it. Anticipation that this is going to happen turns slightly unhappy customers into absolutely furious customers, so one of the most effective ways you can defuse an explosive situation is to immediately promise your personal attention to working something out. When the customer finds a real, live human being who says they will personally take care of the problem, they'll feel a tremendous sense of relief. And, when you actually do solve the problem, they'll become customers for life.

Speaking of stress, it helps to relieve yours if you remember that not every single difficult customer can be satisfied. Sometimes their frustration stems from circumstances beyond your control, the solution is something you can't deliver, and they just can't or won't accept those facts. Or maybe he or she really is that one-in-a-thousand customer whose goal in life is to get the better of you in every deal. If that's the case, just tell them "sorry" and let them go. You'll probably lose a customer but you'll gain a little peace and quiet.

Chapter 44

Case Study: Managing Unhappy Service Customers

"Keep your primary goal in mind: make more sales."

"You can do fifteen or twenty great jobs and have just one job that leaves a sour customer and there goes your word-of-mouth," says Wayne Shelnut, Manager of Carolina Rod Shop in Piedmont, South Carolina. "Even if we know the customer is not right, we try to go out of our way to try and please them," he says. That outlook has kept the full-service street rod, custom, and restoration shop in business for fifteen years.

Most customer problems arise when they think you're trying to deny them satisfaction. They may feel the work you've done on their car or the system you've sold them isn't what they thought they were supposed to get, or that what you are providing doesn't satisfy their needs. Regardless, the first step in reducing the stress level is to find out what's really bothering them.

Stay Off The Defense

When there's a problem at Carolina Speed Shop, according to Shelnut, shop owner Glen Dodd sits down with the customer to analyze the problem. "We let them spill whatever it is they feel they've got to say," Shelnut explains. "We'll hear their side. Then we say 'here's why that might have happened' and then 'here's what we're going to do about it.' If it's something we've done, there's no question about it. If it's something the customer's done or it's just wrong, we may meet him somewhere in the middle, but we try to do it as diplomatically as possible."

That's much easier said than done. All too often, our first reaction to a complaint is to get defensive. The customer makes a less-than-pleasant comment about the spoiler we've slaved over for hours and it's like somebody saw the picture of our family on our desk and told us our youngest son looks like a deformed monkey. How dare they!?

We have to keep our primary goal in mind: make more sales. It's very satisfying to do solid quality work, but the only prize that counts is the one that ends up in your bank account and it's awarded by a very opinionated judge, your customer. Bob Nardine, owner of Bob's Top Shop in Orlando, Florida, agrees: "We strive for perfection. We don't always achieve it, but we strive for it. The secret is, when you don't do something right, to fix it right away. We'll go above and beyond what we probably should fix sometimes." And they do it cheerfully, because growling, "the customer is always right" under your breath just adds to the customer's stress.

Some, fortunately very few, customers try to take advantage of such policies, says Shelnut: "We get bit sometimes, but it's just one of the costs of doing business." There are people who try to get something for nothing, but there are a lot fewer of them than we think. Assuming the customer is trying to take advantage of our good nature is no foundation for a long, happy relationship.

Listen First, Then Talk

If you listen carefully, you might also learn that the customer's complaint stems from their misunderstanding of what's possible and what's not. As Shelnut says, "We have a lot of car enthusiasts who don't really understand what goes on in a project, so it's kind of an education for them as well."

Here are a few ways to improve communication with difficult customers:

- Show the customer you want to hear what they have to say by giving them a chance to say it.
- Examine the situation from the customer's perspective. If you were faced with something similar, what would you expect the seller to do?
- Set limits on the problem by excluding things that happened in the past or aren't relevant to the current situation.
- Break the problem up into smaller pieces and try to reach an agreement on each one.
- Emphasize the things you have in common. "We both want your car to make heads turn," for example.

Nardine recommends trying to anticipate problems before they occur: "We try to catch everything when we estimate the job. We try to keep everything in writing so that there are no misunderstandings." He also, although rarely, refuses a job if it looks like there's trouble on the horizon. "A lot of times," he says, "you can peg that person when they come in. It's very seldom that I turn down a job, but I do once in a while."

"When they ask the impossible, you're never going to make them happy," Nardine points out. He tells about a customer who brought in an old Pontiac scissors-top convertible. "The guy wanted me to fix it, but he didn't want to spend any money. I had to tell him, 'what you want, you're not going to get for what you want to spend.'"

Chapter 45
Finding Prospects

"Think of networking as a public relations campaign for yourself."

Many salespeople truly hate the very thought of prospecting. It smacks of cold calling, door-to-door canvassing, and rude telephone calls during dinner time. Besides, it requires a lot of work that often doesn't result in making a sale. They much prefer to be supplied with "qualified" leads, preferably ones that have requested that a salesperson call. And many companies have systems to do just that.

I suppose if you have a source of leads that supplies you with enough qualified prospects to allow you to earn the kind of living you want, that's great. Keep in mind, though, that your income growth (or lack thereof) will be determined by your lead source. You'll earn no more than what the company allows you to earn and your income will be dictated largely by forces outside your control. Sometimes you have no choice in the matter, but most of the time you do. After all, how many companies will turn away an otherwise qualified order just because it didn't originate with their lead program? In other words, company-supplied leads shouldn't preclude your own prospecting.

The most successful salespeople I know grow their income by assiduously adding new accounts to their lists. They prospect constantly, always looking for potential new sources of sales and commissions. They don't dread the cold call, they thrive on it. They love the challenge of meeting new people, learning about different prospects, and making revenue appear where none existed before. They have a nose for the hunt.

Regardless of which category you fall into, there's a strong likelihood that you'll need to do some prospecting at some time. Let's talk about some of the methods you can use to make the process as painless and as productive as possible.

Cold Canvassing

Cold canvassing is the first method that comes to mind when most people think of prospecting. You go door-to-door or make phone call after phone call until you find someone who might be interested in buying your product. In cold canvassing, you generally make a standard presentation which introduces your company and product to the prospect while getting the prospect to respond with information that will allow you to determine whether they are likely to buy or not.

This is also sometimes known as the "mud against the wall" style of selling. If you throw enough of it, some of the mud sticks to the wall. If you call on enough people, some of them are bound to need your product. Except for salespeople with certain masochistic tendencies, this method is generally not one with a lot of fans.

It takes a lot of energy, effort, and time to make cold calls. And it's about as creative as digging a ditch. The only way to make it work is to just keep doing the same thing over and over. But guess what? The ditch gets dug if you do that. And your muscles get stronger, too. This method would have died out years ago if it weren't successful in producing sales.

Cold canvassing has its place in the Creative Selling System, too. There are some compromises in the system, though, that have to be made. First, while you need to have a concrete needs-based proposal to present on your call, you probably can't have a unique one for every single prospect you see.

The solution is to create a generic idea that reflects the benefits of the best your company has to offer. If you don't have an actionable idea to present, you'll really waste a lot of time and energy making cold canvass calls with no purpose other than to hand out your business cards.

Secondly, you can't have a custom written presentation for each prospect, either, so you put that idea into writing without the prospect's name. Use the standard five-page proposal form outlined in *The Dynamic Manager's Guide To Sales Techniques* and print a stack of them to use on your calls.

Your goal on the cold canvass call is the same as on your first call on any prospect: get information. Since you have an actionable plan to present on the cold canvass call, you should get responses to it that you can use on subsequent presentations to the prospects you qualify during the canvass.

Canvassing Fun

I suggest that you do a little cold canvassing from time to time. Not necessarily every day or even every week, but pick a day once a month or so and set it aside for cold canvassing. Make a game of it, concentrating on the process rather than the result. Take your generic proposal and see how many different businesses you can pitch in one day. Or set some specific goals, like making a pitch to every business on the south side of Main Street between First and Tenth Avenues. Or calling every business in the Yellow Pages from "banks" to "bed and breakfasts."

I've found that a good time to spend the day cold canvassing is when I'm feeling a little down. Maybe things haven't gone too well lately or I'm just a little bored with life. A day of cold calls is a great cure for the "blahs." If it does nothing else, it'll blow out your mental cobwebs and open your mind a little bit.

Don't get too picky about whom you call on, either. This is like brainstorming—quantity, not quality, is what counts. About the only administrative task I suggest is that you keep a list of everybody you call on, noting anything you learned on the call and putting a star next to the prospects that deserve a follow-up call with a custom presentation in the Creative Selling System format.

Above all, try to have some fun. Look on this as an adventure full of unknown people and unexpected events. Don't worry about making a sale. Try out some new "reasons to buy" or that package of services you've been wanting to test. See if that unsold inventory in the back of the warehouse will move at break-even prices. Make it different and make it fun.

Cold canvassing can be a lot more interesting if you do it with other salespeople. You can make a contest out of it, with the winner the person who makes the most calls, or the most sales, or turns up the most prospects. Meet at a convenient coffee shop a couple of times during the day to compare notes and war stories as you go along. It'll make the day go faster and the break will help you keep up your enthusiasm.

Category Canvassing

Another prospecting method which is more consistent with the Creative Selling System is category canvassing. This technique is most often used by salespeople whose products or services can be sold to a variety of different kinds of businesses. If you sell office supplies, for example, or insurance or advertising, you may have clients ranging from grocery stores to swimming pool contractors. When you use the category development technique, you choose one type of business and pitch them all the same thing.

You need to do a little homework when you use this method, following the prescribed routine of researching the prospects' needs, estimating the potential, and preparing a needs-based proposal. This sounds like a lot of work if, for example, you're going to pitch fifteen different funeral homes in your territory.

It's actually a time saving technique, though, because the research you do will reveal pretty much the same needs for every one of the fifteen prospects. And the idea you come up with for the first one is the same idea you pitch to each of the others. All you do is change the name on your presentation.

You then pitch that idea to each one in turn until one of them buys it. The odds are great that you'll never get to the last name on the list because someone will buy the idea before you do.

One of the beauties of this method is that you'll learn something more about the category on every call, allowing you to make each successive presentation more effective. It's a lot like calling on the same prospect once a week for fifteen weeks, only in this case you're calling on fifteen prospects one time each. You add to your store of knowledge with each meeting.

I recommend that you start with the smallest prospects, not the largest, when you use this method. Why? Because you want to do your "learning" before you get to the biggest prospects. Practice and make your mistakes on the small accounts so you have a better chance of closing the largest ones.

If you work with a group of other salespeople, there's a great temptation to divide the category among yourselves. This is a more efficient way to cover the category, but it doesn't help the learning process much because it cuts down on the number of prospects each salesperson is exposed to. If you do decide to work as a team, make sure you get together at the end of each day to compare notes.

Referrals

One of the very best ways to pick up good prospects is by referral. You usually think of getting referrals from your current satisfied customers, but you don't need to limit yourself to that group. One of my good friends and competitors in the consulting field makes it a practice to ask every person he pitches for a referral to someone they know who might be interested in his services. If the original prospect doesn't buy, at least he gets something of value for his time. He gets a lot of business that way.

The best part of getting leads by referral is that you get to draw on the source's body of knowledge about the referral as well as your own. Most of the time, they'll have a different viewpoint than you, giving you some insights you wouldn't normally have right away. They also may identify a prospect that you had never thought of or didn't even know existed.

Most people are happy to do you this favor, at least as long as it doesn't carry too high a cost to them. Never use their name when following up on the referral without their explicit approval in advance. Your referring source doesn't need to write a letter of recommendation for you, either. All you ask for is the name of the person you should see. If your source offers to call them or write a letter to introduce you, all the better, but don't push it. If you can get a name, you have enough information to start the process.

I've done business with the same insurance agency for many years. In fact, since the agency is a family affair, I've literally watched the children grow up and take over the business from their father. From time to time, one of them will call me with the name of someone they've encountered in their rounds who might be a prospect for my company. I do the same for them every chance I get.

Once, when my wife and I sold our home, our realtor brought a couple who were relocating to our area to see the house. The realtor told me afterwards that the prospective home buyer had seen some of my sales literature on my desk at home and asked him what my company did.

The couple didn't buy our house, but I followed up on the lead (which turned into a short consulting project) and gave my new client the name of my insurance agent, since I figured he might need one being new in town.

My insurance agent got the business. I'll have a chance to return the realtor's favor one of these days, too.

Networking

A great form of the referral method is networking. There are lots of ways to do this, with entire books available on the subject. Think of networking as a public relations campaign for yourself. You want your name and reputation to circulate among as many people as possible so that if someone happens to mention that they're in the market for what you sell, one of your network contacts will pass your name on to them, let you know that person is in the market, or both. If you're lucky, you might even get a testimonial or endorsement along with the lead.

Good networkers go to lots of meetings, actively belong to many organizations, and work at the process in an organized fashion. They don't just let it happen. Needless to say, they always have a supply of business cards at hand and are alert to potential prospects that may come from any direction. And they reciprocate.

Speaking of business cards, how do you use yours? Here are some ideas to get them into circulation:

- Don't hand out just one card. Make it a practice to give two and ask the recipient to pass the extra one on to someone else.
- Give one to the customer on every call, not just the first one. Ask them to pass them on.
- Give one to every person in a group presentation, not just the decision-maker.
- Give a card to every receptionist when you ask to see Mr. Big.
- Put two cards in the envelope with every letter, birthday card, or thank you note.

Business cards don't do any good hiding in your desk—they're only useful when they're spread around.

Remember that successful networking requires conscious effort on your part. It's one of those tasks that easily gets pushed aside by more pressing business. It's easy to skip a couple of meetings because you got too busy or put off those networking phone calls you were going to make because you had paperwork that had to get done. It's tempting to rely on happenstance to produce networking opportunities. But the best salespeople are proactive and generate the opportunities themselves.

It's a good idea to budget some time for it. Set aside a specific hour every week (outside prime selling time) to call ten people just to say hello and see how they are getting along. When you see an acquaintance's name in a trade journal, drop them a short note. Every quarter, send a business card and brochure to everyone on your Christmas card list (or address book) with a short note asking them to do you a favor and pass them along to anyone they know who might benefit from your services or products. You never know.

Competitive Monitors

The prospecting method most commonly used in many industries is monitoring the competition. There are companies that provide this service for a fee. At most companies, the salespeople find it in their job descriptions. In some industries, the users of the product or service are publicly known. If you sell car fleet leasing services, for example, you can identify which companies are leasing from your competitors by examining state car registration records. If you're in the ad sales business, you can readily see the prospects who advertise on the competitive media.

A truly aggressive salesperson will make it a practice to monitor competitive activity religiously. Many companies, of course, require competitive monitoring on a formal or informal basis. Even if yours doesn't, you should make it a habit to know who is using your competitor's products so you have a ready source of leads.

Chapter 46
Turning Suspects Into Prospects

"You can't deposit assumptions in your bank account."

In some industries, the prospect list is provided to you or is very apparent. If you sell prescription drugs, for example, your list of prospects consists primarily of the licensed physicians in your territory, since they have to approve your product's purchase before the end user can buy it.

If you sell a service like direct mail advertising, though, any business that you can physically contact can be a prospect. That's a large list, consisting approximately of every business with a telephone or mailing address in the world. What you need is a way to cull that list down to the most promising names.

This part of the prospecting process is the qualifying step. Think of it as pouring gravel through a series of successively smaller-grid screens. You start with a large, mixed up mess going into the first screen and end with a few pieces of exactly the right size coming out of the last one. The information you have or can get about each prospect dictates whether they can go through each screen.

Most prospecting methods are designed to put a lot of gravel into your screen. They generate leads. But leads and prospects are two different things. Leads are suspects, not prospects, until you determine whether they are capable of buying your product or service.

Mathematics And Common Sense

One screen to use is also a good time management tool. It's looking at the size of the suspect's potential order(s). To use this screen, of course, you should do some of the estimating math we explained in *The Dynamic Manager's Guide To Sales Techniques.*

In this screening process, though, you may not need to go into as much detail. You can just prepare some ball park figures to rank the prospects in a given category. Then choose a cut-off at the smallest potential spender you can justify investing your time in. Everyone above that mark moves from "suspect" to "prospect" based on potential order size.

You also will want to screen them on the probability of their purchasing from you. That's why competitive monitors work so well—the prospect has demonstrated a willingness and ability to buy something like your product. To narrow the list of prospects down, you need to qualify them in some (or many) ways. But watch out, qualifying has a lot of pitfalls.

My first sales manager, a man in a plaid sport coat whom I considered to be a sales god, used to say, "Pick the cherries that are ripe," which, of course, meant to call on those prospects who were most likely to buy at a given time. Almost every product or service has a seasonal or cyclical factor that dictates the timing of a prospect's needs. You can screen out until later those prospects who are "out of season" and concentrate your efforts on those most likely to buy today.

Another produce-related axiom he often used was, "Go after the low-hanging fruit." It's more efficient to sell the easiest prospects than the hard ones—the fruit that grows highest on the tree. This too, made eminent sense at the time, particularly since it was telling me to not work as hard.

The pitfall in both of these approaches, however, is that every one of my competitors was doing the same thing. Everybody was going after the easy pickings, to use one last fruit adage.

When I stepped back and looked at them, I realized that these prospects tended to be current users of my products or my competitors' (which is why I knew their buying cycle) and they were easy to sell—and to switch pitch—because they made their decisions based mostly on price. This was easy to do, since all of us were competing for the same business.

I finally learned to devote just as much time to these prospects as it took to get my share of their business, but to devote the bulk of my creative selling efforts to finding and qualifying prospects the competition hadn't gotten to yet. These prospects were the ones where it was hard to get in to see the decision maker, or who didn't appear to have much potential, or who somehow otherwise discouraged my competitors. I suspected that some of those prospects had big potential—and I was right.

Assumptions

Many times you disqualify a prospect based on assumptions you make about them. You jump to a conclusion based on your suppositions and don't do any research on the prospect. As a consequence, you don't have enough hard data to make a decision. Additionally, if a prospect doesn't use a product like that sold by you or your competitors, you assume there must be a reason and you don't pursue them. Sometimes there might be a reason they don't buy, but often the situation becomes a classic self-fulfilling prophecy. Since no one is trying to sell them, they don't buy. Since they don't buy, you don't try to sell them. Or you make assumptions based on incorrect information. You look at the building or the neighborhood the prospect is in, for example, and assume they can't have much potential, so you don't call on them. But you never know until you find out for sure.

I used to travel a two-lane highway every Tuesday, driving between two good customers of mine who were located in towns about thirty miles apart. I sold television advertising at the time. Located about midway between my two customers on the side of that highway was a small farm house with a good-sized metal machine shed behind it. It looked like a dozen other farm houses with sheds just like it on that highway except that this house had a little sign out front that said "Energy Savers" on it. I probably drove by that house and its sign for six months.

Finally, my curiosity got the best of me and I was ahead of schedule, so I stopped to see just what "Energy Savers" was all about. I knocked on the front door of the house and got no answer. I walked around to the back and heard somebody whistling in the machine shed. When I went inside, I found a big beefy guy in overalls laying under a trailer working to get a piece of baling wire unwound from one of the axles. He didn't look much like the "normal" television advertiser.

But it turned out he not only became a television advertiser, he became one of my largest accounts! Like many farmers, he had another business on the side. "Energy Savers" turned out to be an early provider of blown insulation, which offered an inexpensive, non-intrusive way to insulate the side walls and ceilings of existing homes. It was a perfect product to advertise on television and, because it carried such a high profit margin, this guy in the overalls and seed corn cap could afford to buy a lot of TV advertising from me.

If I had continued to judge the potential by the appearance of the prospect, I never would have made that first call on him. Remember, you can't deposit assumptions in your bank account—only commissions.

Prospecting and qualifying shouldn't be a chore to be avoided. It should be the beginning of the creative selling process where you open your mind to the possibilities and then try to make them happen. It's one more adventure in selling.

Chapter 47
Time Management And Sales Priorities

"You can make more calls and work no harder if you improve your sales efficiency."

We are all born with individual levels of innate intelligence, physical strength and coordination, and widely different circumstances of poverty or wealth, to name just a few ways we vary from each other. But we all have the same twenty-four hours and some odd minutes in every day. The different ways you use that asset determines how you grow your personal worth.

There are many valuable things in life that contribute to the quality of your short time on earth. Your relationships with family and friends, the development of your artistic skills and athletic talent, your accumulation of knowledge and the growth of your religious or spiritual faith. All of these things make use of that asset, time. That's not to give short shrift to making money, either, which is the greatest time user of all for most of us.

Since time is an asset, you should manage it to produce the greatest return on your investment of it. That return may be in the form of greater income or it may mean more time available to spend with your family or in other pursuits that give value to your life. But the principle is the same: you should treat time like any other asset. Don't waste it; capitalize on it.

Sales, especially commission sales, is one of the few occupations where you can see a very direct and fairly immediate return on the proper investment of your time asset. If you were to look at thousands of salespeople as I have, you'd see that the way they use their time may well be the single most important determinant of their success. The best and the brightest don't waste a moment. Even salespeople who lack good presentation skills or some other talent can make up for it by efficiently using their time. And, on the opposite end of the scale, the salesperson who is floundering and failing invariably has problems with time management.

Face Calls

There's a simple principle involved in time management for salespeople. More calls means more sales. Simple. As Woody Allen said, "80 percent of success is being there." You're "there" more often when you make more calls. If you learn nothing more than that from this book, you'll be ahead of the game.

Let's define a term. A "call" is a face-to-face meeting where you ask a prospect to buy something. It's not a telephone call to get an appointment or a service call on a current customer, although those activities are certainly important. But when I talk about making more calls in the context of business-to-business sales, I'm talking about asking for orders in person more frequently.

The technological advances of our society are wonderful. You have email, smart phones, instant messaging, video conferencing, and all kinds of other ways to communicate with your prospects. These high-tech wonders can make you more efficient. But they can't take the place of the face-to-face call. The salesperson who tries to substitute electronic "virtual selling" for personal contact is going to be about as successful as the quarterback who tries to run a play from the bench. The rest of the team may run the play, but it won't be the same without him there to handle the ball.

There is no substitute for meeting with the client in person. When you're there face-to-face, you build trust. It's really hard to believe in what someone's saying if you can't look into their eyes while they're saying it. If you've done any telephone sales, you know how hard it is to create a trusting relationship with a prospect who can't see you.

You also demonstrate your professionalism and transmit your enthusiasm much better in person. "Seeing is believing" is more than just a truism when it's applied to a sales call. When the prospect can see your animation, can see how prepared you are, can see the masterful way you control your presentation, you gain tremendous credibility. When you're there face-to-face, you find yourself much more focused on the client, too, which in turn will make your presentation just that much more persuasive.

Personal calls also show the prospect you care. They say you're so concerned about the success of his or her business that you are willing to invest some of your valuable time in working on it with them. Use all the modern technology you want, but use it to get more face time with more prospects and current customers. That's where its real value lies.

Efficiency And Effectiveness

This sure sounds like I'm pushing you to work harder, doesn't it? Add a couple more hours to your 12-hour workday and you'll make more money. Of course, you may lose a spouse or a couple of kids in the process, but hey, that's just part of the price you pay. More calls means more hours, right? Not necessarily.

I'm really not advocating that you work longer hours. I'm suggesting that you find ways to work more efficiently. Because you can make more calls and work no harder if you improve your sales efficiency. And you can make more sales on those calls if you improve your sales effectiveness. You've read several thousand words helping you learn to be more effective, now let's work on improving your efficiency.

There are three steps in building more personal worth through better time management:

1. Set Priorities
2. Plan Activities
3. Execute Effectively

There are many, many tools available to help you do these things, from computerized calendars and contact management software to personal coaching and time management seminars you can attend. But ultimately, time management is just like any other skill: it can't be taught, it has to be learned by practice. And you will only benefit if you are the one practicing the skill.

Keep in mind that the time you are trying to manage belongs to you. It's not your sales manager's time or your company's time, regardless of what they say or think. It's yours. And in the end, you are the only one who can manage it.

Time management is all about mutually exclusive choices. You can only do one thing at a time. You can't be in two places at the same time. No matter how you express it, you have to choose which account to call on at a particular point in time and you have to choose what you're going to do on that call. That's what priorities are all about.

In sales, there are two sets of priorities, account priorities and activity priorities. The relationship between the two—how you manage your activities to produce the greatest revenue from the chosen accounts—determines how successful you will be in increasing your personal worth.

Active Account Priorities

Account priorities are pretty straightforward. Which prospect has the potential to yield the greatest revenue for the amount of time invested in them? Let's start by quantifying the importance of each current account. In most businesses, the major accounts count and they count big. That's where the ever-popular "80/20" rule came from.

Of course, you generally like to think that you give your full attention and top notch service to every account. But in reality, which is where you live and operate most of the time, the constraints of time force you to make choices about how much time and what type of service you render to each account.

I suggest you assign priorities to each of your active accounts based on their potential for contribution to your personal revenue stream. I divide them into three groups.

Must Have Accounts

These are just what their name implies. They represent such a large share of your total business that you must have them or your business' very existence may be jeopardized. Here's a breakdown of the contribution various sized accounts make to a year's revenue for one of my clients:

Five Largest Accounts = 26 percent of total revenue

Next Five Accounts = 10 percent

Next Five Accounts = 9 percent

Next Five Accounts = 7 percent

Total of Twenty Largest Accounts = 52 percent of total annual revenue

My client does business with about 350 different accounts every year, but over half of the revenue comes from just twenty of them—and less than half comes from all of the other 330. Look at the top five! In a very simplistic way, if the company's profit margin were five percent, the loss of any one of these top five accounts could push the income statement into red ink territory.

As a salesperson, you have a few personal Must Have Accounts. I once had a sales position where I handled about 50 different accounts, but two particularly large ones were crucial. The commission on one was large enough to make my mortgage payment each month and the other basically paid the rest of the household bills. If either one of them cut back their spending or, heaven forbid, cancelled their contract, I was in deep trouble. I'm sure you know which ones of your accounts are Must Haves.

Priority Accounts

The second priority group for current accounts are Priority Accounts. These are fairly large accounts now but have the potential to spend a lot more—to become, in essence, Must Have Accounts. In the list above, the accounts ranked 6 through 20 would fall into this category. These accounts are important in their own right but not individually crucial to your company's survival.

The Priority Accounts' importance lies in their potential. They deserve an outsized portion of your time and effort because they could be much larger contributors to the revenue stream. Also, because they are active accounts, they are often the most fertile ground in which to plant new business seeds. They're profitable, they know you and your company's products, and they can grow if you give them a reason to do so.

Other Active Accounts

The third group of active accounts is simply Other Active. These are the accounts that do business with you but are generally limited in growth potential for some reason. They may be small businesses that don't have the capital to grow, or even large businesses with a use for only a limited number of your particular products or services. They may be seasonal accounts for you, buying only during certain times of the year because of some constraint peculiar to their business. For whatever reason, Other Active Accounts don't have a lot of growth potential.

You can't ignore them, though, because they can represent a significant portion of your business in total. The key to efficiently servicing these accounts is to stick to the business at hand with them and not go off on non-productive tangents.

New Account Priorities

The account priority groups I've been discussing consist entirely of current accounts—ones you do business with today. But you have to give some degree of priority to developing new accounts as well, or your business will stagnate. In fact, I suggest you place a priority on new accounts equal to that you give to existing ones. It's the only way to make sure you give them the attention they deserve. Again, I'm going to divide the prospects into three groups.

Target Accounts

The first are Target Accounts. These are prospects who have the economic potential to be Must Have Accounts but who, for one reason or another, don't spend any money with you now. Maybe you sell widgets and they are dedicated woudget users. Maybe your largest competitor has a deep consultive relationship with them. Or maybe no one in your company has yet found the magic button that will convert the Target Account from a prospect to a customer.

You know who your personal Target Accounts are. Most good salespeople have a couple of "dream sales" they'd like to make and they're usually to the great big accounts that no one else has been able to sell. You not only get rich off of them, but you become famous in the sales annals of your company as well. What you have to do is make yourself stop dreaming about that sale and start making it happen.

There is usually at least one if not more major obstacles to selling the Target Account. If it were easy, it would already have been done. So setting a high priority on getting their business—the same time priority you dedicate to working with a Must Have Account—is the only way you will succeed.

Unknown Potential Accounts

The next group of prospects is the Unknown category. I use that name because you don't really know what their actual potential is for any number of reasons. Maybe they are a new business in town. Maybe they have new owners whose plans and policies aren't apparent yet. For whatever reason, you don't really know what their potential is, so your first activity priority with them has to be to find out. But since you already know what the potential revenue is from a Target Account (and it's big) you have to rank them slightly lower.

All Other Prospects make up your final group. These accounts are the ones that you are pretty sure will fall into the Other Active category when they are sold. They'll be small accounts for the same reasons and you'll assign them the same place on the list of priorities.

Activity Priorities

But setting priorities for coverage of your accounts is only half of the process. The other half is determining the priorities of the things you do every day. Again, though, you can set activity priorities according to their revenue producing potential. In general, time spent making specific proposals to buy (face calls) should carry the highest priority while time spent performing non-sales tasks should carry the lowest.

In my grand time management scheme, there are six activity priorities to consider. The highest is making sales calls, or asking someone to buy something from you. As I mentioned earlier, this means face-to-face calls where you lay out a specific proposal to a prospect. These may be cold calls on new prospects or renewal calls on current customers—or any call in between where you make a specific proposal. If you are very lucky and really organized, you may be able to spend 60 percent of your average workday engaged in actual selling this way.

Service Calls

The next highest priority is assigned to service calls. These are the face-to-face meetings with current customers where you take care of their existing business in some way. If you sell retirement plans, for example, you may need to spend time with your customer's controller setting up the payroll withholding procedures. That's time out of your day—maybe a big chunk of time, in fact—that I classify as a service call because the sale has already been made.

Service calls have the second highest priority because of their value in customer retention. Keeping an existing customer is just as important and, in fact, generally more profitable, than selling a new one. And servicing that customer well is usually the single most reliable way to keep them.

Preparation For Calls

The third activity priority goes to preparation for sales calls. The Creative Selling System requires a fair amount of research, proposal writing, and presentation rehearsal, all of which takes time. Much of that time can be invested outside of prime selling time, which I'll discuss shortly, but the investment still has to come somewhere from within that 24 hours you have each day. And the priority for sales call preparation is so high because the activity is important to the successful completion of your highest priority, making the actual presentations.

The fourth item on the activity priority list is preparation for service calls. Someone (you) has to spend some time in the office getting the materials together for your meetings with the current customers.

Even if much of the service work is delegated to other departments in your company, someone has to coordinate it internally—usually the salesperson. In fact, depending on the type of business you represent, your job description may well say that you are the prime contact between the customer and your company before, during, and especially after the sale. This activity, by the way, can be a large black hole into which great amounts of your time disappear.

Sales Support

The fifth activity priority is the large group of those things salespeople generally hate, but like a low-fat high-fiber diet, are good for you. I'm talking about sales support or administrative activities. Sales meetings. Reports. Revenue projections. More sales meetings. Training. All of these things need to be done—like broccoli, they really are good for you and some of them are even important to the company—but they take a bite out of your daily time allotment. If you don't set and observe a priority for them, they'll eat your day alive.

The last priority goes to non-sales activities, or those things you need to do sometime during the daylight hours that aren't actually even remotely related to your job. You stop by the dry cleaners on your way to your first call of the day. You talk to your son's teacher to set up a conference after school (and during the work day). You eat lunch, take a coffee break, chat with your co-workers. These are essential life tasks that you are going to perform one way or the other, so you might as well plan for them as best you can.

One of the exercises I use when giving time management seminars is to ask everyone in the audience to list everything they did the day before in 15 minute increments from 8 AM to 6 PM. I promise them that no one will see the list but me. I can always tell how honest the group is when I see how much non-sales time they list.

The prize for the most egregiously wasted day goes to three salespeople in Mississippi who collectively spent six man-hours helping to unlock one of their cars. The salesperson had locked his keys in it when he got to the office that morning. To this day, I still don't know why it took three of them to get the door unlocked. I would hate to see them confronted with changing a light bulb. I do know they were honest because nobody would make something like that up.

Chapter 48
Time Management And Sales Planning

"Every minute you take away from prime selling time costs you money."

From a practical standpoint, you don't have 24 selling hours in a day. You don't even have eight. I estimate that most salespeople can count on no more than five hours and 30 minutes daily when they can expect to make face-to-face presentations. This is due mainly to the availability of your prospects and customers. Even if you work an 8 AM to 6 PM ten-hour day, you'll probably not be able to get more than five and a half hours in front of prospects.

Occasionally, of course, you'll have breakfast and lunch meetings with customers, squeeze in one last call at 4:45 PM, etc. But for the most part, you'll find it difficult to consistently make appointments with anyone before 9:30 AM because your prospects are busy organizing their own day (which does not revolve around you). Much the same holds true for lunch, which seldom starts at noon or lasts exactly an hour for most decision makers and influencers.

Here's what a typical sales day looks like:

8 – 9:30 AM Arrive at office, attend meetings, organize day, leave for first call

9:30 AM – 12 PM Prime Sales time

12 – 1:30 PM Lunch, return phone calls, paperwork, leave for calls

1:30 – 4:30 PM Prime Sales time

4:30 – 6 PM Return to office, return phone calls, attend meetings, paperwork

As you can see, you have five hours and 30 minutes of prime selling time in the day. How do you maximize it? Using the priority system you've set up, you have to plan your activities.

"Plan your work and work your plan" is yet another "golden oldie" sales adage. And it's a good one because it describes the essence of sound time management. It's not enough to lay out a plan, you have to execute it to get any benefit from it. In fact, if you don't "work your plan," you've wasted the time it took to draw it up.

You can spend a lot of time planning. You can also invest hundreds of dollars in account management software and cross-indexed leather-bound time management systems. Or you can make up a "to do" list on a napkin at the coffee shop where you start your day. These are all planning systems that can work. I suggest trying something in between.

You need both long-term and short-term plans. Or call them strategic and tactical plans, if you have a military frame of mind. Which one is more important? Neither. They serve two distinct but equally important purposes.

Long Term Planning

An annual plan is your long-term strategy. It generally includes activities with accounts with the greatest revenue potential because those are important enough to justify reserving repetitive blocks of time around which you schedule everything else. If you don't set those blocks of time aside, the long-term campaign to sell the Target Account tends to get pushed aside in the daily rush to get everything else done. But the Target Accounts—and Must Have and Priority Accounts as well—are too important to be overlooked.

I like to use one of those great big wall calendars that I can write on with a dry-erase marker and where I can see all 365 days at once. You may prefer a computerized system or a day-timer. At the beginning of each year, I note the times I expect to make presentations to my Must Have, Priority, and Target Accounts. There may be one such presentation each month for each account. If so, I'm going to mark that twelve times for each one on the calendar.

I then note the predictable sales events and sales support activities that I know will happen during the year. These include trade shows and conventions, promotion campaigns, special seasonal offers, sales meetings, report due dates, and anything else of that nature that I have even approximate dates for.

After that, I plug in my vacation (yes—it's important, too) and important personal dates like the kids' school programs, wedding anniversaries, and others that I don't want to forget in the rush of business. These may be non-sales activities, but they're valuable, too, so they deserve a place in the plan. If you have laid out the first two categories of activities ahead of these, you won't have to worry about accidentally being on a fishing trip in Manitoba when your top account's contract comes up for renewal.

Here's what goes on your annual plan:

1. Must Have Account Presentations
2. Target Account Presentations
3. Priority Account Presentations
4. Predictable Sales Events
5. Trade Shows
6. Seasonal Offers and Promotions
7. Report Due Dates
8. Vacation
9. Personal Dates

Advantages of Long-Term Planning

Having a long-term plan like this allows me to further schedule the time to prepare for each event. If I'm planning on making a presentation to a Target Account during the first week of May, I know I need to do the research the first week of April, write the proposal the second week, call the prospect for an appointment the third week, and rehearse the presentation the fourth week of April. And if there are other people in the company who will play a part in this pitch, they have a timetable to refer to as well.

Long-term plans get changed. That's to be expected. In fact, I suggest that you informally review your annual plan every month to see just what adjustments need to be made. A year is a long time and lots of things can happen which may change some of your priorities. So change the plan to reflect those changes.

One of the often overlooked advantages of long-term planning (and even short-term) is that planning reduces stress. Few things cause your blood pressure to shoot up worse than "discovering" that a report is due tomorrow—and you need some information from a co-worker who left on vacation yesterday. I don't know about you, but my life is full of surprises. Some of them are pleasant, but many of them aren't. The bad thing about all of them, though, is that every surprise reminds me that I'm not in full control of my life—a major cause of stress. Planning at least gives me the illusion that I am somewhat the captain of my own ship. This lowers my general stress level and enables me to more calmly cope with the surprises of each day.

Short Term Planning

The basic tactical tool of the Creative Selling System is the weekly plan. This is where you allocate your time assets in detail so that the annual plan becomes real and the events on it actually occur. I suggest you prepare a weekly plan every Friday (during non-sales time, of course). Again, you can use the format of your choice, but I use a very simple three-column sheet of lined paper. Each column is pretty self-explanatory: Account, Idea, Result.

The middle column, the "Idea," is there to remind you to have an actionable idea for every sales call that you make. Whether you're presenting a full-blown five-page Creative Selling System pitch or a "quick and dirty" add-on to an existing contract with a current customer, this column reminds you to build it around an idea based on a prospect need. Attaching an idea to every planned account call also reminds you to prepare for the call, not just try to "wing it" on your good looks and glib tongue. It's great self-discipline.

You start the weekly plan, of course, by listing the annually-planned activities first. Look on that big wall calendar you prepared and see what's there. List those activities first on the form so you remember to do them first. You'll probably find that there's some activity for your Must Have, Priority, and Target Accounts on the plan every single week. And that's as it should be. If they're going to represent 80 percent of your business, they deserve at least that much of your time. Then list all the other accounts you want to see and the ideas you're going to pitch them.

I can't tell you how many calls you should plan for each week because I don't know how big your territory is or how long your presentations take. But you should have a personal goal for the number of sales calls you make each day.

For my business, I generally assume about an hour for each presentation, including local travel time. With a five-and-a-half hour sales day, that means I'm able to get in a maximum of five every day. Quite frankly, if I ever got five solid presentations made in a day I'd be ecstatic (and rich). I can't because too many other things get in the way.

But five is a great goal to shoot for, which means I list 25 accounts on my plan each week.

When you decide on the appropriate number for yourself, make sure you list them in the order of their priorities, so that, hopefully, the ones that get cancelled due to lack of time are those with the lowest potential revenue.

Using Your Weekly Plan

You can undoubtedly do a weekly plan on a digital device of some kind. Feel free to do so as long as it's by your side throughout the week. If the device is going to keep it out of sight and therefore out of mind, however, you'll be better off with a sheet of good old paper. In either case, as the week proceeds, note in the "Results" column the outcome of your calls so that you know what you have to do to follow up on them and which accounts you need to see the following week. Every Friday, then, start a new plan by carrying over the calls that didn't get made or require some follow-up. If you're statistically minded, you can compile the results of several weeks' plans, looking for trends in your performance.

The goal of any time management system should be to produce more revenue, not more reports. That's why I rely on just two pieces of paper—the annual plan and the weekly plan—to cover strategic and tactical plans. You can certainly do more if that's what works for you. But beware of becoming plan-bound, which is that condition where you spend so much time and energy making plans that you can't ever get any actual work done.

One symptom of over-planning is when you make up a "to do" list in the morning with "Make To Do List" at the top of the page. That gives you an item to check off as soon as you're done making the list. It may give you a sense of accomplishment, but I think it's overkill.

Call Reports

I've always questioned the usefulness of post-call reports, which are nothing more than reports to management on what you did all day. As a stand-alone procedure they take up time which could be better spent working on an activity with future benefits, rather than reporting on something that's already done.

In their worst manifestation, the sales manager (or the poor administrative assistant) keeps a tally of the number of calls, sales, presentations, etc., and calculates a bunch of performance ratios. This gives the sales manager a club to use to "motivate" the salesperson. At their best, call reports serve as a source of information on the market for sales managers and the people above them, but this function could be better accomplished in many different ways.

The Weekly Plan treats the salesperson as an adult, capable of making sound business decisions about their work priorities and gives them credit for having priorities which are in synch with the company's. The Weekly Plan also contains all the history you need, which is the information about follow-up calls and actions that need to be accomplished. In other words, the Weekly Plan is designed to improve future sales, not punish past failures.

Preserving Your Assets

Executing the plan is the final step. The only way you're going to get all those calls made during the week is by taking all the little steps necessary to squeeze the waste out of your workday. There are several practices you can adopt to help.

Delegate work responsibly. This particularly applies to service of existing accounts. You have to strike a balance between the need for you to maintain positive contact with the customer and your need to work on other accounts. It's the "can't be in two places at the same time" problem. If you have support personnel to help you, delegate some of that work to them. After all, that's what they're there for.

Those service personnel aren't your slaves, however. Sometimes you forget that they deserve some appreciation for the work they do for us. When one of the support people does something extra for one of your customers, you should do something extra for them. And that something extra doesn't have to be monetary. A short note of thanks—with a copy to their supervisor—goes a long way. It's a matter of selling internally.

Use your non-sales time wisely. While you may have five and a half hours of selling time every day, that leaves four and a half hours of non-selling time during the normal work day. How are you spending it? Chit-chatting about last night's football game? Reading the newspaper? Planning lunch? I've seen plenty of salespeople (and sales managers as well) who start their day in the office that way.

But non-sales time is when you do your prospect research, write your proposals, rehearse your presentations, etc. You must do these things if you're going to be a successful Creative Seller, but they require time. Sometimes you'll need to use evening or weekend hours, but a well-organized salesperson can get them done during non-sales office time.

That's also when you do your call reports, update your expense account, and complete the general paperwork every sales job requires. If you find yourself filling out a report for your sales manager on Wednesday morning at 10 AM, you have a time management problem.

Group your calls geographically. This is one of the more common-sense time management tools. For several years, I lived and sold in a small town where you could drive from one end of town to the other in 20 minutes. You would think that geographically grouping my calls would be more trouble than it's worth. But I soon learned that if I had to make that 20-minute drive between every call, I lost the time for a major sales call for every three calls I made! That's because I spent an hour shuttling between those three calls (20 minutes times 3 calls equals 60 minutes wasted in the car). On my calculator, this meant about a 25 percent reduction in my income! I soon learned to geographically group my calls.

Schedule as much of your telephone work as you can for non-sales time. It's a little easier these days with cellular phones and voice mail, but taking and making phone calls can eat up a lot of sales time. Consider that time before 9:30 AM, during lunch, and after 4:30 PM as your prime phone time. Your customers are in or around their offices then and so are you, so it's actually the best time to make telephone contact.

Use voice mail effectively. To some people, voice mail is one of the unfortunate inventions of the modern age while to others it's a valuable time and energy saver. Use voice mail to its best advantage, which is not simply as a recording device for your pleas to the client to return your calls. Efficient sellers have learned to leave informational messages on the recorder so that the recipient can respond with information of their own. Think of it as email, where the two parties convey information back and forth according to their individual availability. Entire conversations can be held over time in this way and a surprisingly large amount of work can be accomplished.

Work on one thing at a time. You need to focus when you're at your desk during non-sales time doing proposals and paperwork. That's probably one of the hardest things for salespeople to do since much of your success depends on your ability to juggle several tasks at once. But "desk work" is different. The starting and stopping of your concentration on any one task actually adds significantly to the amount of time it takes to do it. And, at least in my experience, the number of mistakes in a given document go up in direct proportion to the number of interruptions you receive while preparing it.

Time Eaters

There are some things (and people) that just seem to devour time. To put a spin on an old saying, change the ones you can, avoid the ones you can't change, and minimize the ones you can't avoid. Here are several items with large appetites for your time.

Meetings. Unfortunately, you almost always have to go to them. They're important to someone important—usually your boss—so that makes them important to you. So do your part to make the meetings useful and efficient. If you diplomatically can, request that they be scheduled in non-sales time. If you are expected to participate actively, be prepared in advance so you don't spend a lot of time during the meeting trying to get your act together. Don't be the person who talks just to be talking, either. If you have something to contribute, by all means do so, but if you're just talking because you think you're supposed to, you're wasting your time and everybody else's.

Reports. These fall into somewhat the same category. Reports are almost never optional, so the best thing to do with them is do them as quickly and correctly as you can. Procrastination is one of the biggest time-wasting habits you can have, and reports seems to bring out the procrastinator in the best of us. The best way to handle an unpleasant task is not to put it off and hope it goes away, but to exercise some personal discipline and just do it. Get it over with so you can get to something you really want to do—like making sales calls.

Morning Syndrome. It afflicts many salespeople. This condition arises when little things just keep commanding your attention in the morning, demanding to be finished before you leave the office. So you attend to them. You return that phone call, step down the hall to talk to the production department, take a few moments to straighten up your desk—and the next thing you know, it's 10:30 AM. Guess what? You've lost an hour of prime selling time. If this happens more than once a week, you've got a serious problem.

One cure for this insidious time-stealing disease is to set an alarm clock on your desk for 9:15 AM. When it goes off, finish whatever it is you're working on (if you can) before 9:30, then leave. If you can't finish it, leave anyway and make arrangements to finish it at noon.

If someone else comes in to see you after the alarm goes off, tell them you have a 9:30 appointment and make an appointment with them to see them later in the day. Don't pick up the phone after 9:15 unless you know the call will take less than two minutes. After a few weeks of practicing this discipline, you'll be surprised at how much sooner you get in front of prospects every day—and how many more sales you make because you were there.

Putting out fires. One of the most common time-related job complaints I hear is that emergencies never stop. Entire days get lost as one "critical" situation after another clamors for the salesperson's attention. It seems like every department in the company brings every smoldering problem to the salesperson to stamp out. What happens here, of course, is that the salesperson essentially lacks the self-discipline to work according to his or her own priorities. He allows or even encourages other people to impose their priorities on him. Then he blames "everybody" for taking up all his time.

Of course, these problems are always emergencies, which can be defined in this instance as situations that someone else believes *you* should tend to immediately. Actual emergencies—which are situations of such enormity that they really must be dealt with immediately—are surprisingly rare. Floods and fires are emergencies. A production line snafu probably isn't. The snafu is undoubtedly important, but your part in untangling it can probably wait until noon.

At least that's what you should shoot for. When the production manager comes barreling into your office with his latest emergency, ask him if you can get back to him at noon because you have an emergency of your own—a customer meeting—at 9:30. Make him take the moral responsibility for canceling a sales call. You'll be shocked at how many "emergencies" will hold for a couple of hours. You'll be even more pleasantly surprised at how many of them seem to get taken care of before your noon appointment.

Pleasant distractions. These are time-killers that salespeople are particularly susceptible to. Do you have a customer with whom you've struck up a strong friendship? Or one who's a fan of the same basketball team you follow? It's really easy to slip into his or her office for a few minutes of "did you see that game last night?" Those few minutes turn into an hour before you know it.

Since that customer is always glad to see you, you like going there. Salespeople are human—if it feels good you keep doing it. Salespeople are also generally pretty gregarious folks; you like to talk to other people. So you almost never pass up the opportunity to do so. What's more, you rationalize it by telling yourself that you're just building strong customer relationships.

Don't fall into that trap. Yes, you should be glad your customers enjoy spending time with you. But you should be more glad when they spend *money* with you. And you seldom make a sale when you're talking about that three-pointer at the buzzer.

What's Your Time Worth?

It may seem obvious, but every minute you take away from prime selling time costs you money. To quantify it, calculate your "sales hourly wage" by dividing your annual income including commissions by 1,270 hours, which is the approximate number of prime selling hours in a year after allowances for vacations, sick days, and holidays. If you gross $63,500 annually, your sales time is worth $50 an hour to you.

I know I'd be pretty upset if I let a $50 bill fall out of my pocket and disappear on the street. But that's the same thing as inadvertently spending an hour of selling time yakking about the movie you saw last weekend. I'd be even more upset if I intentionally spent an hour of selling time writing a proposal. That would be like setting that fifty on fire.

If you want a good reminder to practice sound time management, calculate your "sales hourly wage" and write it on the back of a business card. Then tape that card someplace time wasting might occur, like on your telephone or on your car's steering wheel. Every time you use one of them, it will remind you to ask yourself if what you're doing at that moment is the best use of your time.

For a real eye-opener, do a version of my time management seminar exercise. Track everything you do in fifteen-minute increments for a week. Then add up the actual sales time. Be brutally honest with yourself and only count as time spent on sales calls those minutes where you asked someone to buy something. If that time totals less than twenty-seven and a half hours for the week, you've got a time leak someplace.

If you want to really motivate yourself to plug that leak, multiply the lost time by your "sales hourly wage" and then by the 52 weeks in the year. That's the size of the raise you can give yourself if you work at it.

In sales, time is money—your money.

Chapter 49
Sales And Technology

"Human beings are still the best tools for opening new accounts, introducing new products, and building long-term mutually-profitablecustomer relationships."

One of the earliest debates about technology in sales occurred when cell phones were first introduced. For those of us old enough to remember, the phones weren't cheap, service was spotty, and none of the early models fit in a shirt pocket. Most of them, in fact, wouldn't fit in a briefcase! The alternative technology, which most managers elected, was to issue a roll of quarters and a list of pay phones and to tell their salespeople to "keep in touch." The issues in the debate are basically the same today; there are just more gadgets to choose from.

The debate centers on three essential issues. The first question, of course, is cost. Technology isn't cheap and margins are shrinking, so volume has to increase if the sales technology is going to make economic sense. Cell phones may be cheaper today, but they're still not free. Nor are scanners, PDAs, laptops and tablets, and other accoutrements of the revolution in marketing technology.

The second issue is effectiveness. Not all the gizmos live up to their reputations and just because we *can* do something doesn't mean we *should.* You can, for example take a pretty good picture of a candy bar with your cell phone and email it to the customer along with a proposal—but should you? You might make a stronger impression if you went to his office and handed him a sample while you made the pitch in person.

The largest issue with technology, though, is communication—does it help or hinder the customer relationship? Underlying this question, of course, are some less palatable: do personal relationships really matter when the principle concern of the buyer is to get the lowest possible price to protect their already-thin margins? Are personal relationships even possible when the faces on both sides of the desk change constantly due to employee turnover? There aren't any easy answers to these questions, nor is there anything even remotely approaching a consensus of opinion.

Technology Isn't Free

The cost question looms large for both large and small business operators. For most, slow (or no) growth in many product lines and low margins on nearly everything make technology investments tough to justify. The normal everyday candy and tobacco distributor, for example, is struggling mightily. "The business just isn't there," according to Larry Diamond, buyer for H. J. Bailey & Co. in Neptune, New Jersey.

"Technology gets to be expensive," says Leonard Zlotoff, President of Palisade Wholesale in San Diego. "You have consultants, you have monthly this, monthly that. When you don't have experts in your employ, it can be costly." It's not just a matter of buying equipment, either. There are training expenses, highly specialized (and costly) maintenance, software licenses, upgrades, and more.

But then, salespeople aren't cheap, either, as Shane Segal, a partner in Segal Wholesale in Minneapolis points out: "When you're working on one percent margin like on candy, you can't afford to put a guy out selling, give him insurance, expense money, and a car." Especially when that salesperson's time is devoted to doing something probably better done through available technology. He adds, "For a salesman to walk in and say, 'let's see, you need an inventory of thirty Snickers and you've got twenty…' it's a real waste of time. We do the same old thing every week. A Snicker's a Snicker. He's really not selling anything."

Cost Efficiencies

Checking and refilling inventory, straightening shelves, handling returns are all functions that have to be performed. But they are also functions that take up time and manpower, therefore adding to costs, and do little or nothing to contribute to sales growth. Segal says, "Major chains want the salesperson to straighten up the shelves, unpack the goods, it's a waste of time. That's their responsibility."

Consequently, one area where there is general agreement on the value of technology is inventory management. Hand-held scanners and computerized checkouts help both the buyer and the seller. "All but the smallest customers have a computer system now," according to Segal, "and by tracking in and out sales, it can tell you what you need to maintain inventory levels."

Does this mean salespeople—and their attendant costs—can be taken out of the equation? Segal says, "We've cut way back on salespeople. People fax in their orders; we email them about new products." According to some distributors, though, you can only eliminate those sales people whose sole job description is "order taker." And only if the personal customer relationships don't matter.

Where People Fit

"We've had hand-held scanners for about five years. Most of those are used by the customers themselves, so our guys are in there consulting," reports Tim Arlint, VP Sales and owner of Glacier Wholesalers in Kalispell,

Montana. "They were order-takers before the customer did his ordering himself." As Arlint points out, removing much of the mundane task of filling inventory frees the salesperson to do their real job—sell product.

In this scenario, the technology-assisted salesperson becomes a productive asset to the company, not just a necessary expense item. He or she can consult with the customer. The salesperson can use the time formerly spent processing paperwork to look for product niches, services, promotional ideas, or other ways to help the customer improve their own bottom line. This turns into more sales for the wholesaler and a better-served customer—the foundation for a mutually-profitable relationship.

"We have more volume, we are bigger than we were, that's why we have more salespeople," Arlint says. "There are companies that are doing away with their outside salespeople—and we're getting their customers."

Arlint comes down strong on the side of personal customer relationships. "Electronic communication's just not face-to-face," he says. "That means the friendships that develop over the years can't happen. Customer relationships matter—at least in this part of the country."

Diamond agrees. "You could do away with the salespeople and let the customers do everything by EDI or through a telephone. Let them enter their own orders," then he adds, "But I don't want to lose the personal touch we've had since 1932." He describes what the salesperson should do: "You still need a personal appearance. I like one of my people to walk into an account and say 'How are you doing today? How's everything? Let me show you something new' instead of 'Hey, just send your order in, we'll get it off the machine.'"

How do you open new accounts through technology? "You don't," according to Diamond. And most managers would say that bringing in new business is one of the sales person's prime functions.

Segal agrees. "If you get an aggressive salesperson, they can open up new accounts," he says. "Our sales people are more or less establishing new accounts, keeping old accounts happy, stopping in making good will calls, but they're not writing up orders."

In The Future

Asked if there will come a time when salespeople will be replaced by technology, Arlint replies, "That's not coming for us." He adds, though, that he expects technological advances to continue improving the effectiveness of the sales people on his staff. "Ten years ago, our salesmen didn't have cell phones. That's made a big difference. There are all kinds of technologies that will come along and help."

The Internet is one. "We use email for communication between the customers and their salesperson now," he says. "We also have a website with online ordering."

"For the small company," Arlint recommends, "it's best to incrementally add technology." That allows the costs to be tailored to cash flow and the staff to be trained one step at a time so they're not overwhelmed by a desk full of new gadgets. It also gives them time to adjust their own mental job description to play down order processing and play up pro-active selling. If a salesperson has spent years in a job where ninety percent of the day is spent taking inventory, filling out order forms, and processing returns, they are going to need help adjusting to the new demands. For the technology to fully pay off, the sales staff may need to be trained in business development skills as well as how to operate a scanner.

It's not really an all-or-nothing question of people versus the machine. Investing in technology doesn't mean salespeople aren't necessary, nor does the need for personal customer relationships preclude the use of it. What most small business operators find is that gizmos and gadgets do many things like inventory management just as well and certainly much cheaper than people do. What they also find is that human beings are still the best tools for opening new accounts, introducing new products, and building long-term mutually-profitable customer relationships.

Chapter 50
Persistence Counts

"Sales is a learning process, with the salesperson the teacher."

If you listen to many sales gurus, you might think that making a sale is as simple as saying certain magic words and presto! The customer gives you an order. That's not the way it is, of course, as anyone who sells for a living will readily attest. Getting an order isn't an event; it's a process. And, like any other process, one of the key components is time.

It takes time for you to get to know the needs and desires of the prospect. Time for them to learn to trust you. Time for them to comprehend the benefits of adding your product to their collection of management tools or general life improvement devices. Very few sales happen the first time you see a new prospect. It generally takes three or four—some experts say as many as twelve—meetings where proposals are made before an order is secured.

Which is not to say that you shouldn't try to make a sale on the first and every subsequent call, as I wrote in *The Dynamic Manager's Guide To Sales Techniques*. In fact, the potential length of the process itself is one reason to not dally with "good will" calls or "get acquainted meetings." Get down to business right away—you've probably got a long road ahead of you and the sooner you start, the sooner you'll finish.

Customers Learn To Buy

Sales is a learning process, with the salesperson the teacher. Making a sale, especially to someone who has never bought a product or service like yours is a lot like teaching someone to play the piano. You don't expect them to play Beethoven's Moonlight Sonata after the first lesson. They have to learn how to sit properly, hold their fingers correctly, read the score, and so on.

A new customer has to learn a lot of things, too. They have to learn what role your products can play in their business or their life, how they can use them to build morale, cement customer relationships, or satisfy whatever needs they may have. They also must learn how to buy them; things like what sizes are available, what choices they have in design, how much lead time is required, and how much they cost.

Perhaps most importantly, they also have to learn a lot about you. What kind of person you are, how your company operates, how responsive you are to their needs. They need to learn to believe the claims you make and to trust your company to deliver exactly as ordered and on time. Many of these items are more or less subliminal—the prospect may not even know they're looking for them. But all of them are lessons that have to be learned the way anything is learned: through repetition of the lessons over time.

Why Sales People Fail

Which is where a lot of salespeople fail. They give up after their first few attempts to get a prospect to give them an order. It's tough to hear a prospect say "no" to proposal after proposal. It's even harder in many ways to deal with one who repeatedly says "maybe." So, after two or three seemingly fruitless meetings, the sales person gives up on that prospect. And who can blame them? After all, who wants to keep banging their head against the wall?

Besides, good time management practices would seem to dictate that you should spend that time on other, hopefully more lucrative, prospects. We're always sure the grass is greener on the other side of the fence, especially when it's brown on our side. And so it goes, with the student (prospect) learning the first three bars of the sonata but never having an opportunity to learn the rest of the song because the teacher stops showing up after the first couple of lessons!

Tips For Success

Quitting on a prospect too soon is a major selling mistake, but how do you avoid it? Here are some tips:

- Keep the door open. If you get a turndown, make sure the prospect understands that you will be back—soon—with another one. There's nothing wrong with saying, "Since you didn't care for this idea, is it okay if I come back with another one?"
- After every meeting, review what you learned about the prospect's needs and likes and dislikes so your next proposal will meet them better. Write down your impressions as soon as the meeting is over and they are still fresh in your mind.
- Bring a new gift basket idea to the prospect every two or three weeks. There's no limit to your creativity, so use it!
- Manage your own expectations. Don't look on calls that end with "no" as defeats, but rather as learning experiences for both you and the prospective customer.
- Keep the pipeline full. Always have a number of active prospects at various stages of development—some new ones, some who have seen a few ideas, and some who are just about ready to buy. Con-

stantly putting new prospects on your calendar will help you keep your enthusiasm up.

Is there ever a time when you give up on a prospect? Yes, but only under one of two conditions: First, if you determine that they truly can't afford what you are selling. After all, even the most dedicated piano teacher needs to get paid! Second, if you decide that they have absolutely no need for your product or service. If you diligently do your research and qualify your prospects, though, neither one of these two things will happen very often.

Chapter 51
Self-Motivation And Creative Selling

"If I had just one piece of advice to give anyone in sales, it would be this: don't ever settle for mediocrity."

Do you remember your very first sales call? Strangely, I can't remember my first sale, but my first sales call is etched deeply into my mind. It was a general debacle as sales calls go, but that first call told me why the sales life was the one for me.

I was an eager lad not quite old enough to legally order a beer, working as an announcer for a radio station in my hometown. The general manager of the station called me into his office one day and asked me if I would like to earn some extra money by selling advertising for the station on my own time. I could keep my current job and make some extra money in commissions on the side. What a deal.

So he gave me a list of 20 prospects pulled directly from the phone book, showed me a rate card and told me to go get 'em. The only training he gave me was to say, "Keep asking them to buy until they say 'no' three times, then go on to the next one." This was (and unfortunately still is) pretty standard sales training for the broadcasting industry.

My first call was on a roadside diner in Elwood, Kansas. The only person in the place when I walked through the door was a rather large lady in waitress white holding a big spatula in her hand.

"Excuse me, miss," I said, "Are you the owner here?"

"Yeah, what do you want?"

"I'd like to offer you some radio advertising today."

"Don't want any. Get out."

"But radio doesn't have to cost a lot of money…"

"Don't want none. Get out!"

"Let me show you…."

And that's when she came around the counter taking dead aim at my head with that big spatula, which I assumed was the third "no." I ran for my car and got out of there.

As soon as my heart stopped thumping I started laughing so hard I had to pull off the road. That's when I knew sales was going to be my field. Where else could you get such excitement? Such challenge? Learn so much about other people and human nature and get paid for doing it?

Why Sales?

What attracted me to sales in the first place was the freedom the job offered. I could come and go pretty much as I pleased, work on the things I wanted to work on, and even sort of set my own goals and use the methods I wanted to achieve them. Of course I had to make sure these things didn't contradict the company's policies and practices, but that has never been hard since every company I've ever sold for wanted the same things I did: more sales from more customers to produce more income. I soon found that if I produced those things, all of us would be happy.

But the personal freedom of sales turned out to be just a side benefit to the job. The real source of gratification turned out to be the senior partner of freedom, which is personal responsibility. Selling makes you free to set and pursue your own goals, but holds you responsible to yourself for doing so. When salespeople accept that responsibility, they have taken the first step on the path to satisfaction and success.

Another constant in selling is the need for salespeople to communicate with prospects on a human level. Advancing technology may make some transactional sales functions obsolete, but as long as people make the decisions about what to buy or not to buy, there will be an important place for salespeople in our economy.

And selling will always be a fun thing to do. It combines many of the positive stimulating forces in life: learning new things, facing different challenges, and meeting a wide variety of people. You get to make a pretty good (or even a very good) living and you can take most of the credit for your own success. Above all, you get to take some interesting risks, which adds plenty of spice to your life.

Creativity is a risk-taking enterprise. To endeavor to make something new is to take risks on several levels. Risk might be defined as the ability to fail. You may spend hours, days, even weeks on the project but fail to conceive an idea that's workable. Even if you do create one, you may fail to complete it satisfactorily and have to abandon it. Even if your idea comes to fruition, you may fail to find a market for it. Even if you sell it, your idea may not produce the results your customer expected. Every one of these potential failures wounds your ego and your pocketbook. With all these ways to fail, why try?

Because not every idea fails and the ones that succeed reward you tremendously. The risk/reward ratio is actually stacked in your favor. What's even better, you will improve the odds of success as your professional capabilities grow.

Sales Rewards

Selling offers many different kinds of rewards as inducements for the risks you take. Some of those rewards are very apparent—the income, the tangible achievement of quotas attained, the gratification of closing a deal after weeks or months of work. These are the rewards that you can see and identify.

But many rewards are more difficult to define because they are different for every individual. I think what motivates great salespeople is that they know themselves and the particular rewards they are seeking—and they also know they have the personal abilities and the opportunities to achieve them. Do you know what rewards you want?

Every good salesperson I know sets their own goals and plans their own rewards for achieving them. Sure, they also have company-set quotas and commission plans and other forms of goals and rewards, and they certainly work to achieve them, but they do so because that gives them the opportunity (a sales job) to work toward their personal goals. The real important goals are those they set for themselves. And the truly motivating rewards are the ones they choose to give to themselves for attaining their personal goals.

Those star salespeople make their goals tangible. Their goals are quantifiable in some way so that their attainment can be objectively measured and the salesperson can honestly say, "I did it." They don't allow fudge factors and they don't give rewards to themselves for trying—only for succeeding.

Almost all of the best salespeople set long-term goals. Opening fifty new accounts in the year. Getting promoted to manager within five years. Owning their own business by the time they are thirty.

Some set short-term goals. Completing five Creative Selling System presentations in one week. Closing a deal with the hardest account in town. Earning a particular commission amount in one month.

And they don't let achievement of the goal stand on its own—there has to be a tangible reward, too. I promised myself that the first year I earned $100,000, I would buy a hand-tailored, custom-made Brooks Brothers suit. A salesperson I know gave herself a hiking trip to the floor of the Grand Canyon when she closed her first sale for over $500,000. One of the most distinctive rewards I've seen is when a friend of mine pledged that he would quit his job and start his own company after he lead his sales team to their fifth record year in a row. The company he left after he achieved his goal was darn sad to lose him.

Set Your Own Rewards

If you don't have your own tangible goals and rewards, get some. Take a couple of hours some evening and make a list of the things in life you'd like to have. These are your rewards. List everything you can think of—and it's okay to put a few "if I won the Lottery" items on there, too. Do this first so you get good and fired up about the possibilities.

Now make another list, a shorter one, of some goals you could set for yourself. There are two tests the goals must pass: 1) they have to be complementary to the goals your company has and 2) they have to be just barely attainable—within reach only if you stand on your tiptoes. Now pick one of those goals—just one—and set a deadline for achieving it.

Finally, pick a reward from your first list. The test the reward must pass is that you have to be able to give it to yourself when you achieve your goal. A seat on the space shuttle may not pass this test, but a vacation in the Bahamas might. Now do whatever it takes to fix these two items in your mind. Write them on an index card and put it in your pocket every day. Make a screen saver out of them and put it on your computer. The salesperson who went on the hiking trip kept her goal in mind by hanging a picture of the Grand Canyon over her desk. Do something to keep your goal and your reward dangling in front of you at all times.

Goals and rewards. Scratch a top seller and you'll find them right under their skin.

Money Motivation

Whenever I'm asked to deliver a seminar on motivation, I always ask whether they really mean motivation or compensation. Most companies confuse the two. They think that the way they pay their salespeople will determine how successful those salespeople will be. You and I know that money's only one part of the deal—and one of the smallest parts of all. Motivation is about having goals and rewards in your soul. The money just helps you buy the rewards.

One of the companies I helped start was a nationwide advertising sales organization. I made plenty of mistakes as the project went forward, but I also learned a lifetime of lessons about human nature and motivation. One of the most important things I learned is that the best salespeople aren't motivated purely by money. As a start-up, the company didn't have a revenue stream on which to base commissions, nor did it have the money to promise big signing bonuses or hefty salaries to recruit star salespeople from its established competitors.

What I was able to promise them was a company that would be built around the opportunity to practice creative selling. Since the people I was recruiting were working in an established mature industry, they didn't have a lot of opportunity for creative selling in their present jobs. In fact, most of the firms they worked for measured a salesperson's success purely by the volume of transactions they could handle. Creativity had very little to do with it.

I believed that a start-up built on creating new opportunities would be successful in that industry. I also knew that to make it successful I had to have the best salespeople I could find. I didn't have the time or resources to hire and train rookies, and I knew my concept wouldn't work if I hired anything less than the best that were already working in the industry.

What I had to offer them was the chance to flourish in a very different way. To create sales opportunities rather than process orders. Of course, this meant more work, more risks, and pretty vague monetary rewards compared to what they were doing. I counted on their creative drive to lure them to us.

I was successful in hiring some of the best and the brightest. Maybe they all weren't the "top producers" at their old companies, but they were definitely the ones who had the itch to succeed in a creative environment. And they did succeed spectacularly. The company I started went from zero to $35 million in annual sales in the first year—then more than doubled to $75 million in the second. It produced an operating profit in the first year. And I also proved that selling in musty, old, in-a-rut industries could be fun if the job was redefined as a creative enterprise.

What's pertinent about this story is that the company's sales compensation plan was a simple salary. No commissions, no bonuses, no spiffs. The closest thing I had to monetary motivation was the $100 bounty I offered to the salesperson who brought in the new company's first order. The salaries weren't particularly generous. In fact, some of the people I recruited actually took a slight cut in pay to work for the company. I am convinced that every one of the salespeople succeeded because they were motivated by their personal pride in a job well done.

The story doesn't have a happy ending, though. In our third year the company came under control of a larger firm, which immediately imposed its commission-based compensation plan on my staff. It may have been coincidental, but sales that year grew at exactly the same rate the rest of the industry was growing.

One by one, the salespeople started drifting away to other opportunities and the company settled into the same rut as everyone else in the industry. I very strongly believe that the just average performance was because the salespeople became fixated on their commission checks rather than their personal pride. The company had achieved mediocrity.

Be careful. You may only run a company of one (yourself), but the same thing can happened to you. If I had just one piece of advice to give anyone in sales, it would be this: don't ever settle for mediocrity.

You'll be tempted to allow a little mediocrity to slip in now and then because it takes hard work to be a creative seller. There aren't any magic spells to make it easy, either. If mediocrity has anything going for it, it's that it's easy. But you know as well as I do that the easy things in life and the best rewards are almost never connected.

You don't have to be mediocre. You have a spark of creativity that will grow into raging excellence if you just fuel it with opportunity and a little work.

Resolution

Success requires resolution. If you were to ask my mother why I have been a successful salesperson, she would say it's mainly because I'm stubborn. Maybe she's right. Mothers usually are, aren't they? I hope you are resolute—or stubborn—enough to stick to it until you succeed.

One more story about the power of an idea and the rewards of resolution. Once when I was selling television advertising, I was assigned an account that every salesperson in the station had handled and failed with at one time or another. It was a furniture store that employed a little advertising agency, mainly to screen out salespeople.

The furniture store spent a grand total of $1,000 on our station every year for as long as records had been kept. Never a penny more. Yet this was the largest furniture store in town. It spent hundreds of thousands of dollars in the local newspaper. I knew this was going to be a challenge.

My first call was on the store owner, who, when I called to get an appointment, referred me to his advertising agency. I went there once so I could say I had, then called the owner for another appointment, laying the idea pitch on him as thickly as I could. He must have sensed that I was not going to go away, so he agreed to give me the 15 minutes I asked for.

That first call was a textbook Creative Selling System presentation, although I didn't know that at the time—I was just following my instincts. The store owner didn't say much, though, until I asked for the order, which was for $60,000, or 60 times the amount he had spent with us before.

He didn't blink at the amount, but he told me that he didn't like the idea so he wasn't going to buy it. I asked him if I could come back with another idea and he said something that created a selling monster. He said I was always welcome as long as I brought him a new idea to consider. "You never know," he said. "Someday you just might hit one."

He didn't know my mother, so I'm sure he didn't know how stubborn I can be. I adopted a very simple game plan: I would pitch him a different single idea every week until he bought one of them or until one of us died. I kept the same dollar proposal and developed, borrowed, or otherwise created a new idea for him every week.

That went on for exactly 52 weeks. I didn't want to lose my rhythm, so I even made that one call each week while I was on vacation that year. While I was waiting to see him each week, I came to know everyone in the store. I was there so many times I learned the names of most of his customers. I became a semi-expert in the furniture business by osmosis. And every week he would give me my 15 minutes and end them by saying "no."

The biggest problem I had, of course, was the number of ideas I was using. I couldn't pitch the same thing twice, so I needed a new one every week. The station copywriters and commercial producers started hiding from me. The sales manager refused to let me nominate furniture stores for our weekly brainstorming session. But somehow the ideas came. One every single week.

One day, one of the commercial producers collared me and said he had something to show me. We went back to the master control room, where he loaded a piece of videotape on one of the machines. "I was fooling around last night and this happened, he said. "Watch this monitor." He rolled the tape and I saw the furniture store's logo appear with an electronically-generated moving tail like a comet. By today's standards it would be primitive, but back in those dark ages of analog TV, it was unique. The tape lasted four seconds.

I called the store owner and asked him to come to the station to see something. This was in the days before portable video cassette players. When he saw the logo with the comet's tail, he said just two words, "That's it."

I got the order after making fifty-two presentations—the last one based on a four second idea. That contract made the furniture store the station's largest advertiser that year. My commissions on the account enabled my wife and I to buy our first home. Stubborn? Yes, and proud of it.

On reflection, my biggest reward from that sale was the lesson I learned about the power of selling an idea. The decision maker never would have seen me twice, let alone 52 times, if I hadn't brought him an idea at the beginning and another one on every successive call.

Creative selling celebrates the relationship between buyer and seller. You know your idea is a success when the buyer's eyes light up as you explain it, when they start making suggestions to modify it to even better meet their needs, when they say "yes" and give you the order. Until it is sold, the idea exists only in your mind and on paper. But when the buyer says "yes" the idea comes to life through its execution—the two of you have created something together.

Just like anything else in life that promises great rewards, creative selling takes dedication. You've already demonstrated a great deal of dedication to your art by slogging through this book and enduring my circumlocutions, rants, and war stories. I hope you take the lessons to heart and use the Creative Selling System to achieve your own rewards.

About Dave Donelson

I've had four careers—each building on the one that came before it. The first was in small-market radio and television where I did everything from reporting the news and writing ad copy to selling spot schedules to local businesses. In the process, I learned a ton about how small companies work, how they interact with their customers, and what kinds of challenges they face—not just advertising and marketing problems, but personnel, finance, real estate, insurance, and even succession planning.

My second career was in national ad sales. I honed my selling skills competing for million-dollar budgets spent by the largest advertisers in the world. In addition to working with them and their advertising agencies on locally-executed campaigns in markets around the country, I built management skills as I climbed the ladder to eventually establish and run a nationwide sales organization with eleven offices and several hundred sales and support personnel.

Having built a company from the ground up for someone else, I decided it was time to strike out on my own, an urge that led me to found Sales Development Associates, Inc. (Donelson SDA), a management consulting firm that specialized in helping companies that were going through ownership changes and strategic transitions. My clients included one of every seven commercial television stations in the U.S. as well as companies in fields as diverse as heavy manufacturing and construction, magazine publishing, industrial sales, retail operations, and consumer services. I also took advantage of several opportunities to further test my entrepreneurial mettle by investing in a few select client companies and several successful start-ups.

Those investments allowed me to start my fourth career. For the last several years, I've been a writer and speaker, sharing what I learned with readers of some three dozen national newspapers and magazines and audiences at trade associations, professional group club meetings, and conventions of state and national organizations. In addition to the Dynamic Manager series, I'm the author of *Creative Selling: Boost Your B2B Sales* (Entrepreneur Press, 2000), and two novels. Learn more about me and the Dynamic Manager series at www.thedynamicmanager.com.

also by Dave Donelson . . .

The Dynamic Manager's Guide To Marketing & Advertising:
How To Grow Sales And Boost Your Profits

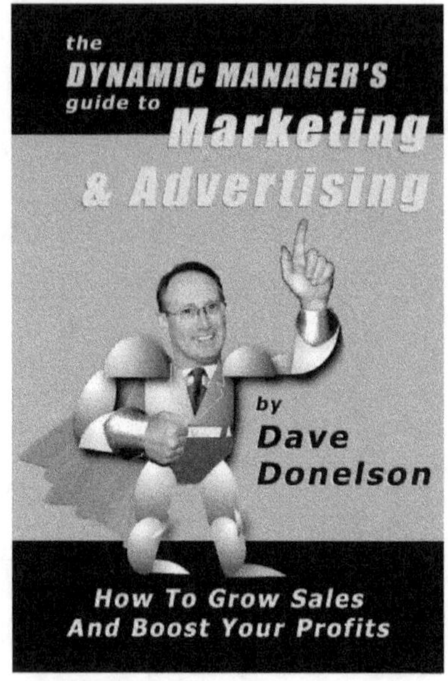

This complete guide includes all three Dynamic Manager eBooks designed to help you grow your business with good marketing, advertising, and sales promotions. Hundreds of entrepreneurs and small business managers just like you tell how they learned to identify their best prospects, define their needs, and design marketing and ad campaigns that make the cash register ring.

Businesses that thrive—and the managers who run them—have one thing in common: they make their decisions based on meeting their customers' needs. They are good marketers. Dave Donelson distills the experiences of hundreds of such business owners—and his own as an entrepreneur and consultant—into this guide to attracting customers, persuading them to buy, and turning them into customers for life.

Learn how to increase the return on your advertising investment by following a few basic rules of the game. Find out what makes your customers tick and why they buy from you—or your competition. Discover how to build your profits on a solid foundation of good marketing skills.

In the first two sections, managers and entrepreneurs just like you tell how they handle the nitty-gritty details of creating ads, buying media, designing promotions, and all the many other tasks of good marketing. Insightful case studies of small companies across the country—retailers, manufacturers, service providers, and more—help you see how marketing drives successful business strategy.

ISBN-13: 978-1453889602

www.thedynamicmanager.com

Dynamic Manager eBooks by Dave Donelson

Guide To Sales Techniques:
How To Create New Prospects And Make More Sales
ISBN 978-1458028556
Amazon Kindle ASIN B004HILRJY

Guide To More Sales:
How To Nurture Customers And Grow Your Business
ISBN 978-1458116499
Amazon Kindle ASIN B004L62BQU

Guide To Creative Selling:
How To Make More Sales And Build A Super Sales Career
eBook ISBN 978-1458114990
Amazon Kindle ASIN B004NNV5L8
Please note – this eBook contains both the *Guide To Sales Techniques* and the *Guide To More Sales*

Guide To Advertising:
How To Grow Your Business With Ads That Work
ISBN 978-1452491011
Amazon Kindle ASIN B003X9786Y

Guide To Marketing:
How To Create And Nurture Your Best Customers
ISBN 978-1452444994
Amazon Kindle ASIN B0044XV0R6

Handbook Of Sales Promotions:
23 Ad Campaigns and Sales Promotions You Can Use
ISBN 978-1452317328
Amazon Kindle ASIN B004A14T8Y

Guide To Marketing & Advertising:
How To Grow Sales And Boost Your Profits
eBook ISBN: 978-1453889602
Amazon Kindle ASIN B004AM5E8C
Please note – this eBook contains the *Guide To Advertising*, the *Guide To Marketing*, and the *Handbook Of Sales Promotions*

In addition to Amazon Kindle editions, all eBooks are available in formats for the Apple iPad, Sony Reader, Barnes & Noble Nook, and other devices.

also by Dave Donelson . . .

Heart Of Diamonds
A novel of love, scandal, and death in the Congo

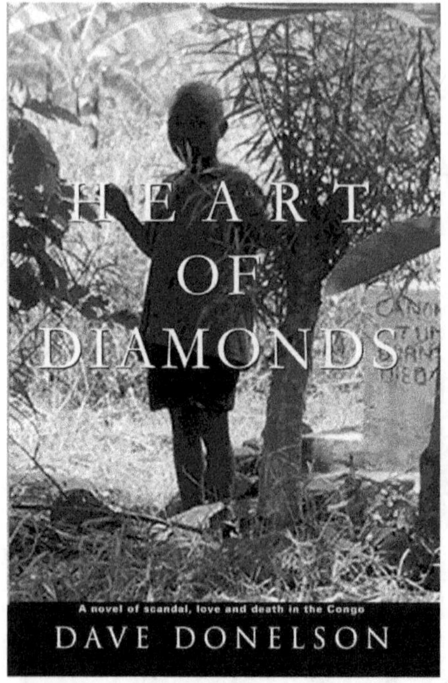

Corruption at the highest levels of government, greed in the church, and brutality among warring factions make the Congo a very dangerous place for television journalist Valerie Grey. Amid the bloody violence of that country's endless civil war, Grey uncovers a deadly diamond smuggling scheme that reaches from the heart of the Congo to the White House by way of an American televangelist. ***Heart Of Diamonds*** is a fast-paced tale of ambition, avarice, betrayal, and love.

"An absolutely brilliant must-read book. Dave Donelson captures the essence of the Congo's challenges. His ***Heart Of Diamonds*** *is the modern corollary to Joseph Conrad's* ***Heart of Darkness****. Dave breaks the silence about the conflict in the Congo and firmly stands with the Congolese people in their quest for peace, justice, and human dignity."*

--Kambale Musavuli, National Spokesperson, Friends of the Congo.

ISBN 978-1449919924
Amazon Kindle ASIN B0032UY4UM

www.heartofdiamonds.com

Available for all ebook readers from your favorite ebook vendor.
Audiobook edition read by the author available from Audible.com and iTunes.

also by Dave Donelson . . .

Hunting Elf
A doggone Christmas story

A puppy for Christmas? What could be better! Dan McCoy and his capable wife June find out when Santa gives them a frolicsome hairball named Elf, a Silky Terrier with champion bloodlines and the table manners of Groucho Marx at a Hunter S. Thompson New Year's Eve party. He's also on the wish list of nefarious dognappers who want to steal him as part of a murderous plot to win Westminster's "Best In Show." Elf foils everybody's plots, though, and brings Macy's Thanksgiving Day Parade to a tumultuous halt in the process. Hunting Elf is a comedic canine Christmas adventure.

"Donelson fills the novel with experiences recognizable by anyone who has ever raised a puppy. Elf lifts his leg in all the wrong places, chews on everything from an heirloom Oriental carpet to the CATV cable, and has an uncontrollable urge to dig up and eat delicacies like kitty paté, which gives a whole new meaning to the term 'doggie breath.'"

--The Larchmont Gazette

ISBN 978-1456315924
Amazon Kindle ASIN B000ZM2HO0

www.huntingelf.com

Available for all ebook readers from your favorite ebook vendor.
Audiobook edition read by the author available from Audible.com and iTunes.

One of the few things I enjoy as much as writing is speaking before groups of all kinds.
--Dave Donelson

"Wow! What a great presentation you made at our Annual Convention last week! We've heard excellent remarks and compliments on your session and hope you enjoyed doing it at least half as much as our delegates enjoyed hearing you."

--Oscar Rodriguez, Deputy Director Texas Association of Broadcasters

"Your seminar was great. Everyone in attendance seemed to enjoy themselves and I continue to hear very positive comments about your presentation. You were successful at interjecting some fun into the day, as well as providing our members with some very useful and much needed information."

--Sue Toma, Executive Director, Iowa Broadcasters Association

"...a timely and compelling presentation. Our evaluations indicate that it ranked high above average. Some of the positive comments we received referred to your upbeat tone, humorous style, inspirational words, and thought-provoking presentation."

--Debbie Griffin, President DFW Society for Marketing Professional Services

For more information

Email dave@thedynamicmanager.com

www.ingramcontent.com/pod-product-compliance
Lightning Source LLC
Chambersburg PA
CBHW071355170526
45165CB00001B/57
9781460929667